Palgrave Macmillan Studies in Family an

Titles include:

Graham Allan, Graham Crow and Sheila Hawкer
STEPFAMILIES

Harriet Becher
FAMILY PRACTICES IN SOUTH ASIAN MUSLIM FAMILIES
Parenting in a Multi-Faith Britain

Elisa Rose Birch, Anh T. Le and Paul W. Miller
HOUSEHOLD DIVISIONS OF LABOUR
Teamwork, Gender and Time

Deborah Chambers
SOCIAL MEDIA AND PERSONAL RELATIONSHIPS
Online Intimacies and Networked Friendship

Robbie Duschinsky and Leon Antonio Rocha (*editors*)
FOUCAULT, THE FAMILY AND POLITICS

Jacqui Gabb
RESEARCHING INTIMACY IN FAMILIES

Stephen Hicks
LESBIAN, GAY AND QUEER PARENTING
Families, Intimacies, Genealogies

Clare Holdsworth
FAMILY AND INTIMATE MOBILITIES

Peter Jackson (*editor*)
CHANGING FAMILIES, CHANGING FOOD

Riitta Jallinoja and Eric Widmer (*editors*)
FAMILIES AND KINSHIP IN CONTEMPORARY EUROPE
Rules and Practices of Relatedness

Lynn Jamieson, Ruth Lewis and Roona Simpson (*editors*)
RESEARCHING FAMILIES AND RELATIONSHIPS
Reflections on Process

David Morgan
RETHINKING FAMILY PRACTICES

Eriikka Oinonen
FAMILIES IN CONVERGING EUROPE
A Comparison of Forms, Structures and Ideals

Róisín Ryan-Flood
LESBIAN MOTHERHOOD
Gender, Families and Sexual Citizenship

Sally Sales
ADOPTION, FAMILY AND THE PARADOX OF ORIGINS
A Foucauldian History

Tam Sanger
TRANS PEOPLE'S PARTNERSHIPS
Towards an Ethics of Intimacy

Elizabeth B. Silva
TECHNOLOGY, CULTURE, FAMILY
Influences on Home Life

Lisa Smyth
THE DEMANDS OF MOTHERHOOD
Agents, Roles and Recognitions

Palgrave Macmillan Studies in Family and Intimate Life
Series Standing Order ISBN 978–0–230–51748–6 hardback
978–0–230–24924–0 paperback
(*outside North America only*)

You can receive future titles in this series as they are published by placing a standing order. Please contact your bookseller or, in case of difficulty, write to us at the address below with your name and address, the title of the series and the ISBN quoted above.

Customer Services Department, Macmillan Distribution Ltd, Houndmills, Basingstoke, Hampshire RG21 6XS, England

Social Media and Personal Relationships

Online Intimacies and Networked Friendship

Deborah Chambers
University of Newcastle, UK

First published 2013 by
PALGRAVE MACMILLAN

Palgrave Macmillan in the UK is an imprint of Macmillan Publishers Limited,
registered in England, company number 785998, of Houndmills, Basingstoke,
Hampshire RG21 6XS.

Palgrave Macmillan in the US is a division of St Martin's Press LLC,
175 Fifth Avenue, New York, NY 10010.

Palgrave Macmillan is the global academic imprint of the above companies
and has companies and representatives throughout the world.

Palgrave® and Macmillan® are registered trademarks in the United States,
the United Kingdom, Europe and other countries.

ISBN 978-1-349-34933-3   ISBN 978-1-137-31444-4 (eBook)

DOI. 10.1057/9781137314444

This book is printed on paper suitable for recycling and made from fully
managed and sustained forest sources. Logging, pulping and manufacturing
processes are expected to conform to the environmental regulations of the
country of origin.

A catalogue record for this book is available from the British Library.

A catalog record for this book is available from the Library of Congress.

Transferred to Digital Printing in 2013

Contents

Series Editors' Preface

The remit of the *Palgrave Macmillan Studies in Family and Intimate Life* series is to publish major texts, monographs and edited collections focusing broadly on the sociological exploration of intimate relationships and family organisation. As editors, we think such a series is timely. Expectations, commitments and practices have changed significantly in intimate relationship and family life in recent decades. This is very apparent in patterns of family formation and dissolution, demonstrated by trends in cohabitation, marriage and divorce. Changes in household living patterns over the last 20 years have also been marked, with more people living alone, adult children living longer in the parental home and more 'non-family' households being formed. Furthermore, there have been important shifts in the ways people construct intimate relationships. There are few comfortable certainties about the best ways of being a family man or woman, with once conventional gender roles no longer being widely accepted. The normative connection between sexual relationships and marriage or marriage-like relationships is also less powerful than it once was. Not only is greater sexual experimentation accepted, but it is now accepted at an earlier age. Moreover heterosexuality is no longer the only mode of sexual relationship given legitimacy. In Britain as elsewhere, gay male and lesbian partnerships are now socially and legally endorsed to a degree hardly imaginable in the mid-twentieth century. Increases in lone-parent families, the rapid growth of different types of stepfamily, the de-stigmatisation of births outside marriage and the rise in couples 'living-apart-together' (LATs) all provide further examples of the ways that 'being a couple', 'being a parent' and 'being a family' have diversified in recent years.

The fact that change in family life and intimate relationships has been so pervasive has resulted in renewed research interest from sociologists and other scholars. Increasing amounts of public funding have been directed to family research in recent years, in terms of both individual projects and the creation of family research centres of different hues. This research activity has been accompanied by the publication of some very important and influential books exploring different aspects of shifting family experience, in Britain and elsewhere. The *Palgrave Macmillan Studies in Family and Intimate Life* series hopes to add to this list of influential research-based texts, thereby contributing to existing knowledge and informing current debates. Our main audience consists of academics and advanced students, though we intend that the books in the series will be accessible to a more general readership who wish to understand better the changing nature of contemporary family life and personal relationships.

We see the remit of the series as wide. The concept of 'family and intimate life' will be interpreted in a broad fashion. While the focus of the series will clearly be sociological, we take family and intimacy as being inclusive rather than exclusive. The series will cover a range of topics concerned with family practices and experiences, including, for example, partnership, marriage, parenting, domestic arrangements, kinship, demographic change, intergenerational ties, life course transitions, step-families, gay and lesbian relationships, lone-parent households and also non-familial intimate relationships such as friendships. We also wish to foster comparative research, as well as research on under-studied populations. The series will include different forms of book. Most will be theoretical or empirical monographs on particular substantive topics, though some may also have a strong methodological focus. In addition, we see edited collections as also falling within the series' remit, as well as translations of significant publications in other languages. Finally, we intend that the series has an international appeal, in terms of both topics covered and authorship. Our goal is for the series to provide a forum for family sociologists conducting research in various societies, and not solely in Britain.

Graham Allan, Lynn Jamieson and David Morgan

Acknowledgements

This book arose from a previous monograph that I wrote in 2006, *New Social Ties: Contemporary Connections in a Fragmented Society*. The earlier book explored how the discourse of friendship fosters ways of managing rapid change in social networks by focusing on personal relationships, community and computer-mediated communication. At the time, social media was embryonic. I wish to thank Philippa Grand, Publisher at Palgrave/Macmillan, for offering me the opportunity to address the transformations in social media and personal relationships since then. I also thank Andrew James, Commissioning Editor, for guidance to completion. I am grateful to Anne Graefer, Newcastle University PhD student, for providing research assistance. I thank the group of anonymous college students in the North East England for discussing their views on social media. Finally, I wish to thank the series co-editor, David Morgan, for his constructive advice on earlier drafts of the manuscript.

1
Introduction

One of the most striking changes in personal life during late modernity is the use of social media for conducting personal relationships. These changes entail a growing significance in the public display of personal connectedness and the importance of the term 'friendship' in managing these connections. Digital communication technologies are contributing to new ideas and experiences of intimacy, friendship and identity through new forms of social interaction and new techniques of public display, particularly on social network sites. This book explores the ways people engage with social media to build, maintain and exhibit personal networks. The aim is to provide an understanding of the *mediated* nature of personal relationships by developing a theory of 'mediated intimacies'. The dramatic changes in rituals of connection brought about by the explosion in use of social network sites compel us to reconsider the concept of 'intimacy' and extend it beyond its former, narrow focus on family life. This book therefore enquires whether digital modes of communication are generating new intimacies and new meanings of 'friendship' as features of a networked society. Key debates and research evidence are assessed about emerging ways that people share their lives with each other in a digital environment and the motives for doing so. New opportunities being offered by social media to transform identities and generate new modes of self-presentation, interaction and etiquette are identified.

With a particular focus on the ways social network sites are being used to support or complicate personal ties, this book explores the intersecting uses of a range of social media. Social network sites constitute a now well-established mode of communication. Yet they only emerged in the first decade of this century. These highly popular forms of social and personal connection continue to be treated, publicly and academically, as an emergent phenomenon. Facebook, for example, now has over 900 million users globally and is regarded as a 'new media' success story. The company states, 'Our mission is to make the world more open and connected'.[1] At the end of March 2012, just before its shares were floated on the market, Facebook was able to boast that it hosted 125 billion total friendships.[2] This detail is simply fascinating, yet in terms of its significance the figure is also totally mystifying. The implications of such an assertion are still being unravelled by those of us engaged in the study of mediated interpersonal communication. How people construct their mediated networks to build their identities and establish intimate relationships is, then, the subject matter of this book.

Social network sites are said to be increasing the number of friends that people have and strengthening ties between families, especially those separated by migration. Yet, at the same time, new media technologies are being blamed for a decrease in close, 'genuine' bonds. A strong belief persists that face-to-face communication is superior to mediated communication, as Nancy Baym (2010) states. This assumption is regularly expressed in news reports and by various experts (e.g. Ferguson 2012; Putnam 2000). It has had a powerful influence on debates about social media, fuelling fears that social network sites contribute to a breakdown of community. Has Zuckerberg's vision of a more connected world transformed into a more alienating scenario with people interacting with their screens and disregarding the people around them? The current hype about social interaction on the Internet conveys some of the public anxieties and moral panics surrounding social media (see Critcher 2008). Fears have been expressed that online social networks cause alienation and uprooting, the breakdown of community, erosion of family values and traditional modes of sociability. For instance, the head of the Catholic Church in England and Wales, Archbishop Nichols, has claimed that Facebook and MySpace can provoke teenagers to commit suicide because such sites encourage them to build transient relationships and dehumanise community life (Wynne-Jones 2009).

Disturbing to some is the image of solitary individuals withdrawn in their private domestic spaces yet simultaneously in connection with a global network. A further media-generated panic includes the idea that young people have no sense of discretion or shame and have grown into the habit of exposing 'their bodies and souls in a way their parents never could'[3] (Livingstone 2008: 397). Users of social network sites are regarded as self-obsessed and narcissistic (Buffardi and Campbell 2008; Carpenter 2012; Twenge and Campbell 2009) or as socially isolated. Sites such as Facebook are also being blamed for damaging time-honoured

conventions of personal communication, for generating shallow relationships and for making us all feel insecure. As journalist Keith Watson
remarks in a light-hearted tone:

> That's the thing with Facebook – it has ripped up rules of social
> intercourse and kidded us with a vision of a bright new smiley
> world where we all *Like* each other. But really it's just cranked up
> our potential for insecurity to a massive scale. Haven't we all got a
> clutch of Friends Requested killing us softly with their rebuffs? Just
> me then.
>
> (Watson 2011[4])

There is, then, a concern that digital media is creating a dysfunctional
society in which past tight-knit communities are being fragmented and
gradually taken over by more dispersed social networks. Exaggerated
claims have also been made in the opposite direction through assertions
that, in the era of 'communicative abundance' (Keane 2009), social barriers and inequalities will be broken down by the rise of a new global
digital network. Within this extravagant scenario, an egalitarian public
sphere is envisaged in which each individual is liberated through digital
autonomy with a shift of control from governments and big business to
individuals. Whether optimistic or pessimistic, such exaggerated claims
suffer from a media centrism: a technological determinism in which digital communication is misrepresented as being at the centre of society as
the determining or principal factor of social change and that we all ori-
ent our lives around it (Postman 1993; Smith and Marx 1998; Williams
1974). In both scenarios, social network sites seem to have become the
index of the progress or collapse of social connectedness.

Changing meanings and practices of friendship

Despite widespread social anxieties about the impact of digital technologies on traditional social ties, emerging findings indicate that social
network sites and other social media have become important sites for
cultivating *personal* relationships. The research addressed in the following chapters contests the view that heavy social network site users are
more isolated than occasional or non-users. Growing evidence suggests
that this technology is contributing to a dramatic reconfiguration of
our ideas about intimacy and friendship. While sites such as Facebook,
MySpace and Friendster are reshaping the landscapes of business, culture
and research, these sites are also forging new ways of being intimate and
'doing intimacy'.

Although research in this field is embryonic, a growing body of scholarship is now assessing the ways that social network sites and other social media are being drawn on to sustain personal relationships. This book engages with the disciplinary traditions of media studies and sociology to explore the key features of changing personal relationships and modes of sociability in the context of social media. The book draws on and combines traditional and new sociological debates about intimacy, family, friendship and new social ties with new media studies of computer-mediated communication and social network sites. Social network interactions and intimacies are examined from a range of theoretical and methodological angles. The aim is to revisit and advance the concept of 'intimacy' through the lens of social media use and to develop a theory of 'mediated intimacy'.

This emphasis on intimacy, family and friendship is something that Facebook is keen to promote in describing its attributes. It states, 'People use Facebook to stay connected with their friends and family, to discover what is going on in the world around them, and to share and express what matters to them, to the people they care about.'⁵ The company is keen to become embedded in our personal lives. It now has strong commercial motives for doing so (see Chapter 9). At the same time, this communication technology is capable of facilitating weak, thin ties of acquaintanceship (Morgan 2009). Close relationships with family, children, lovers and friends are being sustained in concert with loose ties connecting work colleagues, acquaintances, neighbours and also virtual networks composed of shared interests and causes. The transformative potential and affirmative values of choice and agency associated with social media, particularly social network sites, are therefore foregrounded in this book. However, while social network sites offer us opportunities to express our identities and connections online, individuals are subjected to certain social pressures and constraints in the presentation of an online self. The personal profile requires constant monitoring and remodelling. The kind of self-regulation involved in online self-presentations suggests that social network sites can be viewed as sites that cultivate the enterprise of self-improvement (Rose 1999). This issue is explored in Chapter 4 on self-presentation online.

'Friendship' is a major ideal being exploited as a principal feature of social network site communication, within the process of *publicly displaying* connectedness. However, this new, *mediated* friendship is being shaped by conventions that vary considerably from those associated with the traditional sense of friendship formed before Web 2.0. In contrast to the public display of matrimony, for example, friendship has not generally been publicly declared until now in Western contexts (Baym

2010). This digitalised era is the first in which personal connections of friendship become formalised through online public display. The question is whether this emergent ritual of displaying non-familial as well as familial social connections online affects conventional meanings and values associated with 'friendship' and 'intimacy'. Questions about the intensity and speed of self-disclosure online, the unforeseen side effect of constant self-disclosure and how to sustain digital connections are issues that provoke questions about the sorts of skills now required to be 'a friend'. These social skills may include initiation of contact, changing expressions of self-disclosure, rejecting self-disclosure or friendships, self-management of identity and creating social distance from others. The internal rhetoric used by social network sites promotes 'friendship' signifiers and imagery through the choice of terms employed by the sites themselves. For example, MySpace.com has described itself as a place to 'find old friends' and 'make new friends', as a place to 'connect', as a community (Parks 2011: 106).

The design of social network sites, including the software applications or 'tools' of engagement for making personal connections, plays a key role in shaping users' communication. The processes are therefore worthy of some attention here. Participants create an online profile by listing personal information and interest, connecting with other site users and sharing updates about their activities and thoughts in their networks (boyd and Ellison 2007). Sites such as Myspace and Facebook encourage users to publicly display a record number of 'Friends' by offering specific incentives for users to add people to their Friends list. Users are provided with the tools to create an individual web page to post personal information such as self-descriptions and photos, to connect with other members by creating 'friends lists' and to interact with other members. After joining a social network site, users are invited to link up with others on the site that they know. Although the label for these connections differs according to site, common words are used to emphasise the informality, sociability and casualness of the links including 'Friends', 'Contacts', 'Fans' and 'Followers'. On Facebook, individuals invite other users to be 'Friends,' in a relationship that is made visible to others on the site. This enables two users to communicate with each other and share content. The decision to include someone as an online 'Friend' prompts a 'Friend request' which asks the receiver to accept or reject the connection. This generates a further stage of processing or friendship management.

Most sites reveal the list of Friends to anyone permitted to view the profile but several recently launched privacy features enable users to prevent 'non-Friends' from either viewing their profiles, adding comments or sending messages. 'Friend' selection allows choice in excluding people from one's friendship list. Excluding and 'deFriending' a person known to the member can generate offence. This practice is particularly an issue among teenagers for whom the management and public display of Friends can play a major role in peer group interactions. These are often characterised as intense, dramatic and occasionally volatile (see Chapter 5). In addition, a whole range of information about online status and idle status and about 'away messages' can reveal personal information about a person's context and movement (Baron 2008).

While the contact lists on our mobile phones are used as personal reference tools for connecting with significant others, social network sites are unique in publicly displaying personal contact lists to all who have access to our profile. Contact lists publicise our networks as our 'Friends'. Friends have therefore come to function as a key dimension of a person's identity and self-presentation (see Chapter 4) as well as part of the regulation of access to certain features (such as commenting) and content (such as blog posts). The rise of social media has coincided with the introduction of several new words in the English language such as to 'Friend', to 'defriend' or to 'unfriend' a person; 'offline friends' and 'non-friend'. The term 'frenemies' is used in the context of online stalking: 'stalking your frenemies'. The term 'unfriend' was selected as the Oxford Word of the Year in 2009, defined as the action of deleting a person as a 'friend' on a social network site. 'Friending' a person on a social network site presupposes and evokes the idea of a degree of purpose and determination in establishing the connection (Madden and Smith 2010). Following boyd and Ellison (2007), the word 'Friend' is capitalised here to indicate social network contacts and to distinguish the term from conversational understandings of the term.

In a study of friendship in LiveJournal, Raynes-Goldie and Fono (2005) discovered considerable variation in the reasons people gave for Friending each other. Friendship represented content, offline facilitator, online community, trust, courtesy, declaration or nothing. Similar motives were found by danah boyd (2006) in a study of participants' activities on Friendster and MySpace. Thirteen incentives were identified by boyd in descending importance, as follows:

1. Actual friends;
2. Acquaintances, family members, colleagues;
3. It would be socially inappropriate to say 'no' because you know them;
4. Having lots of Friends makes you look popular;

5. It's a way of indicating that you are a fan (of that person, band, product, etc.);
6. Your list of Friends reveals who you are;
7. Their Profile is cool so being Friends makes you look cool;
8. Collecting Friends lets you see more people (Friendster);
9. It's the only way to see a private Profile (MySpace);
10. Being Friends lets you see someone's bulletins and their Friends-only blog posts (MySpace);
11. You want them to see your bulletins, private Profile, private blog (MySpace);
12. You can use your Friends list to find someone later;
13. It's easier to say yes than no.

The first three incentives involve already known connections. The rest provide clues about why people connect to people whom they do not know. Most of the reasons given reveal how significant the technical facilitators are in affecting individuals' incentives to connect (boyd 2006). There is evidence that Friending encompasses a wide range of contact categories and that, as boyd's findings show, not all users view all 'Friends' as actual friends. The implications of these changing practices are explored in the following chapters.

The emerging principles and customs shaping online friendship and intimacy are having a profound impact on the way companionship is practised and experienced offline. This is particularly the case for young people (see Chapter 5). For example, users of sites such as MySpace are invited to rank their 'Friends' in order of preference as a routine feature of engagement. These online customs are also influencing conventions surrounding intimacy for adults. The word 'Friend' is being applied to all declared connections whatever their nature or intensity. Family members, work colleagues, school friends and acquaintances are regularly being listed and publicly displayed as 'friends'. In 2007, Facebook set up a feature for users to group friends into categories. Before that, all contacts were indistinguishable, all being labelled as 'Friends'. MySpace differed, with a tool enabling users to mark out their 'Top 8' contacts.

Modes of online connectivity

Levels of engagement

This section addresses variations in levels of social network site engagement according to social groups and online experiences. It acts as a backdrop to some fascinating details outlined in the following section about *why* and *how* people engage on sites and *who with*, to provide insights into digitally mediated personal ties. In terms of age groups, data from the Pew Internet and American Life Project confirms that more young adults use social networks than older adults in the United States (Lenhart 2009). Among 18 to 24 year olds, 75 per cent of online adults have a profile on a social network site and among 25 to 34 year olds, 57 per cent have a site profile. The number steadily decreases with age with 30 per cent of online adults aged 35 to 44 having a profile, 19 per cent of online 45 to 54 year olds, and 10 per cent of online 55 to 64 year olds. Among those aged 65 and over, only 7 per cent of online adults have a profile. In a study of frequency of use, Joinson (2008) found that women visited Facebook more often than men. White Facebook users tend to have more ethnically and racially homogeneous friendship networks than non-white users (Seder and Oishi 2009). Studies further reveal that different sites attract different social groups (Hargittai 2007). The different designs of sites offer differing modes of functionality and affordances (Hargittai and Hsieh 2011). Some sites are used mainly for maintaining social relationships such as Facebook and others to promote professional networks such as LinkedIn. Significantly, the *personal* use of social networks is more widespread than *professional* use in terms of both the type of networks that adults choose to use and their reasons for using the applications (Lenhart 2009).

Although research on the intensity of social network site use is nascent, certain patterns emerge. Eszter Hargittai and Yu-li Patrick Hsieh (2011) found that some people engage with one site only either frequently or infrequently while others use several sites regularly or infrequently. Based on a study of US college student users, they distinguished between Dabblers, Samplers, Devotees and Omnivores. Dabblers use only one site and occasionally. Samplers visit more than one site but infrequently. Devotees are active users on one service only. Omnivores use several sites and use at least one site intensively. Women are more likely to be intense users than men but only more likely to be Omnivores. There are no gender differences between Dabblers, Samplers and Devotees. No significant differences according to racial and ethnic background were detected except that non-Hispanic African American students are less likely to be Dabblers and non-Hispanic Asian American students tend to be devotees. Students with at least one parent with a college education are more likely to be Omnivores. They are also more likely to be intense users if they do not live with their parents. Users with better web skills tend to be intense users and to incorporate their social network site use into their daily routines. Web skills are likely to be enhanced by the extent of use as well as vice versa (Hargittai and Hsieh 2011).

Types of relationships

Throughout the relatively short history of online communication, a major question for researchers has been whether the Internet is used mainly to sustain pre-existing connections or to establish relationships that start online and then move offline (see, for example, Ellison et al. 2007, 2011a, 2011b; Walther and Parks 2002). For some time it was believed that the Internet would be perfectly designed for forming networks with strangers on the other side of the world, with or without shared interests. It was initially assumed that innovations in digitalised communication activities would essentially lead to an explosion of globalised social contacts. Two key trends emerge from research on patterns of social media use. First, all the digital mediums available to us – such as cell phones, texting, Skype, instant messaging (IM), social network sites, blogging and email – are mainly used to communicate with a remarkably small handful of people, largely made up of intimates. Second, in the case of social network sites, rather than being used for initiating new relationships we find that they tend to be used for maintaining or deepening already existing *offline* relationships and for tracing people already known offline.

Regarding the first trend, in research on interpersonal digital communication across multiple media platforms among families in Switzerland, Stefana Broadbent (2011) found that on average 80 per cent of regular exchanges are with the same four or five people. Whether the exchanges were on IM, social network sites, Skype or mobile phone, the result was the same in all cases. Broadbent's in-depth study involved interviews, observations and surveys of users' homes. Respondents were also asked to produce communication logs to identify and describe the purposes of *all* their communications. Most communication was about the state of loved ones including partners, family and friends. She found that most mobile phone calls are made to the same four intimates. Broadbent (2009, 2011) also discovered particular communication channels are preferred for keeping in touch regularly with intimates and that these are determined by the *level* of intimacy afforded by the connection. She distinguishes between 'synchronous' and 'asynchronous' channels, emphasising the more *intimate* nature of voice communication such as the telephone, Skype and SMS in synchronous media (addressed in Chapter 2).

Despite the asynchronous nature of social network sites, they do involve intimate communication. As Sonia Livingstone (2009a) points out, social network sites are displacing, incorporating and remediating other modes of online communication. The technology is supplanting communication forms such as email, chatrooms and website creation and absorbing others such as IM, blogging and music downloading. Social network sites fuse earlier technologies of communication and involve *multimedia* engagement (Haythornthwaite 2005; Jenkins 2006; Madianou and Miller 2012). The technology provides communication, storage and social applications for hundreds of millions of users. The multifaceted technological opportunities or 'affordances' of this medium make it highly suitable for fostering and maintaining intimate ties. Social network site technology also remediates synchronous forms of communication such as face-to-face and telephone communication (Bolter and Grusin 1999; Jenkins 2006).

Although social network site technology offers a remarkably wide and complex range of affordances to connect with large numbers of people through text, images and News Feeds, the medium is being used by individuals mainly to sustain very close, personal ties. Moreover, political communication is limited. During the year of the US presidential campaign when Barack Obama's success was attributed to the use of social media, research by the Pew Internet and American Life project (Kohut 2008) found that only 10 per cent of Internet users in the US population posted political comments on social network sites and 8 per cent posted comments on blogs. The majority of Internet users (64 per cent) obtained their core information from television websites such as cnn.com or abcnews.com (Kohurt 2008).

While social network sites such as Facebook, Bebo and MySpace have made it easy for users to broaden their range of contacts to hundreds of Friends, most users have an average of five close friends (Binder et al. 2009; Choi 2006; Ellison et al. 2007, 2011a, 2011b; Joinson, 2008; Lampe et al. 2006; Lenhart 2009; Walther and Parks 2002; Wilson et al. 2009). In a large-scale study of user interaction events on Facebook, Wilson et al. (2009) found that the most active users only received photo comments from a small number of their Friends (15 per cent), and most users received comments from only 5 per cent of their Friends. This pattern is reflected on Twitter where 97 per cent of twitterers attract less than a hundred followers while celebrities such as Britney Spears have around 4.7 million followers (Infographic 2010). Moreover, the majority of Facebook interactive events tend to be generated by a small and highly active subset of users, while a majority of users are significantly less active (Wilson et al. 2009). A study of user interactions on the South Korean social network site, Cyworld, reflects this pattern. It was found that Cyworld users with fewer than 200 friends interact only with a small subgroup of friends. Interactions tend to be bidirectional rather than multidirectional (Chun 2008). Significantly, this pattern resonates with conventional offline friendship networks and users of other social media technologies.

With reference to the second trend, a succession of studies confirm that social network sites are being used for sustaining *pre-existing* contacts which have strong offline connections of proximity. For example, a US survey of over 1000 undergraduate college students about offline/online communication by Lampe et al. (2007) found that Facebook profile fields were quite difficult to falsify. Importantly, the software design of sites fosters meaningful or *consequential* ties in the sense that it allows users to identify common ground in offline contexts such as home town, high school and cultural preferences. The researchers found that users of Facebook tend to use online profile details to identify others with whom they have something in common in an offline environment rather than just shared interests. The search for indicators of common ground among other members helps to simplify the process of detecting shared backgrounds, interests and experiences. Lampe et al. (2007) even suggest that simply being aware that a person is from the same town affords a common background and point of reference for people who have not met before. Holding online conversations about having local milieu, events or acquaintances in common can facilitate future contact. Similarly, a related US survey by Nicole Ellison et al. (2007) of 286 undergraduates revealed that users of Facebook connected with many more people with whom they shared *offline connections* such as existing friends, class mates, nearby neighbours or a person they had already met socially than with meeting new people. Facebook users are also much more likely to 'search' for people with whom they shared an offline connection than they are to 'browse' to meet complete strangers (Ellison et al. 2007).

Despite the remarkable technological possibilities for global networking, most people's online connections are, then, generally localised or stem from former local connections. Niche networks can be geographically dispersed but strangers and distant others are far less appealing to users of online social media than initially assumed (Boneva et al. 2006; Mesch and Talmud 2007b). Surprisingly few social network connections are initiated online and there is little evidence that this form of social media is being used to replace existing social relationships with new ones. This range of findings suggests, then, that social network sites are predominantly a medium for *personal* engagement and for maintaining pre-existing contacts with offline connections of proximity. To paraphrase Broadbent,[6] it amounts to a 're-appropriation' or a conquest of *personal* mediated discourse over other kinds of communication. Nevertheless, this does not preclude the use of these sites for the formation of weak ties, as indicated below.

Certainly, social network sites help strangers to connect through shared interests, activities and political views. However, the emphasis on *personal* communication is indicated by the dominant patterns of personal engagement with social network sites and the use of this social medium for sustaining existing relationships rather than linking up with strangers. Given these patterns, the impulse to differentiate between offline and online associates now seems too simplistic. It fails to take into account the intricate ways in which online communication is integrated into everyday personal life (Bakardjieva 2005; Livingstone 2009a; Silverstone 2006[7]). Livingstone emphasises that despite this remarkable range and mix of affordances, face-to-face communication is not being displaced by online connections. Instead, these technological attributes have ensured an *embedding* of this technology in personal life. This is also supported by research beyond Western contexts. In the study of South Korean site, Cyword (Choi 2006), it was found that Cyworld has become embedded in everyday life. Maintaining and reinforcing pre-existing social networks was reported as the main motive for Cyworld use by 85 per cent of users (Choi 2006: 181). This *embedded* nature of the technology indicates that most site users convey information about their own identities rather than inventing new online identities.

'Mass friends'

While social network sites are being used mainly to sustain and deepen *pre-existing* connections formed offline, some users accumulate vast numbers of occasional 'friends'. The average number of online connections generally varies between 120 and 180. Yet certain users of social network sites are accruing thousands of 'Friends' (Golder et al. 2007). This tendency signals a rise in weak ties or acquaintances. Within the motives for Friending others identified by boyd (2006) which are listed above, after the first three, most reasons involve people known to members, the rest provides clues about the incentives for participants to connect to many people that they do not know: popularity, being a fan (of a person, band or product, etc.); expressing one's identity; to make the user look cool; to gain access to several features such as more people or to a private profile or to someone's bulletins and their Friends-only blog posts; to allow others to see one's bulletins, private profile, private blog; to find someone later and finally because it is easier to say 'yes' than 'no'. These incentives for Friending are addressed in later chapters. Speculation about the status of friend collecting and the changing nature of friendship on social network sites has prompted media reports with headlines such as 'Most Facebook friends are false friends'.[8]

The technical facility to generate a large number of online weak ties encourages some users to draw on the software to browse for names online to add to their friend collections (Donath 2007). As indicated by the incentives identified by boyd, this 'mass friend' collecting involves connections with strangers as well as acquaintances. The majority of those who collect large numbers of Friends are often adults such as musicians, politicians, corporations and celebrities. These users depend on wide social networks to advance their status, careers or leisure interests. Most loose connections are likely to be 'trophy' friends such as famous actors, sportspeople and celebrities. The lack of a facility to differentiate between *casual* and *intimate* contacts encourages a blurring of relationship groupings. Social network sites have the *potential* to generate large numbers of positive weak ties, but it raises questions about whether we are capable of handling large numbers of contacts online, whether 'Friend collecting' has social benefits or whether the practice is simply a pretence used to impress others. Research on the theoretical boundaries for the number of stable personal connections that humans are capable of managing suggests that we are unable to handle more than about 150 relationships (Dunbar 1996).

In terms of the qualities and social benefits generated by our social networks, enquiries into the social capital generated by social network sites by Ellison et al. (2011a) suggest that when the number of reported actual friends surpasses 400 to 500, there is a 'point of diminishing returns'. The social benefits to be gleaned from large numbers of Friends are not apparent (see Chapter 8). They point out that, at this size it is likely to be impossible to conduct the kind of relationship maintenance needed to ensure that weak ties provide useful forms of support and information. While some social network site users might have 1,500 friends, the traffic on these sites shows that most people maintain a much smaller circle of about 150 connections (Dunbar 2010). Site users are likely to know little about the lives of more than 150 of their digital contacts. These contacts may range from very close friends to casual acquaintances.

A set of conventions are emerging around the ritual of Friend collecting and gradually being recognised as digital protocols through regular use. Derogatory terms such as 'Friendster whores' indicate the kinds of negative views being associated with indiscriminate Friending activity (Donath and boyd 2004). Young people in particular are scrutinising each others' profiles and judging the number and management of online friendships among their peers (see Chapter 5). In a study of perceptions of social attractiveness on Facebook, Tong et al. (2008) discovered that higher Friend counts corresponded with higher levels of perceived social appeal. Intriguingly, this operated within distinctive limits. Users who accumulated more than 302 Facebook Friends were actually rated lower in terms of social attractiveness, and this was likely to be because they were judged to be 'Friending out of desperation' (Tong et al. 2008: 542) or substituting face-to-face contacts with digitally generated ones. The aspiration to acquire hundreds of friends and the practice of adding relatively weak ties to online friendship lists confirms key changes in the meanings and values associated with 'friendship' in the context of social media.

Weak online ties

The acquisition of large numbers of Friends raises questions about whether online networks are reducing the investment needed in making strong friendships or whether new ties generated online are inevitably inferior ties. Placing multiple postings of information to several people is so simple and fast that the cost of maintaining and forming these weak associations, in terms of time and effort, is being significantly reduced (Ellison et al. 2011b). As mentioned above, social commentators are concerned that IM, texting and social network sites are somehow undermining human intimacy and sociality. Yet others claim that fostering numerous loose ties or 'nodding acquaintances' may have important social benefits.

Mark Granovetter (1973) categorised the members of a social network according to the strength of the ties. He contrasted the effectiveness of 'strong' ties of family and close friends with 'weak' ties of casual acquaintances such as former colleagues or new people whom we meet. Granovetter described the strength of a tie as a combination of the amount of time, emotional intensity, intimacy and reciprocity entailed in the relationship. Our weak ties or acquaintances are less likely to know each other or be socially involved with one another compared to our close friends and family. Granovetter states:

> Thus the set of people made up of any individual and his or her acquaintances comprises a low-density network (one in which many of the possible relational lines are absent) whereas the set consisting of the same individual and his or her *close* friends will be densely knit (many of the possible lines are present).
>
> (Granovetter 1983: 201–202)

Weak ties may offer us access to the kinds of resources and varied social groups and belief systems that close family and friends are unable to supply. Those with extensive weak ties will have access to information, new ideas and tastes from outlying parts of the social system. For example, it gives individuals an advantage in terms of the labour market where employment may depend on knowing of job openings (Granovetter 1973, 1983). Since casual friends and acquaintances often move in social circles that differ from our own, they are more likely to have access to different information and can facilitate information sharing (Benko 2011; Morgan 2009). The benefits generated by weak ties are referred to as 'bridging capital' (Putnam 2000) and are addressed in Chapter 8. By contrast, the strong ties of family and close friends are defined by the frequency of contact and by their voluntary, companionable, supportive and long-term nature (Haythornthwaite 2005). They offer the kind of 'bonding capital' which is not available from weak ties or acquaintances. As Baym (2010: 125) puts it, 'Resources exchanged in strong tie relationships run deep and may be emotionally and temporally expensive. As a result, we cannot maintain too many strong tie relationships at any given time and have many fewer strong ties than weak ones'.

Caroline Haythornthwaite (2005) uses the concept of 'latent ties' to address the ways in which social media technologies create new opportunities for contact between people would not otherwise link up with one another. Latent ties are described as connections 'technically possible but not yet activated socially' (Haythornthwaite 2005: 137). They occur when a new medium of communication becomes accessible, allowing individuals to make contact. The telephone system and phone directory is an example of this. Ellison et al. (2007) emphasise the affordances of social network sites for detecting and identifying people online which might prompt users to initiate latent ties in the future. A 'latent tie' is

...a relationship between two individuals which has not been socially activated. These individuals may have a passing awareness of one another (or may have even met briefly), but the affordances of the social network site serve to enhance and accelerate the relationship development process.

(Ellison et al. 2011a: 877)

The question, then, is whether and what kinds of weak ties and latent connections are being activated in the context of social media such as social network sites, and how they may be contributing to changing personal relationships. This is the subject matter of Chapter 8. Evidence suggests that however small the numbers of connections generated or revitalised through weak ties online, these contacts online can be enormously significant and even life changing (Wilson et al. 2009).

Mediated intimacies

Having outlined some of the broad features of digitally mediated social connectivity, the preliminary characteristics of social network site interactivity can be identified. I shall highlight these characteristics in turn and follow this with a discussion on how they are approached in the following chapters. First, social network sites are, in the broadest sense, (a) *conducive to sociality*. Social network site use corresponds with a growing significance in (b) the *public display of connectedness*. This connectedness is being expressed predominantly through (c) the model of *friendship*. Digitally mediated personal connections tend to involve (d) a small number of *intimate ties* and (e) draw on an informal, *casual* mode of address. This pattern of social media use amounts to (f) the dominance of a *personalised discourse*. Patterns of use also confirm that social network site engagement, alongside all social media, is becoming (g) *embedded* in everyday life. We find that online contacts are largely composed of (h) *pre-existing offline relationships* and related to the way the software is designed, they tend to foster (i) *consequential* or meaningful ties. Finally, social network sites offer the technical affordances to generate and sustain (j) extensive non-personal, *weak* or latent ties.

Engagement with multiple channels of communication – from text messages to social network sites – confirms this pervasiveness and the mediated nature of *all* contemporary personal ties (Madianou and Miller 2012). It indicates the need for a theoretical framework to explain mediated personal relationships, that is, the interconnections between the technical and emotional dimensions of social media in the formation of present-day personal ties. Digitally mediated networks can be approached as 'mediated intimacies'. I use the term *mediated intimacies* to develop a framework to explain the distinctive ways in which new media technologies are being engaged with to sustain personal connections and to understand the nature of these connections. I use the term 'intimacy' in a broader sense than sexual, romantic or familial relationships to include wider ties of friendship (see Chapter 3). In the context of social network sites, *mediated intimacies* configure and are framed within 'networked public culture' (boyd 2007, 2011).

The term 'networked public' is drawn on in the following chapters to describe some of the key ways mediated intimacies are being publicised through social network site engagement. I use the term *'personalised* public networks' to explain the nature of digitally mediated intimacies. The following chapters explore the ways that personal relationships are being *mediated* through digital communication technologies and how media platforms, in particular social network sites, are being *socialised*: that is, the way these technologies are engaged with and become embedded in our everyday lives. This is focused on first in Chapter 2 by examining the distinctive attributes and affordances of the digital mediums that help cultivate an affiliation between technical and emotional dimensions of personal communication as *mediated* interaction. Further characteristics of mediated intimacy are identified in the following chapters and analysed towards a theory of mediated intimacy in Chapter 9.

Approach and overview of chapters

Digitally mediated social relationships are investigated through a series of social and cultural contexts which form the core themes that structure this book. The first part of the book explores relevant theories of mediated technologies and theories of changing intimacies and friendship. How personal connections are being articulated through social media engagement is examined in the second part of the book through a group of five chapters that address key frameworks or contexts of association: the self, youth, families, dating and social capital. These frameworks help to identify the major roles played by social media in transforming personal life. The final chapter identifies the principal features of mediated intimacy. It explores the constitutive features of mediated self and, finally, looks at some of the implications of locating mediated intimacies within commercial frameworks.

Chapter 2 begins by confirming that personal relationships no longer depend on one kind of technology but on a *plurality* of media and examines the implications of this dramatic change. I draw on Madianou and Miller's concept of 'polymedia' which describes this integrated media environment. Polymedia offers 'proliferating communicative opportunities' (Madianou and Miller 2012: 8). This new polymedia environment has led to a major change in modes of interaction from a situation in which the technology dominates to one in which people have a sense of *agency* over the technologies. The concept of polymedia highlights the technological choices offered by social media and the cultural and moral processes involved in the myriad of individual ways of conducting relationships such as through text messaging, Skype, email and Facebook. They describe these new dynamics as a *re-socialisation* of media.

This re-socialisation of media constitutes a significant transformation in the moral framework of personal communication. More personal choice is generated by the multiplication of communication technologies, their convergence (as exemplified through social network sites and smartphones) and the drop in the price of the technologies. The growing diversity of these technologies implies growing control over our interactions. Chapter 2 explains that the choice of medium involves important social and moral questions and not just technical or economic considerations. This choice then becomes a moral issue about the appropriateness of the medium, particularly for dealing with relationship break-ups and family-based misunderstandings (Gershon 2010; Madianou and Miller 2012). Chapter 2 therefore highlights the importance of the concept of mediation (Silverstone 2005) to explain the diversity and complexity of the emotional changes that media sustain. Social media constitute and express the relationships developed in the context of intimacy and friendship. Importantly, these digital technologies of communication offer choice and agency, promoting a discourse and sense of expressive purpose.

The question is why the concept of *friendship* has been adopted to describe this new personalised discourse, and what are the implications for personal life? This is the subject matter of the third chapter. It is tempting to use a media-centric argument and suggest that the nature of the transformation of friendship is being led by the technology, for example by the design of websites and profile pages. Chapter 3 addresses relevant debates about changing intimacies and personal relationships in order to identify the key social trends that precede and therefore underpin aspirations towards the more fluid and more intense personal ties being expressed through social media. It explains how 'friendship' informs the digital era. 'Friendship' has become a key trope in the cultural imaginary during late modernity.

'Intimacy' has emerged as a key area of academic interest in sociology and cultural studies but has generally been situated in the field of family studies. Chapter 3 argues that interpersonal democratisation is ascendant and that, as part of this trend, friendship has grown into a centrally valued relationship that epitomises individual agency and choice. Drawing on Giddens (1992), we can suggest that today's technologically mediated relationships coincide with the quest for choice, equality and emotional disclosure. More informal relationships based on non-hierarchical relationships are being sought after. Social network sites support a new, mediated intimacy which draws on friendship not only to reflect the more flexible and informal qualities of contemporary personal interactions but also to confirm a sense of agency in the use of the technology.

The nature of changing relationships is explored by drawing on the concept of 'personal communities' (Spencer and Pahl 2006) and 'networked publics' (boyd 2011). The *ideal* of friendship is a relationship no longer defined by or confined to ties of duty, but entered into voluntarily in a situation of mutual benefit or well-being. Friendship has extended from a term that describes personal and intimate to include 'network' and 'community'. As such it becomes a slippery concept that can mean many things to many people. As well as being so appealing in the context of social network sites, it feeds into negative debates about fragmentation and moral panics about the superficial nature of relationships, 'too much sharing' in the sense of disclosing too much personal information and eroding the nature of the private and the personal. The following chapters explore these issues.

Chapter 4 addresses self-presentations online by examining the management of self-presentation and the construction of mediated personal identities. It draws on symbolic interactionism to explain the interactive nature of the mediated self, and the challenges of managing the reshaping of public and private boundaries in expressions of self-identity. Following Nikolas Rose (1996, 1999), I argue that the careful management of self-identity required on social network sites can be interpreted as a form of governmentality and self-regulation. Chapter 5 examines the ways social media are used by teenagers to develop and maintain friendships and manage peer networks. It draws on a range of ethnographic studies by Mizuko Ito and colleagues (2010) and also group discussions I held with a small cohort of A-level students aged 17 to 18 in the North East England. The chapter also makes use of a range of survey findings of social media use by young people in the United States and Europe. It shows how teenagers are creating networked publics through social media and how social media are transforming the nature and meanings of friendship for young people. The chapter on home, families and new media (Chapter 6) examines the role that social media plays in sustaining family bonds with a focus on changing meanings of home and changing parent–child relationships. The chapter explains that the relationship between the home and the outside world is transforming in addition to the changes in family dynamics occurring within the home. A variety of strategies are used by parents in attempting to control their children's use of social media and to foster family identities. How social media are used to maintain personal communication between members of transnational families is also addressed with a focus on the combined uses of social media to control the communication process (Madianou and Miller 2012).

Chapter 7 on digital dating begins by examining the way young people use social media for initiating and ending romantic relationships and how they handle mediated break-ups. It also investigates the role of dating forums and social network sites in fostering offline relationships among adults. Patterns of self-presentation and issues of choice and agency are explored in the context of disembodied intimacies. Chapter 8 on virtual communities and weak ties considers the ways in which the concept of 'community' has been used to express mediated networks and asks whether communities are actually being created on social network sites in the context of personalised network publics. This is followed by an assessment of research on the ways in which social network site use may generate bonding and bridging social capital.

The final chapter draws together the key debates in this book to develop a theory of mediated intimacies. It identifies the key features of today's mediated personal relationships by exploring the social consequences of public displays of intimacy and changing personal communities in relation to transforming notions of 'privacy', 'intimacy' and the 'personal'. The chapter also examines the characteristics of the 'mediated self' by highlighting modes of self-regulation involved in new online self-presentations. The final part of the book explores some of the implications of the framing of mediated intimacies within commercial frameworks. How mediated intimacies and related ties are being moulded by commercial agendas is examined.

2
Technologically Mediated Personal Relationships

Introduction

Although social critics fear that technologically mediated communication is eroding 'genuine' face-to-face relationships, several studies indicate that communication technologies are capable of fostering rich, deeper connections by extending intimate contacts across barriers of distance and time. Media richness theorists have compared 'rich' and 'lean' media (Daft and Lengel 1984) and highlighted the richness and speed of certain communication technologies as mediums for carrying information and conveying emotions (Fulk and Collin-Jarvis 2001). Mediated communication is considered to be 'lean' rather than 'rich' and impedes people's ability to handle interpersonal dimensions of interaction (Walther et al. 1994). Yet some of the 'leanest' text messages can cement intimacies (Baym 2010). The rise of the Internet has therefore also generated optimism about the recovery of a sense of 'community' in an electronic form through social network sites such as Facebook and Twitter. As highlighted in the previous chapter, today's social media are facilitating the *informal* qualities of interactions involving personal ties of friendship and intimacy. This and the following chapters demonstrate the ways in which greater possibilities are opening up for more diverse intimate contacts and leading to a re-appropriation of newly emerging media technologies for personal (rather than specialist and professional) ends.

Two important tendencies become apparent in considering the uses of new media technologies for maintaining social ties. First, all digital media have become both more *personalised* and yet also more *diverse* in their use (Baym 2010). Second, as part of that diversity, digital communication comprises a set of mediated interactions that occur in a complex *multifaceted* media environment. The closer the relationship, the more media platforms or channels are involved in supporting the intimate interaction. Today's communication technologies now provide opportunity for individuals to trace, check on and link up with intimate and loose networks through a range of channels. The recent and wide availability of these digital mediums allows us to keep tabs not only on those who figure strongly in our lives on a daily basis but also on those who have figured strongly in our lives at some point in the past: to know where they are, what their circumstances are and to compare them with our own situation. Importantly, this trend of using multiple channels of communication highlights the mediated nature of *all* contemporary personal ties, indicating the need for a theory of mediated personal relationships.

This chapter addresses the changing relationship between technology and social interaction. It describes the personalisation, diversification and multifaceted nature of today's media in order to explain the implications of these changes for personal relationships. The issues explored here and in the following chapters are not only about the ways personal relationships are being *mediated* but also about the ways that media are being *socialised*: that is, the way these technologies are engaged with and become embedded in our everyday lives. The interconnections between the technical and emotional dimensions of social media in the formation of present-day personal ties are examined. To address these themes, this chapter considers the key concepts and theories that explain how present-day relationships and patterns of connectivity are being mediated and articulated through personal technologies of communication.

The chapter begins by focusing on the multifaceted uses of today's digital media to demonstrate how relationships are mediated through new media technologies in diverse ways. This is approached by examining the distinctive attributes and affordances of each medium that foster an affiliation between technical and emotional dimensions of personal communication as mediated interaction. The second section provides an account of Castell's (2009) concept of mass self-communication to highlight the changing quality of communication and develop the notion of media multiplicity. The third section extends the theme by examining the implications of the polycentrality of media. It explains the concept of 'polymedia' (Madianou and Miller 2012) as an integrated media environment. The final section addresses social and moral questions associated with the rise of this polymediated environment. The following chapter then deals with relevant debates and theories about changing intimacies and personal relationships in order to identify the key social trends that underpin aspirations towards more fluid and more intense personal ties expressed through social media.

Mediated relationships

Until recently, technologically mediated interaction has been treated as a substandard form of communication compared to face-to-face communication. Much research on personal relationships has been driven by the conviction that face-to-face communication is superior to mediated communication. This belief was based on the assumption that mediums such as letters or phone calls have greater potential to generate ambiguities and misunderstandings (Baym 2010). The lack of visual cues and agreed norms for organising interaction in mediated exchanges were thought likely to magnify tensions and disagreements. However, research on the social shaping of media technologies – including how they are domesticated and mediated – indicates that mediated interactions are far more complex than first thought (Madianou and Miller 2012). Refuting the assumption that mediated communication is inferior to face-to-face communication, a range of strategies is now used to express emotion. Emoticons introduced in instant messaging (IM) have, for example, become standardised symbols for conveying emotional cues in text-based types of communication to avoid misunderstandings about tone, mood and attitude (Baym 2010: 60–62)

In addition to each medium becoming more complex and efficient in use through agreed protocols, personal relationships no longer depend on one kind of technology but on a *plurality* of media. As Caroline Haythornthwaite (2005) argues, most present-day relationships are characterised by 'media multiplexity' in the sense that they are conducted through more than one medium. She explains the various uses and combinations of mediums in sustaining relationships, asserting that more media are drawn on to sustain closer, more intimate relationships. The number of media used depends on the strength of the relationship bond. Differences in level and intensity of intimacy evoke different types of digital media use. The drawbacks of each medium can be offset by the use of another, often in combination. This means that each communication medium changes its meaning in relation to some other technology that signifies an alternative (Bolter and Grusin 1999; Haythornthwaite 2005; Madianou and Miller 2012: 8). Information and communication technologies are also creating new pathways of communication between individuals who would not otherwise connect with one another. Baym

(2010) makes the important point that as interpersonal relationships become more intricate and multifaceted, so do the media on which they depend. The more personalised and varied the interaction becomes, the more control we feel we have over our interactions. While it appears to extend our control over the relationship, it also increases our potential interdependence (Baym 2010).

Hutchby's (2001) theory of *affordances* identifies the specific functions, attributes and opportunities offered by particular mediums. It conveys the potential for action enabled by a social technology or environment. The term 'affordances' is used to capture the qualities of the medium to understand how the various mediums interact and complement one another when used, that is, how they operate as an integrated communicative framework. The concept of affordances was initially developed in work on visual perception (Gibson 1979) and has since been employed to analyse a broader range of texts, social technologies and social settings (e.g. Fayard and Weeks 2007; Graves 2007; Hutchby 2001). Each medium takes on a position and role in relation to the properties of other media that coexist with it. This approach offers a basis for determining the features of social media that enable personal communication and group interactivity to occur.

Importantly, each channel of communication has a distinctive set of attributes that corresponds with or lends itself to a particular mode of expression or emotional register. This is illustrated by Broadbent (2011), who found that these technological attributes can cultivate or enhance various aspects of social connectivity. People are selecting mediums according to the nature of the message being communicated at the time. For example, the fixed, landline phone has a more public quality. It is 'the collective channel, a shared organisational tool, with most calls made in 'public' because they are relevant to the other members of the household'.[1] Mobile calls tend to be devoted to last-minute planning or to organise travel and meetings, when used by adults. Texting is different again. It is used for 'intimacy, emotions and efficiency'.[2] Email is used not only for administration but also for the exchange of photos, documents and music. Interestingly, in a study of students' attitudes towards online relationship break-ups, Ilana Gershon (2010) noted differences in attitudes to email as a medium according to age. Older people consider email to be informal whereas Gershon's students perceive this medium to be rather formal, sharing the attributes of a letter in contrast to the more casual media young people regularly use, such as texting, mobile phoning and social network site use. This was confirmed by the students I spoke to in North East

England. Social network sites not only contain the potential for vast numbers of contacts but they also facilitate the *informal* nature of inter-actions as an effective and simple way for close friends to keep in contact with one another. IM and voice-over-Internet calls are valued as continuous channels in the sense that they can remain open, in the background, while users are engaged in other activities. As Broadbent states, 'Each communication channel is performing an increasingly dif-ferent function'.[3] When used in relation to one another, these differing affordances can be juggled to match the nature and changing dynamics of the relationship.

Highlighting the distinctions in attributes of media channels, Madianou and Miller emphasise that old and new media forms have differing affordances and dynamics including interactivity, temporal-ity, materiality and storage, replicability, mobility, public/private, social cues and information size. Thus, each communication medium organ-ises communication in differing ways according to social circumstances: 'For example, there is something qualitatively different about commu-nicating though webcam, using Skype, compared to email or phone call. It is perfect for helping kids with home work yet not very good for expressing love' (Madianou and Miller 2012: 14). These distinctions in the attributes of media channels confirm the relational media struc-ture proposed by Madianou and Miller. Building on Haythornthwaite's notion of media multiplexity, they argue that individual media forms are increasingly being defined as *relational* within a wider structure of 'polymedia' (2012: 137). As Madianou and Miller put it:

> Relationships, increasingly, do not depend on one particular technol-ogy, but on a plurality of media which supplement each other and can help overcome the shortcomings of a particular medium. People can take advantage of these different communicative opportunities in order to control the relationship.
>
> (Madianou and Miller 2012: 8)

A feature of this relational media structure is the distinction between 'synchronous' and 'asynchronous' channels of communication. Syn-chronous communication channels are being used increasingly for intimate contact because they involve the voice and therefore require more personal attention than other mediums. Voice communication such as telephone, Skype and SMS signify intimacy. Broadbent (2011) found that regular users of Skype consistently call the same two people. When using these synchronous and mainly voice-based mediums, we tend to negotiate the call in advance because this medium is so intimate that it entails careful relationship management. In the past, when there were no other channels apart from letters, phone call interruption was tolerated much more. In today's polymedia environment, the *unplanned* phone call is potentially intrusive. It becomes a fairly high commitment activity to request a person's immediate attention. It involves close concentration on the person being contacted and signifies the high level of importance of that person in one's life. It implies that the caller's attention is going to be reciprocated or that the seeker of the called person's attention is of a lower status. For these reasons, voice-based mediums of communication are usually dedicated to intimate exchange or exchange with individuals for whom potential status problems have been resolved (Broadbent 2011).

By contrast, Broadbent explains that asynchronous channels are more discreet. They can be employed for larger numbers of wider and weaker, or looser types of contact. These mediums usually entail the written form such as email rather than voice. However, there are significant differences within asynchronous channels. Compared with social network site use, emails tend to be used for more pressing or serious professional, private correspondence such as semi-administrative activities at home (reservations, communication with institutions – schools, associations and so on). But outside the work context, the email remains the channel for sending attachments, including private photos as well as jokes and exchange of PowerPoint themes. Among adults, personal emails imply a mutual commitment: an expectation and moral obligation to respond. Broadbent argues that the more intimate and dyadic the relationship, the more likely the communicators will reflect this by moving in sequence from landline to mobile phone to text and then finally to IM, with each type of communication seen as more intimate than the last in terms of progression. However, asynchronous personal mediums of communication such as text messaging and social network site use transcend this synchronous–asynchronous, intimate/less intimate dichotomy. These mediums are highly flexible and unstable channels which can be used for both deeply intimate communication and factual communication for organising events and meetings (Gershon 2010).

An important quality of social network sites which ensures the medium's popularity and its influence on social interactions is that its technological affordances allow it to be used in a manner that cuts right across the synchronous–asynchronous divide: between apparently 'intimate' and 'non-intimate' technologies. As mentioned in Chapter 1, social network site communication embraces several former mediums including email, text message and IM (see Jenkins 2006). The converged mediated experience is exemplified by the multifaceted affordances of social media that facilitate links to Youtube video, blogs and Twitter and the possibility of sending links from Internet-enabled phone to social network sites.

Depending on website design and technical features, channels such as Facebook, MySpace and Cyworld can be highly efficient at facilitating closer and more intimate communication. Indeed, Broadbent points out that in terms of their affordances, asynchronous channels such as Facebook appear particularly considerate and unobtrusive. They do not demand a person's immediate attention. The person being contacted is not obliged to reply and is not immediately interrupted in the way that they might be by a ringing phone. However, if the person contacted does respond soon, it can be interpreted as a gift (Broadbent 2011). Conversely, there is a risk that the response may be ignored and rebuffed as trivial. A great appeal of this medium, then, is that it seems to be unobtrusive and can foster a strong sense of personal control over the technology in a way that immediate synchronous mediums of communication rule out. Broadbent explains that this is why people often give out their Facebook address to others more readily than their email address. Yet, as detailed in Chapter 7 on Internet dating, the News Feed feature can be especially intrusive and distressing such as when someone is struggling to cope with a relationship break-up and discovers that their ex-partner has changed their relationship status overnight and posted details and photos of their new partner on News Feed to celebrate a new relationship (see Gershon 2010). These details provide important insights into the various affordances and attributes of personal communication mediums.

Mass self-communication

However, the multifaceted nature of social media means that it is not simply a *personal* medium since it contains a public dimension. Castells (2009: 55) reminds us that the multiplicity of the medium highlights the scope of the process of contemporary digital communication which involves enhanced personal power. He explains that three modes of communication coexist in this context: interpersonal communication, mass communication and mass self-communication. Castells defines *interpersonal communication* as distinctive from mass communication in the sense that the designated sender(s) and receivers(s) are the subjects of communication. Interpersonal communication is interactive since the message is sent from one to one with feedback loops. In *mass communication*, which is traditionally one-directional sent from one source to many receivers, 'the content of communication has the potential to be diffused to society at large'. It has the capability of reaching a global audience, for example through the posting of a video on Youtube or a blog with RSS feeds to a range of web sources or a message to a massive email list. *Self-communication* indicates that the message is self-generated, the potential receiver(s) is self-directed and the electronic retrieval is self-directed. Mass self-communication combines these features of mass communication and self-communication. Castells (2009: 55) states:

> The three forms of communication (interpersonal, mass communication, and mass self-communication coexist, interact, and complement each other rather than substituting for one another. What is historically novel, with considerable consequences for social organization and cultural change, is the articulation of all forms of communication into a composite, interactive, digital hypertext that includes, mixes, and recombines *in their diversity* the whole range of cultural expressions conveyed by human interaction.

These three modes of communication and the inherent multiplexity of digital media can be exemplified by the modes of social media engagement during what were labelled the 'Blackberry Riots' in Britain. These riots of 2011 demonstrate in a striking way how social media alters the scale and pace of mobilising social networks through the use of interpersonal mobile media to initiate collective action. In August 2011, angry crowds gathered outside London's Tottenham High Road police station, demanding an explanation for the police killing of an unarmed local black man, Mark Duggan. Riots spread rapidly across London and other major UK cities over five days. The initial *online* gathering of people who grieved Duggan's death occurred on Facebook a few hours after the first public show of protest at the police station. *Guardian* journalist Josh Halliday related the following:

> At 10.45pm, when rioters set a double decker bus alight, the page posted: "Please upload any pictures or videos you may have from tonight in Tottenham. Share it with people to send the message out as to why this has blown into a riot."

(Halliday 2011a)

The Facebook page soon attracted thousands of followers. Halliday further commented:

> ...if there was any sign that a peaceful protest would escalate, it wasn't to be found on Facebook. Twitter was slightly more indicative: tweets about an attempt to target Sunday's Hackney Carnival were spotted by police and the event was abruptly cancelled.

The most powerful and immediate communication method for rallying people occurred on the BlackBerry Messenger (BBM) service which allowed users to send messages, free of charge, to all their contacts simultaneously and instantly in order to draw them to particular geographical urban locations. Twitter was used mainly to spread or deny rumours during the riots. However, unlike Twitter or Facebook, many BBM messages are encrypted and undetectable by the authorities. These mediums were activated as modes of mass self-communication and used in various combinations in this context of media multiplexity.

The police attempted to track communications over the Internet and mobile phones used during the riots. They arrested several people on suspicion of encouraging rioting via social media. Social media became the focal point of public debate in relation to the unrest. For example, an article entitled 'The Blackberry Riots' in *The Economist* (2011) suggested that BlackBerry's encrypted messenger service on handsets was a significant cause of the riots: 'used to summon mobs to particular venues'. The focus on social media prompted Member of Parliament for Tottenham David Lammy to call for BBM to be suspended. It was a view held by many journalists and politicians in the aftermath of the disturbances. Britain's Prime Minister, David Cameron, recommended disconnecting the BBM service to prevent further violence. This new context of media multiplexity involving mass self-communication created profound alarm among authorities and social commentators alike.

However, despite widespread looting and arson, it soon became apparent that a decision to digitally 'disconnect' potential rioters would signify a dramatic change in Britain's Internet policy. Twitter refused to close the accounts of suspected rioters. Free speech advocates accused the government of ushering in a new wave of online censorship. Jim Killock, executive director of online advocacy organisation Open Rights Group, argued that the prime minister risked attacking the 'fundamental' right of free speech. He stated that 'Citizens also have the right to secure communications. Business, politics and free speech relies on security and privacy. David Cameron must be careful not to attack these fundamental needs because of concerns about the actions of a small minority' (quoted in Halliday 2011b).

Academic analyses of the 2011 events have been addressing not only the role of urban street gangs; issues of gender, racialisation and resentment of the police; and government policy but also the significant role of new media technology: the mobilisation, resistance and surveillance of social media and the post-riot rhetoric and profiling of the 2011 rioters (see Briggs 2012). The relationship between the emotional role of Facebook in collectively mourning the death of Mark Duggan and the role of mobile technologies to gather people to particular geographical locations either in revenge or for other reasons raises key questions. Of relevance here is how media multiplexity is exercised through the crossing of personal and public boundaries for mobilising mass sentiments and the creation of public networks through mass self-communication. Stephanie Alice Baker (2011) refers to 'mediated crowd membership' to highlight the mediated process by which people came together to join the disturbances. The digitalisation of social life has rendered 'public space more dynamic' (Baker 2011).

Importantly, the technical affordance of instantly mass mobilising multiple social contacts through multiple mediums thrusts *all* social media technology under a political spotlight. Whether used for personal or collective purposes, social media is now marked out by governments as a potentially dangerous and criminal tool of unrest and political resistance, as exemplified not only by the 2011 riots but also by the 'Arab Spring'. During the 2011 uprising in Egypt, the government instituted a widespread shutdown of communication tools to isolate dissent (Dunn 2011). Studies of the relationship between social media technologies and political resistance (such as the Arab Uprising of 2011), on the one hand, and social media and democracy (such as the 2008 Obama presidential campaign), on the other hand, indicate the growing importance of social media for civic engagement at several levels (see for example, Castells 2009; Lievrouw 2011; Loader and Mercea 2012; Papacharissi 2010; Seib 2011; Smith 2008[4]).

While themes of civic political engagement are outside the scope of a book on mediated intimacies and friendship, the 2011 riots and other forms of social unrest suggest that personal and localised networks can be instantly transformed through mass self-communication into *public networks*. They are generating major debates in political communication and raise questions about how the personal and individuated nature of social media use change social interaction and the so-called private sphere (Papacharissi 2010) and how they *feed into* today's modes of democratic engagement. Not only do the 2011 riots exemplify the multiplicity of mediums and the potential of mass self-communication. They also point to the potential for a *personal register* to be used effectively to communicate public agendas (Papacharissi 2010). Nevertheless, the personalised nature of the content offered by social media and the ability to be private and privately public (Papacharissi 2009) emphasises the self and personhood over citizenship (Fenton 2012).

Polymedia

While the term 'multimedia' describes the simultaneous and amalgamated use of different media platforms, it usually simply highlights the various channels and their ranking. By contrast, Castells' three forms of communication – interpersonal, mass communication and mass self-communication – attempt to build on the enhanced power of the individual generated through media multiplexity. Likewise, Madianou and Miller (2012: 8) describe and develop this idea of multiplexity by emphasising the polycentrality of media. For Madianou and Miller, 'polymedia' is an integrated media environment described as 'the emerging environment of proliferating communicative opportunities'. They argue that the escalation of diverse media corresponds to changes in their pricing arrangement and in users' media literacy. These, in turn, transform people's dealings with and relationships to media. Whereas price and availability influenced decisions about media use in the past, the digital era of polymedia socialises media, according to Madianou and Miller. This shift has prompted a significant change in the conceptualisation of 'mediation'.

In studying the use of different media technologies for sustaining long-distance intimacy among transnational families, Madianou and Miller (2012: 137) identified three conditions for the rise of polymedia. The first condition is the need for accessibility to a wide range of choices, with at least six media to choose from that their household can afford (email, Skype, social network site, mobile phone, texting, landline phone, letter, cassette tapes). Second, users must have the skills to handle the newer, digital media. A third condition is that the main costs should not involve the cost of individual communication but should comprise infrastructural costs such as the initial outlay for hardware and Internet connection cost. However, this new environment of multi-communicative potential is not necessarily available to all social groups in all communities and geographical locations since it depends on access to several media. Nevertheless it represents a dramatic change in the way that technologies *mediate* relationships. For example, in many developing countries such as India, the Philippines and in African nations, governments have made a significant investment in Internet and mobile phone infrastructures as a fundamental dimension of economic development (Castells et al. 2006).

The combination of different media represents, then, a new communicative environment with each medium defined in relation to the other media. The selection of media from a wide range of options has the potential to generate a range of contexts for relationships and differing social and emotional outcomes for the participants. The issue is no longer about treating the channels as discrete mediums but of looking at the impact of polymedia as a whole. This is particularly important in terms of the attributes of (a) convergence of old and new media and (b) mobility of the medium, such as smart phone. Each medium is judged according to how its affordances differ from other media, confirming the relational structures of media. The communication experience addresses personal moods and self-identities as reflexive, mobile and performative (Fenton 2012). Highlighting the importance of personal agency involved, Madianou and Miller (2012: 137) state:

> One of the key attributes of polymedia is that it shifts the power relationship from one in which the agency of the technology is often paramount towards one in which people have regained much of their *control over the technologies*, because they now have alternatives (my emphasis).

As more communication technologies proliferate, the less influential and significant selected mediums become as an underlying factor of a relationship. In a situation of polymedia, there are new association choices that range from media and cultural, moral, social and individual decisions about conducting relationships.

Media socialisation

The notion of polymedia foregrounds the way media are *socialised* by drawing on several traditions. As Madianou and Miller (2012) explain, debates about the socialisation of media are founded on scholarship about domestication of information communication technologies (ICTs) (Berker et al. 2006; Miller and Slater 2000; Silverstone and Hirsch 1992) and the theory of mediation (Chouliaraki 2006; Couldry 2008;

Livingstone 2009b; Silverstone 2005). Mediation is a dialectical notion which describes the diversity and complexity of social transformations to which media give rise. Social media come to support and represent relationships developed in the context of intimacy and friendship. The expansion of multiple media platforms and rise of a polymedia environment shift the situation from one in which the technology dominates to one in which people have a sense of agency over media technologies. This leads to a *re-socialisation* of media (Madianou and Miller 2012). The notion of 'social affordances' corresponds with the 'social shaping of technologies' approach (Mackenzie and Wajcman 1999) to highlight the reciprocal attributes of technology and society particularly for mediated communication. But as Madianou and Miller argue, in polymedia contexts the 'domestication' of the various mediums is significant because technologies are shaped and cultivated through their consumption and use (see Berker et al. 2006; Silverstone and Hirsch 1992). From Skype to social network sites, digital technologies of personal communication are integrated into and, in turn, shape social interactions.

This theme of the social shaping and domestication or socialisation of technology is highlighted in Chapter 6 on media engagement among families and in the home. It describes how social media engagement by parents and children is shaped and negotiated in the domestic context. By applying the social shaping and domestication of technologies approach to interpersonal communication, Madianou and Miller argue that 'mediation provides for a more dialectical sense of the tension between the technical and the emotional' (2012: 142). They also emphasise the importance of media competence and skill in using digital media, in particular, by children and family members (Livingstone 2004).

Debates about media convergence also contribute to an understanding of polymedia. Research about media convergence in the communications and information technology industries shows that the original functions and attributes of certain media can change dramatically by using them in various new combinations: through intersection and hybridisation (Jenkins 2006). Of relevance in this respect are studies that focus on communication between family members and how media convergence has affected families (e.g. Little et al. 2009; see Chapter 6). For instance, social network sites are important examples of media convergence since their use is extending from computing to smart phone platforms (Miller 2011). As such, this medium affords intimate communication as a key feature of engagement, as shown in the following chapters. Convergence also underlines the ways individuals manipulate the media technology in various combinations. Among transnational families who are separated through migration, relatives may text each other to arrange a Skype exchange, send them photos uploaded and sent by email and/or follow family members' day-to-day activities on Facebook (Madiannou and Miller 2012; discussed further, below). In these ways, families and friends who keep in touch across great distances are facilitated by a thoroughly converged media experience.

The concept of *mediation*, as both social and technological sets of practices, allows us to move beyond a technologically deterministic account of social media while acknowledging the combined roles of both technology and social practices in shaping people's relationships (Bakardjieva 2005). Mediation draws attention to the ways in which the affordances and constraints of the mediums influence both the message and the relation between sender and receiver (Hjarvard 2006; Livingstone 2008). Jay Bolter and Richard Grusin (1999) use the notion of *remediation* to explain that the social customs and processes surrounding the use of newer media need to be understood in relation to people's past and present uses of old media (such as landline phones and television). Drawing on the concept of remediation, Gershon (2010: 110) asserts that the socially constructed nature of a new medium is exposed precisely during the phase when etiquettes of engagement are not yet established and are hotly debated – for example, when a person is communicating the ending of an intimate, romantic relationship by text or on Facebook (see Chapter 7).

In their study of how migrant workers in the United Kingdom sustain personal communication with their families in the Philippines, Madianou and Miller (2012) examine the role of different communication mediums for sustaining intimate contact between absent working mothers and their children. The research offers insights into absent 'mothering' in the age of digital media. Mothering is both an experience and normative concept that implies a condition of co-presence. Given the mediation of parenting over great distances through social media interaction, important questions are raised about the social relationship of parenting and the role of technology as mediator. The distinctive qualities of each communication medium can be used to negotiate the familial relationship. In order to avoid an altercation, the adolescent child who is seeking more independence may choose to send an email instead of phoning his or her mother to avoid scrutiny. The multiple media allow relationships to be handled by creating an ideal distance in order to develop a *pure relationship*, one in which the power relations change so that the child can feel a sense of equality (see Chapter 3). In these ways, users of polymedia are able to surmount the limitations of individual mediums through media convergence and the selection of mediums according to their particular qualities in order to manage and fulfil the purpose of their mediated exchange. Madianou and Miller explain that, rather than simply focusing on the individual qualities of each medium in isolation, the idea of 'polymedia' allows us to consider the various ways that different ICTs can be operated or manoeuvred for their emotional and social qualities.

The level of agency of users of communication channels in a polymedia environment is also borne out by the conclusions of a series of studies by Baym and colleagues. Studies of the extent of use of the Internet by 496 college students in their social circles found that the type of medium used had little bearing on the quality or closeness of their relationships (Baym et al. 2007). Particular communication channels were preferred for personal communication and determined by the level of intimacy of the connection but *mediation* did not necessarily enhance or reduce relational fulfilment and intimacy. The most influential predictor of the quality of an interaction turned out to be the type of relationship. The telephone was viewed as equivalent to face-to-face conversation in terms of quality. Online interaction (mainly email) was perceived to be of slightly lower quality, but the differences were very small (Baym et al. 2004). Those individuals in close relationships had high-quality interactions regardless of the medium through which they interacted. This suggests that students are selecting and manipulating the various available mediums to suit their types of relationships in a polymedia setting. It demonstrates a symbiotic relationship between the technology and the personal relationship in the sense that they mutually reinforce each other.

In a related study, in which 51 students kept a diary of their voluntary social interactions, it was found that 64 per cent conducted interactions face-to-face, on the phone and online (Baym et al. 2004). Although there were almost as many Internet interactions as there were phone exchanges, most connections were face-to-face. This complements earlier research findings which demonstrate that the Internet is used on a par with the telephone in intimate relationships (Dimmick et al. 2000; Flanagin and Metzger 2001). It suggests that, as a consequence of the affordances of personal communication on the Internet, distinctions between synchronous and asynchronous communication are important but not primary factors. Other affordances come into play in a polymediated environment.

A further study of the variety of media used by friendship pairs on Last.fm[5] (Baym and Ledbetter 2009) found that while a third interacted with one another only on Last.fm, most pairs used between two and three other ways of interacting with one another. Many of the pairs additionally made use of IM (42 per cent), other websites (34.7 per cent) and email (31.3 per cent). A third of pairs also interacted face-to-face. This confirms that a wide range of media is being used to sustain friendships. Baym et al. (2007: 18) state:

> Hence, rather than replacing, revolutionizing, or reversing the impacts of other interpersonal communication modes, communication technologies may be appropriated to supplement these means of meeting the goals of personal relationships (Katz & Rice, 2002; Kavanaugh & Patterson, 2002). In general, our study demonstrates the importance of contextualizing communication technologies vis-à-vis more traditional means of accomplishing the same ends.
>
> (Baym et al. 2007)

People maintain meaningful personal relationships online and, importantly, the online medium is employed as part of a multiple media framework by being used as part of an intricate range of other modes personal communication that involve synchronous, asynchronous and face-to-face modes of interaction. The concept of polymedia captures this tendency of emphasising choice and agency in combining mediums.

Moral imperatives

This re-socialisation of media constitutes a major transformation in the moral framework of personal communication. Since the multiplication and convergence of communication technologies lead to more choice, the act of deciding the medium through which to communicate increasingly involves *social* and *moral* questions rather than just technical or economic considerations. The feeling of participation within the communication experience seems to offer a sense of control that sustains emotional involvement (Donath 2007) through a shared understanding of the conduct and protocols that frame the network. In a situation where the cost or other outside forces no longer determine the selection of medium, this choice becomes a moral evaluation about the suitability of the medium (Gershon 2010; Madianou and Miller 2012). In these ways, media are configured by the demands of a particular culture or

social situation such as migration and by particular kinds of relationship, whether friendship, family or between young people, and whether
starting or ending a relationship.

These moral imperatives are brought to the fore by Gershon (2010)
in her exploration of the way young people end relationships. Young
people who dump their girlfriends or boyfriends are increasingly held
responsible for choosing inappropriate media to convey the information. Synchronous modes of communication such as phone, Skype or
face-to-face are regarded as morally acceptable while texting or using
Facebook for ending a relationship is viewed as morally reprehensible
(see Chapter 7). In her work on media love, Gershon uses the term
'idioms of practice' to explain the lack of shared norms around the uses
of certain new media technologies. Gershon describes a woman who, in
the act of being dumped by her boyfriend through a text message, felt
almost relieved to have the boyfriend's lack of worthiness confirmed.
The implication is that in conditions of 'polymedia', with a choice
of multiple media forms of communication, the selection of media is
perceived as a moral act to be judged.

In the context of breaking up, the question of morality is framed by
issues of power, humiliation, sensitivity and emotion. It also reflects the
lack of norms for both guiding choices about which medium to use and
the assumptions to be made by receivers of messages about what the
communicator *means* by these choices. To explain the preferences or
idioms of practice that people have for certain mediums over others,
Gershon (2010) refers to the term 'media ideologies'. Media ideologies
comprise 'a set of beliefs about communicative technologies with which
users and designers explain perceived media structure and meaning'
(Gershon 2010: 3). Understanding these ideologies provides a critical
way to gain an insight into technology use. The notion of individual
media ideologies reflects people's preferences for the various attributes
and affordances of various mediums, depending on the quality, phase
and intensity of the particular relationship. Thus, for example, some
people prefer email because it is less disruptive and intrusive than calling someone on the mobile phone. Others find the very interactivity
and synchronicity of the mobile phone to be the appealing quality of
the medium.

As Gershon argues, the differing ideologies about a medium's qualities
and attributes drawn on by users can provoke confusions and resent-
ments. In the British press in 2012, Prime Minister David Cameron was
both ridiculed and condemned for frequently using what is considered
an intimate channel – texting – to communicate with Rebekah Brooks,

formerly chief executive of News International. He was also scorned for using and misinterpreting the shorthand term 'LOL' (laugh out loud) in his messages to her, which Brooks admitted he thought stood for 'lots of love'. This was during the run-up to the Leveson inquiry (2011–2012), a public inquiry into the culture, practices and ethics of the British press following the News International hacking scandal. It was during a time when Cameron was expected to show a sense of professional distance from Brooks who was subsequently charged with conspiring to hack the phones of more than 600 people. Cameron's mobile phone conduct was viewed as inappropriate because it implied the crossing of a professional boundary.

Importantly, then, the polymediated nature of contemporary personal communication means that the focus of analysis needs to shift from the *technological* to the *social* and *moral* implications of media use since the individual is now judged according to which media they select. As we become less and less constrained by price and accessibility, '[T]he choice of media and the combination of various media that is found in the development of any given relationships is itself a major communicative act' (Madianou and Miller 2012: 139). The choice in medium for intimate communication conveys a strong message in itself.

Conclusions

This chapter has addressed a range of approaches that contribute to an understanding of features of diversity and multiple uses of what we can call 'personal media' in a mass self-communication framework. Evidence suggests that the influence of media on personal relationships is being dramatically altered by the advent of complex *multiple media use* in personal settings with the potential for instant, interactive mass communication in public settings. The concepts of media multiplexity and polymedia allow us to focus on the unparalleled diversity and propagation of media and the social consequences of using different mediums in various combinations. The various attributes of the mediums are now more widely accessible to users and have important implications for the reshaping of personal communication. The level of interactivity of each medium, temporality, storage, replicability, mobility, social cues and information capacity are all significant in deciding on the medium to be used to match the particular relationship and mode of interaction. However, wider accessibility to the tools of social media tends to obscure widening social class and racialised gaps between the rich and poor (Thorne 2009).

Notwithstanding issues of access, the polycentrality of media can cater for different emotional registers and thus highlight the social and moral basis of choices about which media to use. For those who do have wide access, these choices can no longer just be blamed on issues of access and affordability. New media are now technologies capable of managing complex emotions and negotiating fundamental ambivalences. However, as polymedia corresponds to a more general re-socialisation of media, the centre of attention extends from the media themselves in terms of their opportunities and limitations, to the moral and social matters that form all relationships. This new polymedia environment therefore highlights issues of power and morality in relationships. The desire to either engage with or avoid certain forms of emotional connection throws up moral dilemmas. People can choose the immediacy of the phone or the delay of email or the playful interaction of texting. Decisions have to be made about how to exploit the major differences in mediums for the various tasks in relationships (Madianou and Miller 2012: 148).

The attributes of these mediums have implications for the reshaping of public and private social boundaries. This chapter has explained that the personalised nature of social media content and the facility of private and privately public communication (Papacharissi 2009) correspond with the idea of mass self-communication developed by Castells (2009). The affordances of social media emphasise the value of *self*-expression. The following chapter explains why friendship has become a model for personal, mediated networking and how this process may be changing the meanings, practices and experiences of intimacy, friendship and networking. Recognising the major role now played by social network sites like such as Facebook in maintaining personal ties, this broadening of the debate about the mediation of personal relationships foregrounds the quintessentially mediated nature of intimacy and friendship and, therefore, the need for a reconsideration of the concept of 'intimacy'.

3
Conceptualising Intimacy and Friendship

Introduction

The relationships being negotiated through today's social media are forcing us to rethink and re-envisage the nature of intimacy, personal connections and wider issues of relatedness. Personal bonds appear to be developing or sustained on new virtual frontiers, no longer originating solely from domestic and familial settings or exclusively located in spatial community boundaries. A reconsideration of debates about intimacy is required in order to understand the mediated nature of today's personal relationships. As Chapter 2 explains, a key change is the shift towards a polymediated environment in which digitalised technologies of communication are becoming more diversified and being combined in various ways to sustain social ties of a personal nature. The emergence of new technologies for connecting people has led to key changes in informal rules and norms governing social contact and encounters. A further trend is the increasingly *informal* and casual nature of the discourse being used across all types of connections to manage contemporary interaction. Whether they are strong, intense and intimate ties or weak ties of acquaintanceship, an informal style is being adopted in many mediated contexts.

The ideal of friendship seems to have particular resonances with social media affordances and modes of engagement, particularly social network sites. For example, the kinds of relationships being articulated on social network sites, such as Facebook, are drawing on and firmly promoting a friendship model. The aim of this chapter is to find answers to the following questions: 'what makes the relationship of 'friendship' so special in contemporary society?' and 'what are the distinctive features of mediated relationships that lend themselves to the articulation and advancement of this friendship model'? The use of 'friendship' to describe a remarkably wide range of relationships online suggests a significant shift in the meanings and conventions of interaction associated with intimacy and personal life in late modern society.

Having outlined some of the key features of social connections online and the ways in which multiple media forms are used in personalised and diverse ways, this chapter examines theories and debates about intimacy and friendship to identify changing meanings and practices and provide a broad conceptual framework for the following chapters. The chapter then addresses boyd's (2011) notion of 'public network cultures' to explain the particular ways in which personal relationships of intimacy and friendship are being articulated through social network sites. The aim is to contribute to an understanding of the transformations being generated by social media, with a focus on social network sites, as contexts for maintaining intimate and wider friendship contacts.

'Intimacy' has traditionally been fixed in the realm of the private and the personal and viewed as physical contact within a sexual discourse, often characterised by romantic or passionate love. More recently, the concept has extended to refer to a wide range of relationships that question the public/private divide, associated with commitment and responsibility. It has been used to embrace wider and more fluid ties of friendship and 'personal communities'. 'Intimacy' has generally been used in contemporary sociology to describe family-like relationships in order to avoid using the term 'family' and to specify or include more fluctuating and flexible associations of affection and care. Intimate behaviour is now acknowledged to include close friends and family as well as passionate and sexual love. For example, Morgan (2011) speaks of 'intimate practices' which can be distinguished from wider family practices through their extension to friends and non-heterosexual partners. However, the recent explosion in social media draws attention to dramatically changing conventions in representations and expressions of intimacy. The increasingly permeable boundaries between close, intimate ties and loose, personal associations on social network sites raise issues not only about the nature of friendship, trust and acquaintanceship but also about the changing relationship between *intimacy* and *privacy*.

Conceptions of intimacy

In Western societies, the notion of intimacy was traditionally associated with the personal, privacy, individualism and the domestic realm and thereby contrasted with civil society, community, the public and public access (Heath 2004). In classical sociology, intimacy was based on exclusivity, where the two individuals reveal their emotions to each other and nobody else (Simmel 1950: 126). Lynn Jamieson (1998) explains that a historical shift in the value of social ties from the emphasis on a sense of 'community' to a sense of 'intimacy' occurred during modernity, leading to a perception of kinship and friendship as corresponding relationships. Kin and friends have been drawn together, as powerful ideals, to be viewed 'as potentially constitutive of a community of people bound by shared sentiments' (Jamieson 1998: 74). However, this shift from notions of the public, the community and the collective to the personal, the private and the intimate has been complicated by the rise of social media. Meanings and practices of intimacy are being reconfigured as they move beyond the 'family' and challenge conventional boundaries between 'private' and 'public'. Conventional dichotomies of public/private that historically governed relationships are now being disrupted and undermined by the articulation of personal relationships through social media technologies such as social network sites (see Chapter 4 for examples in the context of self-presentation online).

This section charts the history of the concept of intimacy to assess how it has shaped an understanding of 'friendship' and changing social ties in general. Jacqui Gabb (2008) has produced a comprehensive study of the concept of intimacy in her book, *Researching Intimacies in Families*. I draw on aspects of her work here to address changes relevant to the study of changing personal connections in relation to social media. Three key stages in the sociological study of intimacy are of relevance here: first, the democratisation of interpersonal relationships, leading to transformations of intimacy; second, chosen or elective intimacies and non-conventional partnerships; third, the friendship paradigm. How social media, such as social network sites, are affecting intimate practices is a fourth stage that then needs to be explored, forming the subject matter of the following chapters.

During the 1970s, 'intimacy' tended to be addressed in the narrow context of family, gender and sexual identity and was uncritically linked with sexuality and sexual/sensual relationships. The focus was initially on the patterning of intimate behaviour through reproduction and parenting. As same-sex relationships, lesbian and gay parenthood were judged as deviant or anomalous; intimacy research was criticised for focusing too heavily on heterosexual couple relationships in this phase (Deegan and Kotarba 1980). However, diversity in the sphere of intimacy is now a familiar theme being investigated by academics.

Transformations in personal life that represent a shift in meanings and practices of intimacy include the rise in single-person households, rising divorce rates, greater physical distances between kin, wider social distances between neighbours corresponding with more privatised and individuated home units and a readiness to include friendship as a major tie of intimacy (Chambers 2006). In the 1980s, intimacy studies extended to the study of gay and lesbian intimacy. Although this remained narrow in its reach, it challenged the overemphasis on marital relationships and heterosexuality (Gabb 2008).

From the 1990s, debates and research widened to address issues of autonomy, equality and emotional interdependence as major influences in the thesis of democratisation. This thesis constituted a foundational principle in contemporary sociology (Giddens 1999; Plummer 2003). Mutual disclosure was identified as a significant formative site for constructions of intimacy and most notably used in the social theorising of Anthony Giddens (1992) and the materialist feminist work of Jamieson (1998). During this period, the ideals of democracy and intimacy were increasingly being linked through the new, popular ethos of mutuality and equality among partners and families (Solomon et al. 2002: 965). Family members would aspire towards intimacy, affection and equality within their relationships by conforming to the principles of openness and honesty (Gillies et al. 2001). This set of concerns then widened beyond family relationships to include work on *friendship* and *community*.

The detraditionalisation of intimacy

Significant changes in intimacy and interpersonal relationships which began to take place in the mid–late twentieth were represented not only by the rise in divorce, more diverse family types and less personal contact with wider kin but also by social aspirations to reshape personal relationships through elective bonds. A detraditionalision of intimacy occurred which was associated with a range of broader social transformations including second-wave feminism and the rise of female autonomy, individualisation and the emphasis on personal autonomy (Beck and Beck-Gernsheim 1995) and postmodernity (Bauman 2000). More fluctuating social attachments becoming commonplace began to draw on and privilege 'friendship' as an important intimate connection. However, by the 1990s, 'friendship' was being reconfigured within new kinds of intimate relationships that emphasised individual agency and choice. Moving beyond the narrow structure and values associated with the heterosexual nuclear family, terms such as 'friends as family', 'families of choice' (Weeks et al. 2001) and 'personal communities' (Pahl and Spencer 2004) were being used to privilege new kinds of connections and living arrangements as close and meaningful bonds within a new discourse on intimacy. These shifts in significations and practices of intimacy were theorised in the 1990s through the theses of detraditionalisation and democratisation advanced by Anthony Giddens (1991, 1992), Ulrich Beck and Elizabeth Beck-Gernsheim (1995, 2002).

Giddens (1992: 3) uses the concept of individualisation to identify and explain how transformations in intimacy correspond with a widespread democratisation of the 'interpersonal domain'. Emphasising the reflexive nature and active agency of individuals, he identifies family and friends as sites for the democratisation of intimate relationships. Individuals are using 'free' choice in the sphere of intimacy by forming and acting on their own personal preferences about friendships, romance, sexual encounters and partnerships. Modern confluent relationships promote companionship and friendship, emphasising *choice* and *compatibility*. Scholars refer to the rise of a new integrity and equality in relationships prompted by the wider choices available, particularly for women. While former interpersonal relationships were configured within a familial and sexual discourse, this new affective choice requires the individual to proactively manage the parameters of their continuously fluctuating intimate landscape.

For Giddens, the individual is now viewed as a 'reflexive subject', someone who is able to create and move within a 'narrative of self' (Giddens 1992: 75). Importantly, individuals are able to effect 'free' choice in the sphere of intimacy through personal options not only about romance, sexual encounters and partnerships but also about friendships (Willmott 2007). The notion of the 'pure relationship' addresses men and women as equals and is based on confluent love: the relationship is based on conditional love, continued as long as both parties are in agreement that the relationship is delivering enough satisfaction to continue (Giddens 1992: 58).The pure relationship forms part of a broad reorganisation of intimacy which supplanted traditional familial ties of obligation in the context of everlasting bonds. The emphasis on choice opens up new, more fluid forms of intimacy including the emergence of new and diverse forms of social dependency based on friendship and 'families of choice' as well as blood relatives and current partners (Roseneil 2000; Weeks et al. 2001).

Moreover, intimate relationships are being judged by a culture of self-fulfilment, supported by therapeutic ideologies. Sexuality is decentred, highlighting the flexible and changeable nature of all modes of intimacy. It opens the way to more flexibility and choice. In late modernity, intimacy is based on *pleasure, autonomy* and *freedom from constraints*. As part of this, a plastic sexuality emerges which functions as a symbol of individual identity and radical sexual choices. This approach establishes the temporary nature of relationships, the conditional nature of commitment and a disconnection of sex from reproduction and family duty. Looser and more transient social ties are now acknowledged as equally significant in the personal lives of individuals. In this way, Giddens makes a major contribution in advancing the idea of interpersonal democratisation.

The democratisation of interpersonal relationships corresponds with the social impulse towards the more informal and diverse types of personal relationships that characterise today's digital social networks. These late modern ideas about transformations of intimacy resonate with aspirations of agency, autonomy, choice and flexibility associated with mediated personal relationships. Drawing on Giddens, we can argue that today's technologically mediated relationships give rise to a new, mediated intimacy which incorporates friendship and reflects the fluid, diverse and informal nature of contemporary personal interactions. The notion of choice and agency corresponds with the characteristics of affordances (Hutchby 2001) associated with the technological potential and attributes of social network sites and the multiplexity and polymediated nature of social media (Hayworthwaite 2005; Madianou and Miller 2012; Chapter 2). Individuality corresponds with the construction of one's personal narrative. As a 'reflexive subject', the individual is able to pursue 'narrative of self' through the technological affordances offered by social network sites in which a profile can be created (see Chapter 4).

In the positive sense used by Giddens, individualisation entails identity, agency, self-actualisation. However, since the foundations to this new approach to intimacy depend on the notion of an erosion of past traditions and democratisation, it has provoked pessimistic responses by social theorists such as Bauman (2001, 2003), Beck and Beck-Gernsheim (1995) and Putnam (2000) who fear a crisis in personal relationships and communities. In its negative sense, used by Beck, Bauman and Putnam, the emphasis is on self-interest. This group of scholars expresses anxieties about social bonds being weakened, ephemeral and lacking in commitment. Bauman refers to more 'liquid' relationships, meaning more fleeting social attachments. These scholars point to the rise of a self-absorbed, individualistic narcissism and social isolation at the individual level and a lack of social responsibility, social cohesion and collapse of community at the societal level. Individualisation and the new, coinciding form of elective intimacy are said to lead to a destabilisation of traditional social relations including a decline in the importance of duty and obligation in family relations. Beck and Beck (1995) claim that new choices have given rise to anxieties over child welfare and the welfare of the elderly. And for Bauman, intimacy in contemporary society arises out of an emotional precariousness leading to a sense of social decline: insecurity, instability and temporariness. The question is whether personal responsibility and collective interests can ever be achieved through individualistic expressions or the quest for self-fulfilment.

Thus, the theses of individualisation and democratisation of relationships in late modernity have generated a deep sense of nervousness and uncertainty about the rise of a new affective fragility within personal relationships. This anxiety is also echoed in relation to social media. Rather than leading to greater participation, there is a fear that social media are destroying human interaction by undermining face-to-face communication and encouraging anti-social, solitary behaviour. As mentioned in the previous chapter, mediated relationships are considered by some scholars to be characterised by 'lean' rather than 'rich' communication, thereby blocking people's ability to handle interpersonal dimensions of interaction (Walther et al. 1994).

Elective intimacy

The democratisation of intimacy thesis allows us to analyse the fluctuating context of online intimacies. However, while a new kind of *elective intimacy* is characterised by equality and mutuality in relationships, it remains a theoretical account of interpersonal democratisation (Jamieson 1998). Aspirations towards interpersonal democratisation may shape personal desires about intimate relationships, but Jamieson (1998: 12) reminds us that there is an acute disjunction between the *aspiration* for choice and equality in disclosing intimacy and the *reality* of today's often confusing and frustrating relationships. There may be a wide gap between people's aspirations and their actual lives.

Lynn Jamieson addresses the emphasis on the notion of 'disclosing intimacy' as a contemporary structuring principle of personal intimacy involving *reciprocity* and *mutuality*. Self-disclosure has become the engine that drives new relationships. This is exemplified by the increasing readiness with which people are prepared to open up and reveal their personal lives. In early stages of relationships, self-disclosure becomes a marker of intimacy as trust: a demonstration of love and affection through shared secrets. The demonstration of love and affection becomes paramount, with friendship and sexual pairs expected to develop *mutual understanding* through 'talking, listening, sharing thought and showing feelings' (Jamieson 1998: 158). Importantly, as the following chapters show, social network sites open up further opportunities for self-disclosure. Thus, today' intimacy contains the following attributes: being no longer authoritative or compulsory, it is comprised of choice, equality and emotional disclosure. While everyday 'family practices' constitute a sense of relatedness and have defined and delineated wider 'intimacies', as Gabb (2008) says, intimacy is now determined and articulated by its *emotional connections* rather than ascribed relations of kin.

In the context of social media, new modes of personal intimacy based on affective and communicative disclosure are identifiable. Social network sites have become an important forum for the disclosure and display of emotions, particularly for the young. These digital media contexts signal the social aspiration for more open relationships. On social network sites, individuals engage in self-disclosure, 'the sharing of inner experiences, mutual self-exploration and the expression of emotional attachment' (Oliker 1998: 20) as powerful signs of intimacy in situations of trust. In this mediated framework, disclosing intimacy functions to distinguish close ties of affection and mutual understanding from weak ties of acquaintanceship. Weak ties can translate into strong ties through stages of gradual self-disclosure through the use of various different social media – from social network sites to texting to mobile or landline phone calls (Baym 2010, see Chapters 5 and 7). Disclosing intimacy acts as a marker that defines authentic friendship and differentiates this relationship from 'artificial' or superficial online friendships.

In this online framework, intimacy as *disclosure* becomes a marker of authentic, *bona fide* intimacy in a broad sense. It performs a symbolic role as an indicator of closeness and trust. This sense of intimacy through disclosure does not preclude rapid fluctuations in friendships. In a situation where 'for ever' is no longer a defining feature of commitment, friendships may be long term or temporary. But while they are active, they are likely to be open and sincere. This new discourse of personalised mediated conversation has generated new regimes of intimacy and truth (Schwartz 2011). New and anonymous audiences are introduced to what were previously defined as intimate situations for the purpose of real-time consultations (boyd 2011). As Schwartz states, intimacy was traditionally based on exclusivity in access to events and information. It is now reconstructed under new conditions as 'network intimacy'. Interpersonal spheres are reshaped.

However, Jamieson reminds us that, within theoretical accounts of democratisation and mutuality, the messiness of everyday lives gets expunged by a lack of understanding of micro-personal worlds. The discourse of disclosing intimacy masks the power relations that operate in interpersonal relationships. Tensions around communication, disclosures, secrecy and surveillance are common (Gillies et al. 2001). As the following chapters indicate, these tensions are exacerbated by social media-generated misuses and misunderstandings, given the moral imperatives now associated with the use of mediums in a polymediated environment (Madianou and Miller 2012). For example, despite parental aspirations to treat children as assumed adults, the desire to protect and control them can lead to an exploitation of disclosed information. This is typified by the excessive online surveillance and even online shadowing or 'stalking' engaged in by anxious parents, jealous partners and ex-partners to check up on children and intimates' social media contacts in a context where deep and less exclusive forms of intimacy can coexist online. Online stalking is particularly common in the context of dating and break-ups, as described in Chapter 7. The affordances of social media and nature of many online intimacies can breach time-honoured conventions of 'privacy' and 'publicity', 'intimate' and 'civil', which in turn lead to deep unease about the accessibility, intensity, speed and reach of online relationships for those who are socially vulnerable.

By emphasising the diversity in emotional intimacy, the democratisation of intimacy thesis has underpinned a related advancement within a 'queer sociology'. The concept of 'friendship' has been highly influential in retheorising personal relationships in relation to 'non-standard intimacies' (Berlant and Warner 2000) and non-conventional partnerships (Budgeon and Roseneil 2004) to emphasise that they have chosen ties and 'elective affinities' (Allan 2008; Beck-Gernsheim 1999; Weeks et al. 2001). Networks of friends and non-resident partnerships are increasingly being cited as a contemporary source and repository of care and intimacy (Roseneil and Budgeon 2004). Friendship is viewed as a central source of consistency and support (Roseneil and Budgeon 2004). Families of choice (Weeks et al. 2001) and 'families we choose' (Weston 1997) or 'friends as family' imply diversity in relationship patterns. These include voluntary affective attachments within which friendship networks can become 'de facto families' (Altman 1982). Central to this friendship ethos is the idea that individuals have the capacity for a much wider range of intimacies than those anchored in a family context (Gabb 2008: 77).

Friendship as personal community

A major advancement in the conceptualisation of intimacy was made at the start of the twenty-first century through studies that confirmed the significance of friendships for personal and social well being. A need was identified to explore broader notions of *personal life* rather than focus narrowly on family-centred couples so as to acknowledge the fluctuating networks of intimates that included neighbours, friends and lovers (Budgeon and Roseneil 2004; Pahl and Spencer 2004; Roseneil and Budgeon 2004; Savage et al. 2005; Spencer and Pahl 2006). This new set of emphases allows us to identify the complexities of relationships of intimacy, friendship, community and acquaintances which are mediated through online connections. With studies now recognising the 'community-like properties' of friendship (Wilkinson 2010: 458), the term 'friendship' is being used to bridge the boundaries between intimate, personal relationships and public, networked community relationships.

The approach to 'friendship' advanced by Spencer and Pahl (2006) highlights the construction of individual networks and 'personal communities' which are relied on for social support and companionship. In their empirical study of family and friendship in the United Kingdom, they identify 'personal communities' as significant dimensions of people's lives, defining them as the 'intimate and active ties with friends, neighbours and workmates, as well as kin' (Pahl and Spencer 2004: 74). They distinguish between 'given' and 'chosen' ties and identify friend-like qualities in the broader sense. Pahl and Spencer found that personal communities entail the interconnection of *chosen* friendship ties with more *compulsory* family ties that involve duty. The 'repertoires' of personal communities can change depending on the ratio of friendship, family and neighbour ties (Pahl and Spencer 2004: 74). These attachments are voluntary and freely chosen within a framework of individualised belonging. Thus, the increasing emphasis is on choice in personal relationships. Yet they also argue that these personal communities have the potential to foster the 'hidden solidarities' needed for social cohesion and support. Their interest is in the role that friendship plays in providing 'a type of social glue' (Pahl and Spencer 2004: 71). In this they also include 'friendship-like relationships'. They explain the meanings of these relationships as individuals' 'micro-social' worlds which are comprised of the range of significant others in our lives. This broadens ideas of intimacy and sociality to allow us to address the social benefits of these new, fluctuating relationships.

Based on the notions of *choice* and level of *commitment*, the boundaries between the categories of 'friend' and 'family' are undergoing suffusion (Pahl and Spencer 2004). Relationships are no longer simply 'given' or 'chosen'. Certain family members are considered to be friends, and friends take on family-like status. Family and friendship ties start to resemble one another by drawing on attributes of commitment and choice. For Pahl and Spencer (2004), the 'repertoires' of an individual's personal community can change depending on the ratio of friendship, family and neighbour ties. Pahl and Spencer do not argue that infinite and unrestrained personal choice operates. Rather, our choice of intimates helps to reshape personal life (Wilkinson 2010: 458).

This stress on choice and agency across contemporary Western societies has negative consequences, according to certain scholars. While certain scholars detect a crisis in personal relationships and society, Spencer and Pahl found little evidence of a decline in the quality of personal and communal life in their empirical research on friendship. By emphasising the importance and enduring nature of friendship ties that contribute to the foundations of social solidarity, Spencer and Pahl (2006) challenge the notion of a 'liquidity' of personal relationships and community expressed by Bauman (2000, 2003, 2007), for example. Their approach provides a counter argument to the pessimistic tenor of sociologists such as Bauman (2001, 2003) and Putnam (2000), who triggered a public discourse about a weakening of social bonds.

Friend-like ties are important and often unacknowledged sources of social support, happiness and well-being. By offering insights into the 'solidarity' of friendship ties, Spencer and Pahl demonstrate that 'friendship' forms a key part of social integration, social capital and the conditions of community. While personal communities now involve greater choice, they are also explained by Spencer and Pahl (2006: 29) as forms of social capital to emphasise the social value of these hidden solidarities and small 'micro-social worlds'. Social capital describes the conditions in which individuals can secure benefits from their membership in groups and networks (see Chapter 8). In terms of personal communities, this works through informal, casual and private forms of social support. Generally, trust and commitment reside alongside duty and obligation where friends are perceived to be family-like and family as friend-like. The implication is that these small circles of micro-social worlds comprise solid and enduring forms of social capital in contemporary society.

The identification of new forms of social cohesion questions the assertion of an alleged lack of commitment and trust in declining personal relationships. Hidden solidarities and the dynamics of friendship that socially cement the fabric of society are effectively brought to the fore of concerns about intimacy and new social ties (see Chapter 8 on social capital). Pahl and Spencer are not arguing that friends are becoming *more* important than family and wider kin during late modernity but that family and friendship are converging, in terms of meanings, expectation and behaviour. Importantly, they found evidence that friends are taking over some of the functions of family, with friends now more important in support networks than in the past. A blurring of the categories of family and friends is being experienced with individuals becoming more selective in choosing the kin with whom they socialise and keep obligations.

Pahl and Spencer found that family members are seen as equivalent to friends if the relationship is perceived as *chosen* rather than a *duty* or if there are strong emotional bonds. Significantly, members of family are also viewed as friends if the relationship involves *disclosure*. The intimate practises engaged in by individuals and the everyday meanings of intimacy that they articulate support the contention that 'family' and 'friends' are converging categories. These research findings confirm that agency, choice and equality are highly valued attributes being aspired to in intimate relationship as exemplified by Gidden's notion of elective intimacy. This favouring of the elective, democratic qualities of personal relationships over compulsory relationships explains the rising significance and popularity of personal communication technologies that foster attributes of choice, agency, equality and pleasure. This trend forms part of an inclination towards what Misa Matsuda (2005) refers to as 'selective sociality' which is being practised by young people who can act on choices about whom to associate with through the affordances of new social technologies (see Chapter 5).

Importantly, Pahl and Spencer's findings confirm that 'friend-like relationships' have come to represent the most *sought after* relationship in late modernity. Despite the unstable and slippery nature of the concept of friendship, its deployment as a metaphor for social cohesion indicates that the relationship has tremendous cultural appeal. Its non-hierarchical, informal nature corresponds with today's ethos of equality. The implication for the advancement of friendship metaphors on social network sites is that social media are aspirational. These social technologies express deep-seated aspirations for intimate connections of choice based on trust, sharing and reciprocity. Paradoxically, while the concept of intimacy has been interrogated through the lens of friendship, friendship has come to be idealised and venerated. Thus, late modernity brings with it a new kind of intimate relationship and culture which draws on the *ideal* of friendship: a relationship no longer defined by or confined to ties of duty but entered into voluntarily in a context of mutual benefit. Friendship signifies less formal, more casual companion-like bonds. The concept of friendship mirrors the 'pure relationship' by signifying the desire for equality and choice in *all* relationships. The variability and emphasis on choice involved in this kind of intimate relationship corresponds well with social media by promoting a sense of choice, control and reciprocity at the same time. This corresponds with the idea of social network sites such as Facebook as more casual, immediate, informal modes of communication. These personal networks can involve self-disclosure, shared secrets and a sense of exclusiveness. Individuals can construct their own narratives of self through fluid, flexible ties.

From personal cultures to networked publics

Contemporary intimate ties can now be described in terms of personal communities or micro-social worlds to underscore the changing nature of intimacies and the importance of friendship in shaping personal relationships. The previous chapter addressed the affordances of social media that foster connections of a personal nature. Having highlighted the ideal of friendship as a late modern social connection, in this section I extend the study of mediated relationships by asking what kinds of connections are being expressed through the ideals of friendship. The question that now needs to be posed is: how is this emphasis on 'the personal', as a personal community or micro-social world being mediated, reconfigured and articulated in the public realm formed by social media? This is addressed by exploring the distinctive ways in which digital technologies now frame personal networks within public or semi-public settings. For example, Barry Wellman (2002) uses the concept of 'networked individualism' to describe the computer-supported social networks through which individuals become connected as thin ties, emphasising that individuals are heedless of spatial boundaries. His analysis of online associations therefore emphasises the individualistic nature of mediated communication: 'this is a time for individuals and their networks and not for groups' Wellman (2002: 2). Wellman's networked individualism thereby questions the idea of a strong sense of collectivity. Computer-communication networks are characterised as loosely structured forms of interpersonal networking, rather than tight-knit and bounded social groups.

'Network public culture' is a term used by danah boyd (2007, 2011) to highlight the way that personal culture has now extended into 'public' culture (boyd 2007; Ito et al. 2010). The relationship between the personal and the public is addressed by boyd (2011) by approaching social network sites as a genre of 'networked publics'. For boyd, 'networked publics' are publics that have been reorganised by networked technologies. They comprise the social space created through networked technologies and the imagined collective that occurs from the interconnection of people, technology and practice. She explains that networked publics share purposes similar to those of other types of publics by providing opportunities for people to come together for social, cultural and civic objectives and foster connections with people beyond their immediate family and friends. To be explored here is the nature of the connections in social media contexts such as social network sites to find out how the groupings assemble and come together and are linked or bound together. Technology structures these publics in distinctive ways by providing new affordances that influence how people interact.

By approaching social network sites as networked publics, we are able to consider the online interactions of social network sites as modes of communication facilitated by the affordances and shared dynamics of *public* interconnectivity. As boyd says, 'Networked public' affordances do not dictate participants' behaviour, but they do configure the environment in a way that shapes participants' engagement.' (boyd 2011: 39).

She points out that the word 'publics' is a contested term with various meanings. Drawing on Livingstone (2005), boyd approaches 'public' as a collection of people who share 'a common understanding of the world, a shared identity, a claim to inclusiveness, a consensus regarding the collective interest' (Livingstone 2005: 9). Thus, a public can comprise a local collection of people or a broader group. Referring to Benedict Anderson's work on nation (2006), boyd approaches a public as an 'imagined community'. This is significant because it highlights the socially constructed nature of that network and the aspirations embedded within it. This is picked up in the following chapter in the study of self-presentations and the ways in which participants in social network sites conceive of their 'audience', their 'community' or their 'public'.

The idea of 'public' is associated not only with a community but also with media audiences, texts and the production and consumption of cultural objects. For example, Mizuko Ito (2008: 2) emphasises the creative dimensions of social media by highlighting the links between networked publics and social and cultural developments associated with digitally networked media. Ito (2008: 3) argues that 'publics can be reactors, (re)makers and (re)distributors, engaged in shared culture and knowledge through discourse and social exchange as well as through acts of media reception'. For boyd, networked publics are not only publics networked through media but publics restructured by networked technologies in terms of space and collection of people. Thus, the concept of networked publics allows us to make a distinction between *personal* and *public* cultures.

Personal cultures encompass cultural forms and meanings such as family albums and snapshot photos, home movies, diaries and other mementos. These personal cultures correspond with 'personal communities' by representing the relationship between the self and our individual network of friends and family. *Public culture* traditionally comprises popular media such as newspapers, magazines, cinema and television (Russell et al. 2008). Yet the notion of *networked* publics identifies the manner in which the personal and public have been brought together through digital technology. Today, many features of personal culture draw on or are negotiated through a public lens. For example, uploading personal and family photos on Internet-based photo-sharing and video-sharing websites and social network sites is now common practice. In other words, the ideas of a 'networked individual' and 'networked public' come together to underline the process of mediation involved in the technological expression of the familial, the personal and the emotional in a public or semi-public setting.

The various features of social network sites are identified by boyd to explain the way these new, mediated interconnections create new kinds of 'publics'. While social network sites share features with other online communities, this genre of website is distinctive in combining features that offer individuals three distinctive sets of opportunities: (1) to assemble a public or semi-public profile in a bounded system, (2) to communicate a list of other users with whom they share a connection and (3) to view and traverse their list of connections and those made by others in the system (boyd and Ellison 2007). Four tools are identified by boyd that play an important role in constructing social network sites as networked publics: profiles, Friends lists, public commenting tools and streambased updates.

Profiles not only represent the individual but also serve as the site of interaction. Participants consciously craft their profiles to be seen by others and, as boyd (2006) says, 'profile generation is an explicit act of writing oneself into being in a digital environment'. Users must decide how to present themselves to viewers. Design, taste and style are therefore important in profile construction. Since profiles constitute a forum where people come together to interact, participants do not have complete control over their self-representation. While many welcome images and comments are contributed by others, profiles are also sites of *control*. Although personal control is never absolute, most participants value the ability to restrict the visibility of their profiles, making them 'semi-public': that is, available to an audience of friends, acquaintances, peers and interesting peripheral ties. Profiles are therefore 'where the potential audience is fixed, creating a narrower public shaped by explicit connection or affiliation' (boyd 2011: 43, see Chapter 4).

Through *Friends lists*, participants on social network sites display who they wish to connect with and endorse ties with those who wish to connect with them. A profiler's Friends' lists are visible to anyone with permission to see that person's profile. Most sites require these connections to be mutually agreed before being put on view. This public expression of friendship and interconnectivity is undertaken by listing and quantifying contacts as Friends but it is much more than a record of friends since a Friends list usually constitutes more than one's 'closest and dearest friends'. The selection and listing of Friends is both political and social. Participants have to consider the implications of excluding or explicitly rejecting a person, as opposed to the benefits of including them. While some restrict their list of Friends, others companionably seek to add anyone. Some include all who they consider to be a part of their *personal community*, but as boyd points out, the majority of participants simply include those they consider to be part of their wider social world. This may include current and past friends, acquaintances and weaker or peripheral ties, people that participants barely know but feel compelled to include. The most controversial actors that may be listed are those who hold power over the participant, such as parents, bosses and teachers. For many participants, it is more socially risky to include these individuals than to include less intimate ties comprising significant others who may well be judgemental.

Importantly, boyd (2011: 44) argues that this public articulation of personal connections on social network sites can be interpreted as an expression of a 'public'. In this way, 'Friends' become the participants' 'public'. Drawing on Pahl and Spencer (2004), we can say that a 'public' is the display of one's personal community. The participants see themselves as connecting with a group, *en masse* as a collective, or what Pahl and Spence might call a 'social convoy'. Modes of selection differ. Some select their Friends from the same social context; others combine various differing contexts. Important with respect to self-presentation and impression management is that the way participants approach the matter of social context or audience determines who they may or may not select as Friends (see Chapter 4). The list of Friends that participants choose to connect with online becomes a person's imagined or intended audience since participants expect this audience to be accessing their content and interacting with them. The list of Friends becomes the *imagined audience* (see Chapter 4). They serve as the intended public. Although some may not interact, participants adjust their behaviour and self-presentation to suit the intended norms of this imagined public or collective.

Public commenting tools refer to the range of devices used to support these public or semi-public interactions (boyd 2011: 45). For example, group features allow participants to congregate around shared interests. A tool commonly used for public encounters is the commenting feature. This tool displays conversations on a person's profile (called 'the Wall' on Facebook and 'Comments' on MySpace). A Facebook Wall is the area on a page or a profile where friends and 'fans' can post their thoughts and views for anyone to read. Walls have three viewing settings: user plus others, just user and just others. The settings can be altered but most users automatically display the 'user + others' option so that they can show posts, links, tagged material and other information posted by both the page user-owner and their Friends. Walls also incorporate the News Feed to display updates made by the user-owner including links, pictures and other information. The commentary is accessible to anyone with access to that person's profile. Participants use this space to communicate with individuals and groups. The content formed by teenagers is repeatedly defined by adults as banal but it constitutes an important ritual, a form of social grooming. 'Through mundane comments, participants are acknowledging one another in a public setting, similar to the way in which they may greet each other if they were to bump into one another on the street. Comments are not simply a dialogue between two interlocutors, but a performance of social connection before a broader audience' (boyd 2011: 45).

Facebook and Myspace instigated features that provide users with opportunities to broadcast content to Friends on the site through *streambased updates.* MySpace initially offered a feature called 'bulletins', which allowed for blog-like messages to be distributed. Facebook implemented 'status updates' to persuade participants to share pithy messages, and then MySpace set up a comparable tool. Through these features, participants can add to content which is then broadcast to Friends mainly through a stream of updates from all of their Friends. Again, 'While individual updates are arguably mundane, this running stream of content gives participants a general sense of those around them. In doing so, participants get the sense of the public constructed by those with whom they connect' (boyd 2011: 45).

In these ways, profiles together with Friends lists and various public communication channels form a range of features which signify social network sites as *publics*. As boyd states:

> In short, social network sites are publics both because of the ways in which they connect people en masse and because of the space they provide for interactions and information. They are networked publics because of the ways in which networked technologies shape and configure them.
>
> (boyd 2011:45)

The use of the term 'public' moves networks beyond the idea of physical space. It no longer emphasises the physicality of 'public' with the distinctions between private and public as private 'home' and public 'outside or beyond the home'. 'Public' no longer means 'outside the home': it now occurs beyond the home/outside home dichotomy. Instead, it becomes a technologically mediated mode of communication which occurs in a complex mediated environment of polymedia (see Chapter 2).

These networked publics correspond with personal communities by functioning as personalised networked publics. The emphasis on the personal highlights the individuated nature of the network, the idea of personal control, yet also the real or potential public quality of the interaction. These networks can, then, be described as *personalised networked publics* (see Chapter 7). The notion of 'personalised networked publics' emphasises the personal control yet also the problem or challenge of the public nature of the interaction. Importantly, the notion of friendship is functioning to bridge the boundaries between intimate, personal relationships and public, networked community relationships.

Conclusions

These debates outlined above about democratising intimacies and unconventional relationships have highlighted the importance of friendship as a social marker of equality and reciprocity rather than authority, hierarchy and duty. This chapter has identified four key trends in late modern society that characterise transformations in intimacy and form the foundations to the ethos and cultural practices of digitally mediated relationships. First, the democratisation and discretionary nature of interpersonal relationships are predominant. As part of this democratisation, friendship has grown into a centrally valued relationship that epitomises individual agency and choice and yet also the caring qualities of intimacy. Second, through this tendency, familial and friendship associations are being combined to form *personal* networks that have the potential to foster social cohesion and support and characterise today's modes of interaction. It is characterised by the desire for informal, non-hierarchical sets of relationships, offering individuals the potential to reinvent narratives of self. This is the subject matter of the following chapter. These new ways of thinking are prompting academic speculation that social ties are becoming more intimate, private and personal yet fluctuating and transient.

Thus the third trend, framed within this late modern emphasis on the personal, challenges distinctions between former notions of public and private. This trend comprises the rise of *personalised networked publics* in the context of social media, epitomised by social network site connections. Importantly, then, the reframing of 'intimacy' beyond as well as within family and the private sphere to include friendships and the public spheres open up a debate about personal relationships. This allows us to explore changing practices of intimacy online and, equally, the ways social media mediate conceptualisations and practices of intimacy and friendship. A fourth trend involves the emphasis on choice within mediated intimacies. Importantly, the notion of *choice* and *agency* idealised in the concept of friendship corresponds with the media characteristics of technical affordances (Hutchby 2001) and polymediated contexts (Madianou and Miller 2012), conceived as choices associated with the technological potential and attributes of social network sites. Thus, the affordances of social media that create personalised networked publics entail choices.

The employment of the term 'friendship' to describe all social connections on social network sites is, then, no accident. The appeal of the concept of 'friendship' is that it is particularly fluid and malleable.

It corresponds with a particular set of tendencies in late modernity. The personal values and ideas of self increasingly rely on friendship as a powerful metaphor through which one can explore new modes of intimacy and individual identity beyond as well as through family. The concept of friendship embodies key aspirations. The disclosing, confiding nature of 'friendship' endorses a new project of the self in an era when 'self' identity, rather than family or community identity, becomes a primary constituent of society. Thus, the positive qualities of friendship – conviviality, equality, choice and mutual disclosure – have been reconfigured in late modernity through social media discourses to validate personal life and mediated self-identity. In the context of social network sites, listed 'Friends' become personal 'publics'.

However, a weakness in the idea of this 'pure relationship' of friendship is not only the presumption of egalitarianism but also the promise of collective purpose. The fusion of the terms 'personal' and 'community' implies collective intent and the promise of social benefits. The idea of an individuated network in a more public setting raises the question of whether it is possible to fuse individual and social concerns together through interpersonal connections within a public realm. While friendship was initially regarded as a chosen, affective relationship, the idea of an *individualised* relationship underestimates the value of friendship in building *social* connections by treating it as just a set of voluntary attachments (Allan 1979; Eve 2002; Wilkinson 2010). The concerns about social fragmentation and alienation raised by authors such as Bauman, Putman and others are echoed in debates about online friendships. Questions are raised about whether social network sites build *community* or promote the *self* in a narcissistic manner (Buffardi and Campbell 2008). Although the attributes of *individualism* and *community* are assumed to be conflicting, the studies outlined above by scholars such as Roseneil and Budgeon (2004) on 'non-standard intimacies' challenge this dichotomy. Chapter 8 explores the issue of weak ties in this respect to uncover their importance.

The following chapters explore the ways in which intimacies are being mediated through social media contexts with a focus on social network sites. They ask whether these new technologies have the potential to disturb and challenge conventional notions of intimacy through various levels of display and expression or whether they reinforce established norms in an online setting. The potential to reinvent narratives of self in the context of the informal, egalitarian relationships being sought through social media is explored in the following chapter by examining the presentation of self on social network sites. The chapter looks at the ways participants adjust their behaviour and self-presentation to suit the intended norms of the imagined public or collective established within personalised networked publics. We find that the technological mediation of intimacies is a process that problematises conventional boundaries of public and private and therefore has consequences for the construction and presentation of the online self.

4
Self-Presentation Online

Introduction

The previous chapter suggests that friendship has become a power-ful emblem of interpersonal democratisation during late modernity. 'Friendship', as an idea and set of practices, is used to navigate both inti-mate and casual ties in the framework of increasingly diverse channels of communication. Social network sites have further reconfigured the apparent flexibility, informality and conviviality of friendship through the public display of personal connections. The type of social media engagement articulated on social network sites promotes a new form of friendship administration (Ellison et al. 2011b). This chapter explores the ways people are managing their personal connections online within personalised networked publics by investigating the ways in which sites are used by participants to present the self. It considers the techniques available to users for managing the public display of the personal and to navigate the uncertain and often risky boundaries between 'personal' and 'public'.

Studies of the display of the self on individual site profiles high-light the challenges of balancing private and public information. Styles of self-presentation and the formation and organisation of tight or loose social settings become paramount (Papacharissi 2009). To address these issues, this chapter explains the significance of personal identities being extended digitally into public cultures. The concept of networked publics helps to understand how personal communities are articulated online as public modes of interaction. The chapter shows how social network sites mediate interaction and facilitate the creation of personal identities and networked publics.

The public presentation of personal associations on social network sites has come to represent an individual's social identity and status

(Donath and boyd 2004). Yet, unlike an ordinary web page, the identity might be contested and modified by interactive onlookers. Conceptions and changing presentations of 'self' and 'other' are analysed in the context of these new kinds of mediated personal ties. The work of Mead and Goffman is drawn on to understand the reconstruction of the 'self' and 'other' in the framework of online social ties. This chapter explains how a symbolic interactionist approach can inform debates about networked identity by assessing Mead's concept of the 'generalised other' and Goffman's idea of the self as a process of dramatic interaction. Given that the self is being articulated and negotiated in highly visible ways through online media, the 'public personalisation' of the self almost inevitably involves the renegotiation of the boundaries between personal and the public.

Imagined audiences and third-party information

As social network site engagement generally entails semi-public messages of mutual acknowledgement, status confirmation and relationship affirmation (boyd 2006b), it can be assumed that a 'public self' is being displayed mainly for one's own social circle. However, site participants are also regularly tracked and 'checked out' by a range of former acquaintances and looser associations. In these ways, sites are designed to display real-world identities. This doesn't mean that it is impossible to invent an online identity but, importantly, the site tools encourage us to communicate features of our offline selves. This process contrasts with the virtual identities constructed in certain online networks such as massively multiplayer online role playing video games where players are expected to assume the role of a character or avatar. Self-representations formed on social network sites are generally constructed to reflect offline selves. Public access to personal and looser connections inevitably involves a staging of personal status and identity (Donath and boyd 2004). For instance, in a study of Twitter, Alison Hearn (2008) found that social media is used to carefully construct a 'meta-narrative and meta-image of self'. Personal profiles are expected to be highly managed as multimedia online identity presentations.

Social network site engagement can, then, be viewed as a form of impression management that involves an explicit construction of the social self (Tufekci 2008). Interestingly, these practices of online self-presentation 'heighten people's consciousness of the ways in which their identities are socially constructed' as Stefanone, Lackaff and Rosen

(2011: 43) state. Users actively participate in forms of impression management that were once the preserve of celebrities, politicians and others in the public eye. This self-presentation is conducted through the organisation of their profiles, the display of their contacts and the tracking of other people through the profiles of 'Friends', their 'friendship' links, membership of groups and the public presentation of their likes and dislikes (Lampe et al. 2007; Tufekci 2008). The tools being employed which were formerly associated with celebrities include: 'Airbrushed photos, carefully staged social interactions, strategic selection and maintenance of the entourage are now in a sense available to everyone with a computer' (Stefanone et al. 2008: 1).

Online Friends provide a context for self-presentation by offering users an *imagined audience* that guides behavioural norms (boyd 2011). Our lists of Friends become our imagined audience, serving as the intended public. Participants modify their self-presentations to fit the norms of this imagined collective. Even though the focus is mainly on close friends or family members, users tend to approach their profile as presentations constructed for a potentially unlimited and undefined public (Schau and Gilly 2003: 391). Several categories of imagined audiences may be evoked through personal impression management: intimates and current offline friends, family members, former friends, employers, professional links, casual acquaintances and latent or dormant ties. Yet this imagined audience is also highly manipulated. 'Friends' are often being carefully selected for display according to their appeal and status, as shown by Facebook's 'Wall' feature, and MySpace's 'Comments'. On this section of a person's profile, others can write messages or leave icon-like images. It forms a public message space as others can see what has been written on a person's Wall. The messages can be seen by all visitors with access to that profile (see Chapter 3). Papacharissi describes the personal profile as a 'controlled performance' in self-presentation (2002: 644). Likewise, Friendster Testimonials are frequently used as self-presentational devices (boyd and Heer 2006). Friendster users confirm that impression management is one of the criteria they use for choosing particular friends (Donath and boyd 2004). These 'public displays of connections' serve as key identity markers that guide people's navigation of the networked social world and serve to validate identity information presented in profiles (Donath and boyd 2004).

Earlier research on relationships has revealed that individuals invest a great deal of time and effort in forming and managing impressions, particularly during the initial stages of interactions (Berger and Calabrese

1975; Goffman 1959). The ability to present oneself in an assured and positive way has been associated with social, and even physical, survival (Hogan et al. 1985; Walther et al. 2008). However, when we meet someone away from other known connections, the claims they make are often exaggerated and not verifiable (Goffman 1959). Important cues for forming an opinion about a person can be identified by finding out whom they know, how they relate to others and how others relate to them (Holland and Skinner 1987). More recent research has distinguished offline from online impression formation. From the late 1980s onwards, researchers proposed that computer-mediated communication (CMC) hampers interpersonal impressions because non-verbal cues are absent in mediated text-based communication. However, this idea was challenged by social information processing theory of the early 1990s which speculated that CMC users may be fairly skilled at interpreting the emotional dimensions of messages within exchanges (Walther 1992). The multi-modal and interactive nature of contemporary social network sites such as Facebook entails the provision of a richer and more informed social context for people about whom we otherwise have cursory knowledge.

Creating and networking online content has become a fundamental resource for managing one's identity, lifestyle and social relations (Livingstone 2008). Nowadays online impressions are often highly managed by participants to enhance the self-image by carefully selecting favourable information for display. Inflating one's positive qualities and downplaying any flaws is a self-presentation practice that profile audiences have come to expect. The inflation of personal qualities even occurs regularly when there is likelihood that observers will meet them offline (Ellison et al. 2006). Yet social network sites such as Facebook are intrinsically *interactive* and embedded in public networks. A unique feature of these sites is the extent to which certain information about the self is disclosed by *others* and may be out of the profiler's control. The combination of interactive and static features in a person's profile impacts directly on self-presentation. In offline communication contexts, individuals make their own choices about how and when to disclose personal information and control their self-image (Petronio 2002). Social network sites challenge this control by providing the tools for interactive audiences to thwart the rules of disclosure that individuals establish to protect private information that they are reluctant to divulge. Insulting messages and reports of misdemeanours are often placed on users' Facebook pages by interactive groups whether light-heartedly or maliciously (Mazer et al. 2007: 3).

It has been argued that social network sites are structured to foster narcissistic skills of self-promotion (Buffardi and Campbell 2008; Carpenter 2012; Twenge and Campbell 2009). However, the interactive nature of information can provide crucial checks and balances against overblown self-promotion, given that details can be posted on to a person's profile by others in that individual's network. Importantly, social network technology is distinguished from others – such as Web pages, email, or online chat where the creator has control over the content – by its high level of interactivity. This information might include details about the profiler's character or about his or her behaviour. It can also include details about the character and conduct of the individuals who post the comments and observers' reactions to both. The profile maker does not initiate or necessarily condone such postings. The prospect of being evaluated according to the conduct of others indicates that, on social network sites, we may be 'judged by the company we keep' (Walther et al. 2008).

Third-party information is usually thought to be more dependable than self-disclosed assertions. In the case of a Facebook profile, observations made by others may be more believable than those made by the profiler. The information retained on a person's profile site that is generated by friends becomes a significant measure of personality. Through intersecting social networks, participants can track one another and try to find out information about each other via mutual connections. A US study found that one in six searchers goes online to seek information about the relationship status of someone they know (Madden and Smith 2010). It becomes a significant part of online dating rituals, for example (see Chapter 7). The purpose of this practice is to reduce any doubts a person might have about the character and trustworthiness of potential or actual partners. To gauge the profilers' character, observers check a range of features displayed both intentionally and unintentionally by the profiler (Vazire and Gosling 2004).

Walther et al. (2008) examined how contributions to a person's own online profile by other people affect observers' impressions and evaluations of the profile maker. They conducted an intriguing original experiment that involved mock-up Facebook profiles alternately featuring attractive or unattractive features surrounding preset central profile material. These variations affected observers' impressions of credibility and attractiveness, all without the target of these judgements having changed. Walther et al. (2008) found that positive and favourable comments made by friends about profile owners enhanced the profile owner's social appeal and credibility. Moreover, having photos of good-looking friends on one's Facebook profile enhanced the physical attractiveness of the profile owner. Yet, surprisingly, it was also found that there is no advantage to be gained from looking better than one's friends.

The researchers further observed that the effect of negative statements on a person's profile depended on the sex of the profile owner, reflecting wider gender-bound norms and sanctions (Walther et al. 2008). The researchers found that respect or admiration was more likely to be conferred on men involved in sexual or drunken encounters while women were more likely to be denigrated for the same actions. This kind of judgement is confirmed in a wide range of other research (see, for review, Crawford and Popp 2003; Marks and Fraley 2006). Walther et al. (2008) confirm that these responses reflect the sexual double standards that influence social attitudes to men's and women's behaviour when people are making judgements about character. These gendered codes, which tend to endorse greater sexual freedom for men than for women, have a significant influence on impression formation in general. The findings draw attention to concerns about the potential of Facebook dynamics to perpetuate double standards of sexual behaviour, reinforce gendered and other social stereotypes and also encourage social practices that may be harmful to groups such as college students (see, e.g., Haley 2006; Walther et al. 2008).

The online self

Although symbolic interactionism assumes that the primary form of interaction is face-to-face, the work of Mead (1934) and Goffman (1959) casts light on the process of digital self-presentation. Symbolic interactionism foregrounds the inherently interactive nature of online communication. For Mead and Goffman, the self is not viewed as a bounded, fixed entity. It is a reflexive construction which is constantly being renegotiated through interaction within the social world (Andersen 1997; Holstein and Gubrium 2000). Mead's concept of the 'generalized other' is addressed in the first section followed by an assessment of Goffman's notion of the self as a process of dramatic interaction in the second section. These symbolic interactionist conceptions contribute to an understanding of processes of online self-presentation.

The 'digital other'

Mead (1934: 138–140) explains that, in terms of experience, the self is inseparable from the 'generalized other'. For Mead, the self is continuously constructed and reconstructed through interaction with others. Our sense of self is composed within a relational process through our interactions with other people and through more abstract ideas of collectively endorsed social customs and values. Mead explains that the self is made up of the 'I' and the 'Me'. 'I' becomes 'Me' by internalising the attitudes of others. The 'me' is consequently able to imagine how a 'generalised other' would see its actions and to evaluate these in relation to the group's norms (Mead 1934). In the case of self-presentation on social network sites, the construction of the self through a personal profile assumes a virtual 'generalized other' (Robinson 2007: 104).

The notion of the generalised other is explained by Mead by referring to the differing characteristics of 'play' and 'the game'. In play, a person adopts the role of someone else. In the game, we must understand the perspectives and attitudes of all other participants. This allows us to understand other peoples' standpoints and how the conventions or rules of society work (Mead 1962[1934]: 154). These 'generalized others', like 'participants in the game', can be described as a 'community' or network. Thus, a person's subjectivity can be seen as the organised response to the network or the 'Me'. Individuals learn to adjust their behaviour to the social context that they find themselves in by taking into account the role of the other. In terms of norms and expectations, we present ourselves in differing ways according to social context and whom we are communicating with. On social network sites, the 'generalised other' is an imagined yet potentially *interactive* audience or network and may be experienced as an online personal community. In this way, the online generalised other, which we can call the 'digital other' complements the idea of the *imagined audience* employed by boyd (2011). Given that this imagined online audience is inherently interactive, Mead's approach offers an important insight into the presentation of the digital self as socially constructed through online interaction. This is not a process confined to the construction of the offline self. Whether online or offline, Mead's other-oriented self is an inevitable product of socialisation (Robinson 2007).

Holdsworth and Morgan (2007) draw on Mead's notion of the generalised other in their study of transcripts of interviews with young people in the process of leaving home. They were struck by the frequency of interviewees' often subtle references to 'others' in their everyday conversational practices. Holdsworth and Morgan (2007: 403) argue that 'the generalized other is a process by which people incorporate notions of what others say, think and do into their judgements'. They identified three distinctive but intersecting levels of meanings associated with the generalised other which correspond with online contexts. The first level of meaning is defined in terms of 'generalizations about social processes, influences or social currents' (2007: 408). The expression 'people say' is an example of a reference to issues outside the individual yet which wielded some influence on their behaviour or views. In the case of the presentation of the online self, this level corresponds with the idea of the more generalised, *imagined online audience* of the kind that boyd (2011) refers to. The second level represents more particular yet still generalised 'others' such as friends, and this may correspond to the Friends, acquaintances and *weak online ties* we adopt and network with. The third level comprises identifiable, named 'others' who could be described as 'significant others'. These significant others may include parents, sibling or influential friends, for example. This corresponds to the closer, *intimate online ties* we form on network sites. Thus, these three levels of referencing a 'generalised other' indicate how ideas of self and personal identity are linked to the generalising process.

These distinctive levels of 'others' have the potential to exercise some constraint on their thoughts or actions through broad standards of comparison (Holdsworth and Morgan 2007). When referring to their family obligations, actors frequently make use of 'moral tales' in order to place themselves within some kind of moral order. In the same way, social network sites position individuals in some kind of moral order through a continuous self-monitoring. Interactions are continually evaluated, compared and reflected upon. As Mead explains, 'other' people being compared with or referred to may not be entirely abstract but may relate to a group or community with whom the individual has some affinity – such as people in one's neighbourhood, friends and colleagues. There is likely to be some common ground and connection between the self and the network of others for these comparisons to be meaningful. References to other people not only are sometimes used to judge one's own actions but also involve judgements of others. As Holdsworth and Morgan (2007: 414) state, 'Through identifying who generalized others correspond to, we can gauge a sense of the varied constituents of individuals' communities'. The 'generalized other' is therefore relevant for an understanding of processes of comparison and judgement. The generalised other – the 'me' part of the self – evokes the idea of a reference group and therefore of some form of generalised collectivity rather than specific individuals. By broadly identifying who generalised others relate to, we can gain a sense of the differing constituents of individuals' networks (Holdsworth and Morgan 2007).

These categories of generalised 'digital others' are relevant for an understanding of online self-presentation. However, while the same techniques are used online to address multiple audiences, the notion of generalised others can be more difficult to handle online. The presentation of an online self may entail heightened risks associated with the speed and scale that information can go public via the features of networked publics (boyd 2006, 2011): profiles, Friends lists, public commenting tools and streambased updates (see Chapter 3). While the online self is embedded in interaction, offline cue systems are redefined in online settings (Robinson 2007). Importantly, then, since online selves are connected to offline worlds, these online selves are involved in modes of interactivity which are embedded in offline power relations – with *offline* as well as *online* consequences. This 'digital' other is derived from and embedded in offline contexts.

In a study of teenagers' self-presentations and self-expressions online, Livingstone (2008) draws on Mead to explain that 'selves are constituted through interaction with others and, for today's teenagers, self-actualization increasingly includes a careful negotiation between the opportunities (for identity, intimacy, sociability) and risks (regarding privacy, misunderstanding, abuse) afforded by internet-mediated communication' (Livingstone 2008: 407). Livingstone discovered that strategies for presenting the self varied dramatically among teenagers. For example, she describes one teenage girl's profile as having 'a big welcome in sparkly pink, with music, photos, a "love tester", guestbook, dedication pages, etc., all customized down to the scroll bars and cursor with pink candy stripes, glitter, angels, flowers, butterflies, hearts and more (because "you can just change it all the time [and so] you can show different sides of yourself")' (Livingstone 2008: 399). A contrasting example was a boy who did not complete the basic Facebook options of recording his politics, religion or even his network ('I haven't bothered to write about myself'). Livingstone explains that most profiles are designed in varying ways to provide 'a way of expressing who you are to other people', as one teenage girl expressed it simply. However, Livingstone also noted the concerns reflected by teenagers when talking about the continuous *revision* of the self involved in social network site personal profiles (Livingstone 2008: 403).

The performance of the self

Goffman builds on Mead's approach by drawing on dramaturgy in his expanded metaphor of the self (Lemert and Branaman 1997). Following Mead, Goffman (1959) approaches the self as the process of dramatic interaction that produces multiple selves for multiple performances. For Goffman the self draws on unwritten social rules to present a moral self. A sense of belonging is partly accomplished by knowing these unwritten rules and by being able to conduct oneself in an 'acceptable' manner before others (Fortier 2000). From Goffman's perspective, the network site user's profile is constructed by the 'I' through the choice of text, photos and formatting which are all selected to seek the other's presence, anticipate their response and consider their reaction. The construction of profiles on more than one social network site to serve differing selves and differing audiences reflects this process. Ljung and Wahlfross (2008: 102) explain that a person is performing a certain *face* of their identity on a website. The nature of the 'face' being performed differs considerably according to the intended audience. One face may be more work-related by being staged on a professional site such as LinkedIn while another face may represent more social dimensions of the self on a site such as Facebook. Through its various performances, the self attempts to express a plausible identity that fits in with audience expectations and with the circumstances that frame the interaction (Goffman 1959).

To participate effectively in society, the self is invited to cooperate with other selves to stage interactions that form 'front stage' and 'backstage' (Goffman 1959). Front and back stage equate with private, semi-public and public displays of online networked interaction. These articulations and performances contribute to the construction of a self-identity that meets the audience's expectations and fits the meaning of the situation or event. The performer relies on two types of communication to create this persona: deliberate and often verbal signs and gestures, and the signs and symbols communicated unconsciously which are often non-verbal (Goffman 1959). Deliberate expressions are viewed as 'given' and unconscious ones are 'given off' and often unintended. Social network site users recurrently give off unintended expressions not only through their Friend lists and Wall posts but also through the genre and pose of their photos, their musical tastes and the topics and tone of their written interactions. These cues are saturated with traces of their social distinctions (see Bourdieu 1986). The unplanned nature of unintended expressions means that the audience is likely to interpret them as genuine. This notion of the self is a symbolic interactionist self in the sense that the performer's role cannot be distinguished from the audience's anticipated response.

Significantly, the interactive nature of social network sites can encourage the view that a profile is a valid and genuine persona, since audiences can add to and comment on a person's profile. For Mead (1934), this kind of interaction comprises and reflects the self. The self has no essential characteristics as it does not exist outside of society and interaction. To paraphrase Laura Robinson (2007) in her study of the cyberself, once the 'I' sees the networked other's reaction, this reflexive composition produces the online, 'networked me'. This online self-ing is located in an interactive setting. It is a continuously fluctuating process since profiles can be regularly modified. They are modified through a stream of communication that comprises action, reaction and counter-action which generates the online 'me'. The profile modifications become part of the self-ing process. With bodily cues unavailable online, textual and visual signals are used to interpret the digital expressions. Through these means, 'the cyberself masters virtual cuing systems' (Robinson 2007: 105).

Robinson (2007) identifies the differences between Goffman's symbolic interactionist approach and postmodern debates about online identities which highlights the nature of today's mediated interactivity. She argues that postmodern theories of self-ing dismiss symbolic interactionism by referring to virtual environments and imagined spaces that *free* the self from Median socialisation processes. Postmodern theorists claim that virtual reality environments no longer comprise other-oriented selves produced through socialisation. However, these postmodern predictions were drawn from role playing in multi-user domains (MUDs). From a postmodern perspective, immersing the self in online worlds allows the emergence of an ephemeral and decentred self that can create multiple online identities. For example, Turkle (1995) found that keen MUD users created unconnected and multiple identities in several virtual settings beyond offline interactions. However, as Robinson (2007: 99) argues, this multiphrenic self-ing and liberation from the body is misleading: 'Rather, the cyberself seeks re-embodiment as a means of identity signalling and as a medium of interaction'. Cyberidentities have to claim a gendered, raced and aged identity in simulated bodies that often idealise real-world bodies.

Robinson contends that a basic problem of postmodern interpretations of cyberself-ing is the attempt to generalise from early studies of MUDs. Although the accounts were thought to characterise identity in cyberspace (Turkle 1995), they were derived from (MUDs) used by white, college-educated, technically expert males. Robinson asserts that it is important to bear in mind the recent dramatic expansion in Internet user populations that superseded postmodern approaches and generalisations. Maintaining largely personal and intimate networks on these sites depends on the generation and effective management of trust and identity. As the authenticity of the user is validated through interaction, the success of these technologies depends on trust between the user and the site (Chen et al. 2011). In turn, this depends on the creation of a *moral community* that agrees to construct accurate and genuine self-representations by participants.

Of course, some participants find elaborate ways of circumventing the regulations that promote accurate profiles (Marwick 2005). However, most social network site users are keen to present their own selves, and in a positive light, rather than create wholly invented identities. As mentioned above, social network sites therefore differ considerably from online role playing games in virtual worlds such as World of Warcraft or Second Life. Nevertheless, research on Teen Second Life has shown that teenagers tend to make friends with users who live nearby offline which suggests that even invented online identities are interconnecting with and reflecting offline life and expressions of identity (Foucault et al. 2009). And Robinson reminds us that for most users the online self is an extension of the offline masterself. She states, 'In creating online selves, users do not seek to transcend the most fundamental aspects of their offline selves. Rather, users bring into being bodies, personas, and personalities framed according to the same categories that exist in the offline world' (Robinson 2007: 94).

Goffman's (1959: 35) concept of dramaturgy contributes to an understanding of online interaction as a performance continually adjusted to respond to the communication. The choice of words and content of postings become a *performance of identity*. The purpose of a performance is to confirm the shared moral values of the community or network. The language communicates 'given' and 'given off' expressions. Robinson (2007) refers to the 'cyberperformer' who becomes conversant with the shared values, linguistic markers and expressions of the community (Donath 1999). These shared codes endorse the groups' sense of shared identity. Thus, from a symbolic interactionist perspective, the online self on social network sites is unequivocally a *socialised* self, produced and negotiated in much the same way as the offline self. The social network site self is embedded in interaction like the offline self, in Mead's sense. Significantly, online settings uphold and enhance the dynamics of interaction that have been established offline. Thus, Mead's concept of the 'generalised other' contributes to an understanding of the online networked self. And, Goffman's expanded metaphor of dramaturgy, with expressions 'given' and 'given off ' remain significant for an analysis of the online self.

Publicising the personal

By mediating the self through symbolic interaction, online social media such as social network sites can be seen as ideal tools for managing 'personal communities'. Yet in terms of its potential, the technology goes much further than this. It provides the affordances not only for interacting but also for broadcasting the information and expressions that emerge from these multiple interactions. By connecting people *en masse*, it creates and sustains intersecting networked *publics*. With regard to boyd's (2011) concept of 'networked publics', addressed in the previous chapter, she emphasises the importance of the content of these networked publics by comprising what she calls 'bits' of information through texts, images videos and other media. These small, manageable chunks of 'bit'-based information require little effort to create, store and distribute. They can be generated instantly and communicated speedily through self-expressions and interactions between people. Through ease of use, networked technologies create new affordances for amplifying, recording and spreading information and social acts (boyd 2011). These technological affordances can shape publics and how people negotiate them. It is worth outlining these affordances since they generate the opportunities, challenges and risks associated with self-presentation and personal reputation management in an interactive environment.

Four kinds of affordance emerge from the properties of content according to boyd, which play a key role in configuring these networked publics: persistence, replicability, scalability and searchability. *Persistence* refers to the automatic recording and archiving of online expressions; *replicability* refers to the potential for these bits to be duplicated; *scalability* refers to the potential visibility of content in networked publics; and *searchability* refers to the way content in networked publics can be accessed through search. In terms of *persistence*, networked technology transforms recording into a common, everyday practice. As boyd points out, tracking down and deleting content that has gone public can be futile. The content is often exchanged across contexts beyond the one in which it was created, thereby raising new concerns when consumed outside its original context. *Replicability* allows these 'bits' of information – texts, images videos and other media – to be shared across the networked publics and also to be altered in ways not always easily recognised. *Scalability* is about the potential for high visibility such as the 'micro-celebrity' (Senft 2008) of a niche group. However, the potential of broadcasting content and creating publics is often not realised. *Searchability* refers to the way that these new technologies are leaving traces, making it easier to locate people in networked publics. Thus, the technological affordances that comprise networked publics introduce new dynamics which participants have to contend with. The attributes of social network sites can change social environments and influence people and their behaviour. For boyd, these affordances comprise *invisible audiences, collapsed contexts* and the *blurring of public and private.*

One of the risks associated with self-presentation on social network sites is that not all audiences are visible when a person is contributing online and they are not necessarily co-present. People can lurk undetected. *Invisible audiences* become a regular issue as part of the imagined audiences. Knowing ones' audience turns out to be vital, given that potential employers and college recruiters scrutinise applicants' profiles. Concerning *collapsed contexts*, the lack of spatial, social and temporary boundaries makes it difficult to juggle and maintain distinct social contexts. Networked publics force people to contend with colliding audiences. Unwanted audiences can appear, bypass or be disruptive. Audiences that were traditionally segmented come together as a 'public'. Formerly distinctive social contexts often collide and generate awkwardness. For example, employers track employees' or prospective employees' profiles; parents come across their children's profiles, often making children feel uncomfortable (see Chapters 5 and 6) and individuals' love lives are often tracked by ex-partners (see Chapter 7).

With regard to the *blurring of public and private*, boyd (2011) explains that 'public' and 'private' become meaningless binaries as they get scaled in new ways. Without control over context, they are difficult to maintain as distinct social realms. Networked publics bring the dynamics and attributes of broadcast media to everyday people. Participants have turned their social curiosity towards those who are part of these more bounded networks (Solove 2007). Some scholars contend that privacy is now dead and we should learn to cope with a more transparent society (Garfinkel 2001). However, for boyd 'privacy' is in a state of transition as people try to make sense of how to negotiate the structural transformations resulting from networked media. Moreover, there are important issues concerning power relations in everyday life which change as a result of social media and can often amplify the power relations beyond. Examples of the potential amplification of power abuse may include surveillance and stalking which usually affect the vulnerable and are often related to relations of gender, age, sexuality, race and religions. They involve racism and sexism; the sexual exploitation of children and young adults and peer bullying. In these ways, networked publics reproduce many of the social injustices that exist in other kinds of publics: social inequalities, including social stratification around race, gender, sexuality and age are reproduced online (boyd 2011; Chen and Wellman 2005; Hargittai 2008). As boyd puts it, 'privacy' potentially involves power and control while publicity potentially involves risks. This technology complicates people's ability to manage *access* and *visibility*.

Affordances of networked publics reconfigure publics more generally. In the face of privacy complications, people use various strategies to gain control. And the dynamics that emerge from these privacy complications are often unforeseen. Thus, the changes brought about by networked technologies are more pervasive than those of earlier media precisely because the content and expressions feeding into networked publics are persistent, replicable, have possibility of being scaled, searched and therefore heightened. The asynchronous nature of social network sites means that people can work around physical barriers to interaction and can connect over vast distances. In other words, 'publics' are being radically redefined as are the dynamics generated by them in relation to the construction of self online.

Managing personal boundaries

This sharing and exchanging of personal information and opinions in a substantially public context has created profound challenges for the management of personal boundaries. Like search engines, social network sites perform a crucial role in creating personal reputations online. As well as connecting with close friends, intimates and wider acquaintances, social network sites are often used for communication between work colleagues and for making comments about their work environments and attitudes to work. Time-honoured divisions between public and personal dimension of everyday life can be breached in a flash through the blurring or blending of personal and formal, work-related spheres. As Madden and Smith (2010: 6) state, 'Personal information has become a form of currency that is shared and exchanged in the social marketplace today.' In a 2008 study of the top 500 US colleges, it was discovered that 10 per cent of admission offices checked on applicants' social network profiles. Thirty eight per cent found information that impacted negatively on the applicants' admission prospects (Kaplan 2008; and see Hechinger 2008). Once a college student was reportedly accused of underage drinking when campus police found photos of the student holding a beer on Facebook (Lang 2009 cited in McLaughlin and Vitak 2012).

Online adults are realising the need to be more cautious, with 44 per cent of them having sought information about individuals in a professional context (Madden and Smith 2010). More and more employers are developing policies about how employees should present themselves online, and businesses and professionals increasingly check one another out. Among employed adults, 12 per cent claim the need to market themselves online as part of their job. Individuals who are dating are also highly likely to be searching for information about their prospective partners. Equally, neighbours who are inquisitive about one another's lives are accessing details about one another. Even those individuals who are protective about their own revelations are under pressure to remain vigilant about detecting information that others may have posted about them on social network profiles, Twitter, blogs and photo- and video-sharing sites. Yet most people who search for information about others online believe that it is unfair to judge people based on the information they acquire online (Madden and Smith 2010).

A profusion of media reports reminds us that employers check blogs and social network sites for personal information that might be relevant in judging the suitability of job applicants. Daniel Bohnert and William Ross (2010) undertook an experimental study of the ways that the content of social network site pages influenced others' assessment of job candidates. They asked 148 students to evaluate the suitability of imaginary candidates for an entry-level managerial job with some résumés marginally qualified and some well qualified for the job. The printouts reflected one of three orientations: an emphasis on drinking alcohol, a family orientation or a professional orientation. Participants in a control group received no web page information. Applicants with either a family-oriented or a professional-oriented page were regarded as more suitable for the job and more diligent than applicants with alcohol-oriented pages. These were more likely to be interviewed and if hired, they were also likely to be offered significantly higher starting salaries.

Dramatic examples of public–private boundary breaches are often reported in the news. For instance, a teenage employee in England was reportedly dismissed in 2009 because she wrote that her job was 'totally boring' on her Facebook status ('*Facebook Remark Teenager Is Fired*,' BBC News 2009[1]). In response to this incident, TUC General Secretary Brendan Barber was quoted as saying that employers needed 'thicker skins' in relation to social network websites. He also stated: 'Most employers wouldn't dream of following their staff down the pub to see if they were sounding off about work to their friends.'[2] Another work-related incident involved the sacking of an employee in 2011. This example highlights the infringement of what were once seemingly clear-cut boundaries between public and private domains. The worker involved criticised his employing company on Facebook. The employee worked in a retail store owned by the American computer giant, Apple. The incident was reported in the press with the headline 'Apple fires employee over iPhone Facebook rants.'[3] However, an employment tribunal ruled that Apple was right to dismiss the worker who criticised his iPhone and job in a series of Facebook posts. Commenting on one particular app, the employee apparently said, on his Facebook page: 'F***ed up my time zone for the third time in a week and woke me up at 3am? JOY!!'. He also poked fun at one of the company's taglines on iTunes. The tribunal panel acknowledged that Apple had a clear social media policy that banned unfavourable comments about the brand because the 'image is so central to its success'. The panel stated that 'We take into account their position that the Facebook posts were not truly private and could in fact have been forwarded very easily with the claimant having no control over this process.'[4] This case, together with a growing number of reports documenting commercial and government data breaches, exemplifies the struggles individuals and organisations experience in controlling the ways that 'public' and 'private' dimensions of life are being reconfigured by social media use.

A further case, thought to be the first of its kind in the United Kingdom in 2010, is that of a 16-year-old worker who was informed through Facebook by her line manager that she had been sacked. The headline 'Café girl becomes first in UK to be sacked on Facebook' was followed by the message she had been sent via Facebook:

> hiya Chelsea its Elaine from work. Sorry to send u a message like this but bin tryin to ring u but gettin no joy. I had to tell the owner bout u losin that tenner coz obviously the till was down at the end of day. She wasn't very pleased at all and despite me trying to persuade her otherwise she said I have to let u go. I'm really sorry. If u call in in the week with your uniform i'll sort your wages out. Once again I'm really sorry but it's out of my hands. Elaine xx.

The sacked teenager's mother stated, in response:

> I'm absolutely fuming, it's disgusting. To sack a young worker via Facebook is appalling and heartless – and the way it was written was

dreadful. I just can't believe they didn't even have the decency to tell her over the phone, let alone in person. And to have the message all mis-spelt with capital letters and apostrophes missing is simply disrespectful and sets no example to other employees.

The implication, regarding the medium of the message and the spelling, is that a *personal* and *social* medium is being used inappropriately for a public, *formal* purpose. Thus, social network sites are being viewed by some as a social and private leisure context for personal display while others – particularly employers – treat them as a highly public domain that has the potential to damage an organisations' reputation. These examples draw attention to the extensive influence of large corporations in curbing the expression of personal views, as in the case of Apple, and the moral imperatives associated with mediated relationships in a polymedia environment (see Chapter 9). Given the pressures of public surveillance, it is not surprising that the vast possibilities for self-expression are often replaced by carefully controlled impressions of self, often structured around class affiliation (Papacharissi 2009) and cultures of taste (Liu 2007).

The choices made by users of social network sites about publicising their identities and how they use information that others impart about themselves can, then, have enormous consequences for personal reputations. Given the uncertain consequences of breaching traditional boundaries between the personal and the public, and the precarious demarcation of these borders, it is not surprising that most users of social media carefully monitor their digital footprints. In the United States, Madden and Smith (2010) undertook a comprehensive study of users' choices in displaying and managing online identities. Reputation monitoring increases as users become more familiar with the mechanism of online reputation management. Within a longitudinal frame, they found a number of emerging trends. Nearly two-thirds of adults now restrict access to their online profiles (Madden and Smith 2010). Over half of adult Internet users (57 per cent) used a search engine to look up their name to check the information publicly accessible about them in 2009 compared to 47 per cent in 2006. The high level of usage including features such as News Feed makes it particularly difficult for the young to opt out of the social network site rat race. As Tufekci puts it, 'If anything, it's identity-constraining now... You can't play with your identity if your audience is always checking up on you' (Tufekci 2008).[5]

Conclusions

This chapter demonstrates the relevance of Mead and Goffman's ideas for an understanding of the nature of self-presentation on social network sites. Highlighting the importance of the relational, symbolic interactionism constructs a model of self as inherently interactive and socially embedded. Following Mead, we can say that the process of self-presentation on social network sites is the result of the collective construction of the online 'I' and 'me' with the generalised digital 'other'. Highly coded cultural conventions and specific technological affordances may govern these online conventions alongside social and personal preferences, as the following chapters explain. Drawing on the work of Holdsworth and Morgan (2007), three levels of referencing the generalised, 'digital other' can be identified: a generalised imagined audience; more particular Friends and weak ties of acquaintanceship and 'significant others' comprising intimate ties of close friends and family.

When 'cyberspace' emerged in the early 1990s, it was venerated as a forum where people could reinvent their identities to become someone completely new. In the context of virtual worlds, such as the persistent worlds of massively multiplayer online video games, this has been achievable through the invention of online characters. But in contemporary social media contexts such as social network sites, online personas are not the norm. The overall design aims of social network sites are to ensure connections between profiles that reflect offline identities. Users of sites are likely to imagine rather abstract categories of audiences. This is because the ease with which individuals' profiles can be tracked and scrutinised constrains much identity construction, given the potential surveillance by employers and others in authority. The symbolic interactionist framework advances our understanding of the process of online self-presentation because the online self is constructed and negotiated in the same interactive way as the offline self.

Two sets of issues concerning online identities emerge from this chapter, first relating to *privacy and control* and second concerning *choice and agency*. First, several problems are thrown up by the challenges of privacy and self-presentation online. While the opportunities afforded by networked publics reconfigure publics more generally (boyd 2011), there are unexpected side-effects associated with constant self-disclosure through invisible audiences, collapsed contexts and the blurring of public and private. As boyd states, the dynamics that emerge from these privacy complications are often unforeseen. These outcomes also raise questions about perceptions of who 'owns' the comments that appear on a person's Facebook Wall: whether the owner, friends or both. This issue may become more important as these websites become increasingly interactive and participatory. Matters about authorship and control are growing more complex and ambiguous. These issues are of rising significance in the context of impression formation and management given that impressions are dependent on the perceptibility of independence or collusion in the creation of peoples' profiles. The self-management of mediated identities is becoming more and more complicated. The Facebook 'News Feed' element that updates users on their 'friend's' activities, views and moods contributes to this complexity. A conscientious balancing act is involved in negotiating intricate, multidimensional relationships. In this way a social network site profile becomes an evolving and fluctuating site of social interaction that reveals the various forces of networked publics.

Regarding the second issue about choice and agency, the accounts of impression and reputation management in this chapter not only confirm the symbolic interactionist constitution of the online self, with adults and teenagers negotiating 'Friends' to stage their identities (Livingstone 2008) but they also uncover wider questions about how people present themselves and gain a sense of control in these networked publics. Affirmative values of *choice* and *agency* coincide with positive visions of a new kind of sociality. They correspond with the characteristics of social network sites through their technical affordances of persistence, replicability, scalability and searchability. This personalised yet public medium of communication evokes powerful notions of personal autonomy and also of self-improvement and self-regulation. The public presentation of personal associations on social network sites has come to represent an individual's social identity and status (Donath and boyd 2004). In these circumstances, friendship is being reconfigured as a symbol of status.

As well as offering choices, these networks require careful management and promotion of the self within potentially precarious, risky public contexts. This technology exhibits features which reflect neoliberal ideologies and the thesis of individualism advanced by social theorists such as Giddens (addressed in Chapter 2 on theory intimacy). These resonances generate a critical tension. On the one hand, social network sites can be viewed as liberating acts of empowerment and as a mediator of new flexible modes of sociability. The interactive qualities of the medium offer multiple opportunities to express identities online and form wide networks, evoking the idea of a new and better kind of 'self' and better kind of network 'community'. On the other hand, the affordances of this personalised technology can be interpreted as exemplars of governmentality and self-regulation.

Social network sites have become prime sites of self-management and self-regulation. Neo-liberalism expresses a mode of governmentality that operates across a range of social spheres and constructs individuals as the entrepreneurs of their own lives (Rose 1999). The emphasis on individualism highlights the idea that the individual is constantly subjected to pressures and constraints from beyond the self. Individuals are expected to work on their self-presentations and mould their conduct and identities according to socially acceptable standards while always presenting their actions as freely chosen. In this respect, social network sites are settings for the exploration of the continual enterprise of self-improvement (Rose 1999: 4). In this context, the unmediated subject is a fractured subject who is made whole again through new media. It is an identity that needs to be constantly reinvented to keep up with the times and achieve personal and professional success. The affordances of social network sites fit neatly into these preoccupations of late modernity in which the subject is constantly updating itself.

Notwithstanding the pressures of self-regulation involved in the construction of the mediated self, adolescents are forging creative ways of dealing with these affordances. As the following chapter suggests, teenagers are developing various strategies for managing the social complexities of social network site environments (boyd 2008). Teens are likely to be more prepared to tolerate or welcome networked publics because many are coming of age during a time and in circumstances when networked opportunities are embedded in and accepted as part of everyday life. The following chapter addresses the multifaceted ways in which young people use social media to mediate their intimacies and wider social networks.

5
Social Media and Teenage Friendships

Introduction

After Facebook expanded its membership in September 2006 to anyone aged 13 and older, the majority who joined the site were defined as 'young profiles', including teenagers, students and young adult professionals (Lenhart et al. 2010). These so-called young 'digital natives' have been contrasted with older 'digital immigrants': older people who have learned to use the technologies as adults. However, this emphasis on 'natives' and the idea of having been 'born digital' naturalises young people's link to new media (Thorne 2009; see Palfrey and Gasser 2008). Nevertheless, 14- to 19-year-olds continue to dominate among users of social media, and the evidence suggests that they are using the technology intensively to foster and enhance friendship and intimacy online.

This chapter examines the role played by technology in enhancing and also disrupting social bonds between young people. In their pioneering collection of ethnographic studies of young people's emerging media practices, Mizuko Ito and colleagues (2010) have identified a number of important themes that shape young people's digital worlds. The authors found that youth participation with new media is motivated by friendships and shared interests. I draw on these rich ethnographic accounts, other key studies and group discussions I held with a small cohort of white middle- and working-class A-level students aged 17–18 in North East England. The chapter considers online social conventions, the management of friendships and peer group alliances, the social ranking of Friends and 'social drama' generated by teenagers about online chat, gossip and intrigues. The chapter also refers to survey findings from Europe and the United States. Several American studies of young people's engagement with social network sites have focused on MySpace as well as Facebook. However, MySpace changed its focus in 2010 from its original site content to entertainment content by targeting music, films, television and games, promoting bands and emerging trends in popular culture, all aimed at a young membership. Most research findings based on MySpace use cited in this chapter refer to the period before these changes took place.

The explosion in sites such as Facebook, MySpace and Bebo has been widely regarded as an exciting opportunity for youth. However, public anxieties have been generated by the apparent lack of privacy and teenagers' narcissistic fascination with self-display in their use of social network sites (Livingstone 2008). Social network sites have been blamed for causing teenage addictions to social media and for isolating adolescents from both their peers and their family. As such, new digital technology has become a major site of struggle – involving parents, teachers, the media and the state – about how young people's use of digital technologies should be regulated (Thorne 2009). Reviews of teenagers' engagement with social media are divided between those who regard youth as exploited and controlled by new technologies (see Schor 2004) and those who reserve judgement and highlight young people's creative and analytic skills (Buckingham 2000; Ito et al. 2010; Livingstone 2008). Issues such as privacy, online opportunities and risk in relation to youth intimacies are examined. As young people are viewed as particularly vulnerable to online bullying, the risks associated with online bullying are addressed. Parental concerns and control of youth online practices are significant issues in debates about mediated teenage friendships and intimacy which are discussed in the following chapter on home, family and new media.

Mediated teenage social worlds

Complementing the findings of ethnographic studies, large-scale surveys in the United States and Europe confirm that digital media use is now embedded in the daily lives of adolescents. Teenagers are more likely than adults to visit a social network profile persistently with 48 per cent visiting their profile at least once a day, according to a survey by the Pew Internet and American Life Project (Lenhart 2009). A further 32 per cent of teens visit their profiles weekly, and 20 per cent visit less often. Similar results were found in the recent EU Kids Online Survey (Livingstone et al. 2011) which was conducted in 25 countries and involved over 25,000 children aged 9–16 and their parents. The results demonstrate that young people are high, regular users of social media with 93 per cent of young users going online at least weekly and 60 per cent of them logging on everyday day or almost everyday. The survey also found that children are going online at a very young age. In Denmark and Sweden, the average age of first Internet use is seven and in many Northern European countries the average age is eight. Across all EU countries, a third of 9- to 10-year-olds who use the Internet go online daily and this increases to 80 per cent of 15- to 16-year-olds. Interestingly, young people not only continue to be more likely to log on at home (87 per cent) but they also engage with social media at school (63 per cent). The diversification of Internet access is also exemplified by the finding that 33 per cent of young people use mobile or hand-held devices (Livingstone et al. 2011).

Social media are embedded in young people's extracurricular, cultural and leisure activities. Digital communication may be a major feature of today's escalating global culture, yet for adolescents this technology is experienced as much more *local* mediated communication. Social network site engagement tends to involve co-present relationships within peer groups, confirming the *spatial* embeddedness of online social ties for teenagers. Importantly, these new modes of sociality remain firmly part of and derived from traditional spatial contexts of family and school. The wider social context of mediated friendships among youth provides important clues about how they use new media technologies. Theorists such as Giddens (1991, 1992) and Beck and Beck-Gernsheim (1995) maintain that youth embody the late modern emphasis on choice and diversity in intimate relationships (see Chapter 3). This trend of individualisation corresponds with the expanded educational and occupational prospects for young people from the late twentieth century onwards.

Individualisation coincides with the emergence of 'young adulthood' as a new distinct life phase in which adolescence shares characteristics with adulthood through increased agency and personal autonomy. The paradigm of childhood studies of the 1990s advanced the idea of childhood as a life phase shaped by children's own agency (see James and Prout 1997; James et al. 1998). These changes in the lives of youth correspond with the growing significance assigned to friendship in people's lives (Roseneil and Budgeon 2004; Spencer and Pahl 2006). Social media technologies are providing a vital cultural framework for young people through which one can explore the sense of choice and diversity in relationships. The increasing technological affordances of digital media have changed young people's transition to adulthood.

The rise of personalised digital communication in the early twenty-first century has meant that, for the first time, young people can interact almost exclusively with one another. Associations between adolescents have taken priority over intergenerational familial ties. This forms part of the move towards 'selective sociality' (Matsuda 2005) in which teenagers can act on personal choices about whom to associate with. This emphasis on agency and selectivity corresponds with Spencer and Pahl's notion of 'personal communities' (see Chapter 3) in which voluntary, freely chosen ties are privileged over ties of duty while simultaneously fostering solidarities within individuals' micro-social worlds. Conversely, although youth have cultivated a distinct generational identity, the phase of financial dependence on parents has lengthened through extended education (France 2007; Livingstone 2009b). Contemporary patterns of youth sociability are, then, both distinct from yet also reliant on adult social worlds. With limited social power or economic resources, peer status among teenagers becomes paramount (Buckingham 2006; Ito et al. 2010; Livingstone 2009b).

The range of studies about teenagers' use of social media by Ito and colleagues (2010) confirms that the social relations developed in the school environment are the most significant in defining young people's peers and friendships. The researchers conducted 23 case studies that documented the views and experiences of digital and networked media use among young people across the United States ranging in age from 12 to 18. The authors confirm that social media is providing a vital platform for adolescents and even younger children on which they can stage their status negotiations in and beyond school. Today's personalised communication tools allow youth to challenge the school system of adults controlling young peoples' *object of attention*: adolescents can select whom they listen to and whom they address, even in a classroom where they can now easily text one another. Thus, peer groups at school and related contexts remain paramount in the formation of friendships online and offline.

Similarly, in her extensive research on teenagers' use of MySpace, danah boyd (2007) observed that when using the Internet in the adult-controlled and private context of home, they are creating the public digital spaces that she refers to as 'networked publics' (see Chapters 3 and 4). These networked publics are vital contexts for negotiating teen identities, gaining status and forming intimacies away from adult attention. Within youth-mediated social relations, adults tend to play a secondary rather than a central, participating role. Rather than being addressed as participants of *equal* status, adults are often consigned to the role of financing and supervising youth media practices. Indeed, teenagers' engagement with social media is part of a longer history of intergenerational tensions over parental authority, youth culture and peer relations fostered at school (boyd 2010a: 82; Livingstone 2009b; Postman 1982; Thorne 2009).

Digital media technologies have, then, presented children and teenagers with a focused yet pervasive 'private sphere' in which they can communicate mainly with age-related friends and wider contacts beyond the scrutiny of parents or teachers. Yet these technologies throw up enormous challenges about the negotiation of privacy in a public context. As indicated in the preceding chapters, 'network public culture' refers to the way that personal culture has now spilled over into public culture (boyd 2007, 2010a). Many teenagers have entered this networked public culture through social network sites such as Facebook, Bebo and MySpace (boyd 2010a). The personal and public dimensions of culture permeate one another through the extensive reach of sites with their easy links to fashion, celebrity and sport cultures. The affordances of persistence, searchability, replicability and invisible audiences affect the ways in which youth interact with one another. In this networked public culture, personal culture is now being conducted under a public gaze that can be scrutinising and judgemental as well as convivial and reciprocal. Thus, while these technologies offer a feeling of privacy, seemingly beyond adult surveillance, the public nature of this network culture throws up risks. Today, young people find that they are actually negotiating their friendships in a very public arena, often under the watchful eyes of their peers and parents.

Youth networks

Within today's polymedia environment, teenagers sustain multiple channels of communication with intimates by using three main technologies: mobile phones, instant messaging (IM) and social network sites (Pasco 2010: 121). Mobile phones enable adolescents to use private channels of communication, to maintain contact and monitor one another. IM technologies are used to sustain continual casual contact with intimates. However, email is diminishing in popularity among the young. Like Gershon's (2010) university student respondents, the group of school students I spoke with in North East England said they rarely use email and some have never used the medium. Email is perceived as a highly formal way of communicating and equated with letter writing. Some admitted they simply don't know how to write an email, in terms of style. For this group, email communication lacks the sense of casualness, playfulness and spontaneity sought from social media. Social network sites such as Facebook are, on the other hand, highly popular. They afford a networked public of broad peer groups.

Site profiles constitute major contexts for representations of intimacy. Textual and visual symbolism is used to publicly display the level of seriousness or superficiality of particular relationships. Facebook is prominent, mainly as a result of its News Feed feature which broadcasts information about participants' personal lives to a wide network of people. As Gershon (2010: 77) states, 'people can know about friends' love lives even though they haven't spoken to that friend in months'. One student, 'Yi-Lun', expressed her dislike for Facebook because, as she said, it 'defines my relationships' (Gershon 2010: 64). The privacy issue is also illustrated by another example from Gershon about the problems of texts and blogs getting in the wrong hands: Rose's boyfriend may think the texts he is sending are secret, but Rose admits to showing extracts to her friends, especially when seeking relationship advice. Similarly, when Frank discovered his parents were avid readers of his blog, he said it was like their 'finding condoms in his wallet' (Gershon 2010: 166).

Teenagers' online connections usually correspond with offline associations but digital sites also offer young people the tools to transcend traditional and institutional barriers in forming romantic associations. When used together in a polymediated framework, these communication technologies enable teenagers to engage in regular and continuous exchanges with each other, described by Ito and Okabe as 'telecocooning in the full-time intimate community' (Ito and Okabe 2005: 137). This polymediated cocooning evokes the sense of being enveloped and immersed in a bubble of peer group intimacy. For example, boyd quotes an 18-year-old interviewee from Colorado who emphasised the significance of new media for the daily lives of young people: 'If you're not on MySpace, you don't exist' (boyd 2010a: 80).

Social media performs a vital role in maintaining contact between young people at times and in situations when face-to-face contact is restricted. Teenagers gather in networked public spaces in the same way as they have gathered in shopping malls and on the streets (boyd 2007). In this way, social media is providing tools that enable youth to expand social exchanges beyond physical boundaries. This mediated interaction projects features of communication explained by symbolic interactionism (see Chapter 4). Young people establish their relations, construct their status and generate a social 'me', an identity in the sense described by Mead (1934). This type of mediated interaction has become all the more significant for young people who find themselves under increasing surveillance in public spaces, often being moved away from streets, parks, shopping precincts and libraries (Buckingham 2000). Networked publics either replace or supplement the street as a crucial site for socialising with friends (boyd 2007). Yet many of the main motives for interactions remain the same. For most youth, the main practices are motivated by friendship with an emphasis on participation described by the Ito team as 'hanging out' (Ito et al. 2010).

Four types of everyday peer negotiations associated with social network sites are identified by boyd: making friends; performing friendships; articulating friendship hierarchies and rankings and navigating issues of status, attention and drama (boyd 2010a). The social interactions occurring at school spill over and extend into social media contexts and then extend back to offline spaces. As a consequence, online and offline friendship-driven practices cannot be treated as separate worlds (boyd 2010a). Knowing the codes for the relevant settings and performing the necessary shifts in public and private personas mark the acceptable social citizen from the anti-social 'others' (Goffman 1959). A shared understanding of friendship and romance is being constructed through social network sites by uploading images, videos, comments, sayings, words of encouragement, inspirational quotes and images taken from websites such as Photobucket on their profiles (Martinez 2010: 85–88). For example, one MySpace user explained that she participated in 'MySpace parties', consisting of sleepovers with friends involving dressing up, dancing, impersonating celebrities and taking photos of each other to be uploaded on to their MySpace pages (Horst 2010: 92–93). Events such as proms, graduation parties and graduation ceremonies are also recorded on Facebook and MySpace so that spaces of networked public culture become major chronicles of the initiation and coming-of-age processes for teenagers.

Young people are using texts and images from established website collections of images indicating that youth's friendship maintenance typically occurs within a dominant discourse of love and friendship which is regularly represented and circulated among friends. Some teenagers collect images and texts in Photobucket albums which are drawn on to post on bulletins to indicate the significance of friendship and romance. For example, 'I want to love somebody like you', 'I want to be your favourite hello and your hardest goodbye', 'Texting is love', 'Cell phone love', 'My cell phone is love', 'Best friends' (Martinez 2010: 87). The images and words tend to be conventional, conforming to traditional gender roles. Yet some move beyond conventional and consumerist rep-resentations of teenage intimacies, for example, by exploring gay and lesbian websites (see Gray 2009). As rituals of heterosexuality may be highly structured, gay teenagers may prefer to explore the Internet for like-minded networks.

Choosing and managing Friends

Although Facebook and MySpace are usually depicted as sites for initi-ating new connections, teenagers emphasise the opposite that IM and social network sites are mainly used for socialising with people they already know from school, religious centres, summer camps and other leisure and sports activities. Like adults, adolescents are grounding their online relationships in offline contexts. Survey findings of US teenager online activities confirm that most use social media to socialise with people they already know or are already loosely connected with (boyd 2010a: 89; Lenhart and Madden 2007; Subrahmanyam and Greenfield 2008). This appears to be a transnational trend among youth. Studies of patterns of Internet use by Singaporean youth show that they tend not to use the Internet for replacing existing relationships. Instead, they use it to expand their groups of friends and to sustain existing friend-ships (Waipeng Lee and Brenda Chan 2003). Likewise, a survey of Israeli teenagers suggests that those who do develop friendships online tend to develop less homogenous connections than teenagers who build con-nections with existing friends and acquaintances (Mesch and Talmud 2007a). While the social contexts of schools have a strong influence on the ways that teenagers select friends, these institutions tend to segregate young people by age, social class, gender, religion, ethnicity and race. This segregation can foster relatively homogenous friendship groups with similar aged people who share interests, identities and ideals (Ito et al. 2010).

The design and organisation of the social network sites guide young people towards publicly recording and displaying their personal con-nections. The public presentation of Friend lists influences the processes and performance of friendship in everyday life, online and offline. Through public endorsements of personal connections, this public shar-ing of personal associations signifies identity and status (Donath and boyd 2004). Choice of Friends functions as a symbol of a person's self-representation on the site as well as part of the regulation of access control to certain features (e.g., commenting) and content (e.g., blog posts). Teenagers are intentionally using listed 'Friends' to express their identities (Livingstone 2008). The need for approval to list one another's names is an important stage of friendship processing on most sites. Since the term 'Friend' is used to signify *all* categories of associations including members of family as well as conventional peer group friends, this selection process can create anxieties for teenagers. So they draw on a wide range of strategies to select and manage associations as their online Friends. In addition to including their friends and some wider peers, they may exclude people they know intimately. They may be reluctant to display intimates such as parents or siblings on a public site. Conversely, they may accept requests from contemporaries that they know of but are not intimate with, in order to avoid offence. Friends of friends are encouraged by the social network sites to consent to peers' requests to keep the channels of communication open (boyd 2010a; Pascoe 2010).

Most sites persuade users to add Friends who are not intimates, but privacy features can block people who are not listed as friends from accessing profiles. Many teenagers are using this and other privacy features. For example, the EU Kids Online survey found that among European children aged 9–16, 43 per cent of social network site users maintain private profiles so that only their friends can see it, and 28 per cent report that their profile is partially private so that friends of friends and networks can see it. Yet, significantly, 26 per cent report that their profile is public so that anyone can see it (Livingstone et al. 2011). Early users of MySpace adopted broadly convivial conventions by receiving anyone as Friends. However, online social customs soon altered with most teenagers now declining these requests as routine practice, thereby reflecting offline customs. Those who are more receptive to strangers in their Friends lists are often criticised for trying 'to seem more popular to themselves' (boyd 2010a: 96) and treating sites such as MySpace as a popularity contest by adding strangers. For example, Mark, a white 15-year-old from Seattle, complained that,

> [t]here's all these people that judge [MySpace] as a popularity contest and just go around adding anyone that they barely even know just so they can have like, you know, 500,000 friends just because it's cool. I think that's stupid, personally.
>
> (quoted in boyd 2010a: 96)

Some teenagers do use network sites to foster links with complete strangers. Thirty per cent of Internet users aged between 9 and 16 have communicated with a person they have not met face-to-face according to the EU Kinds Online findings (Livingstone et al. 2011). However, it is atypical for young people to meet the new contacts offline. Only 9 per cent had met an online contact offline in the past year. Yet a US survey found that as many as 43 per cent of teenagers with a social network site profile reported being contacted by a person who had no prior link to themselves or their friends (Lenhart and Madden 2007). Teenagers who tend to be excluded or bullied by peers often take the chance to network outside their school contexts. Moreover, those with distinctive leisure activities or unusual, specialised or 'geeky' interests that may not be catered for in school often develop online friendships through shared pursuits (boyd 2010a).

Similarly, lesbian, gay, bisexual and transgender (LGBT) teenagers can often feel marginalised at school and may discover valuable social media connections with other LGBT youth (Gray 2009). Many, particularly in small rural communities, learn to be cautious about whom they reveal information to. In these ways, social media seem to offer young people opportunities to manage their sense of emotional risk. However, adolescents who search for communities that share intimacies in common such as gay youth may be more susceptible to unwelcome approaches from strangers. Although social media offer prospects of developing virtual communities with gay youth, it exposes them to risk. Some teenagers who participate on chat room websites or on MSN Messenger in search of like-minded communities may find themselves on non-age graded sites which can be a shock (Pascoe 2010).

Thus, a significant minority of teenagers is developing new online associations through social network sites, but this occurs in a culture of disapproval. This practice is condemned by most teenagers. Classmates tend to view teenagers that meet new people online as peculiar or 'freaky' (boyd 2010: 91). This activity is seen as a failure to make friends at school and also perceived to be risky. Evidence suggests that a moral panic has emerged around 'stranger danger' online, reflecting the general concerns young people have in initiating contact with strangers in unmediated public spaces (Levine 2002; Valentine 2004). School assemblies routinely address issues of online dangers with an emphasis on sexual predators. Although public fears about online 'predators' do not match the extent and realities of risky online behaviour, when they occur they can be serious and are often widely reported in the press (Livingstone et al. 2011). These concerns fuel parental inclinations to restrict young people's online behaviour (boyd 2010a; Livingstone et al. 2011; Wolak et al. 2008).

Nevertheless, the accumulation of 'mass Friends' which involves connecting with strangers can be quite tempting to teenagers if it enhances their status. Young people may accumulate Friends for amusement or rivalry rather than for the sake of developing valued friendships. The practice of collecting attractive women as Friends is so widespread among boys that profiles of attractive women are being provided by spammers to entice men. Adolescents regularly send Friend requests to bands and celebrities and value the connection as a fan and the intermittent comments from them. Such connections serve as a public display of taste and identity, forming an important dimension of self -presentation (Donath and boyd 2004; Goffman 1959; see Chapter 4).

Young people may also use the Friending category to establish networks not based on intimacy and friendship but on specific connections and relationships such as religion, sexuality, nationality or ethnic identity. Although some go on to develop personal relationships through these networks, this is unusual. Connecting to these virtual networks can offer individual opportunities to participate in a networked public of people that share identities (boyd 2010a). Some add to their Friends list people they are attracted to in the hopes that a connection might develop into a more intimate bond. Yet this custom is often contentious. However, there is little social reprisal in rejecting Friend requests from strangers. Teenagers worry more about rejecting individuals that they already know. To avoid the tensions in relationships that can be generated by this practice, young people often accept friend requests from recognised peers including friends, acquaintances and classmates no matter what the quality of the relationship.

When teenagers meet new people 'offline', they often check over their network site profiles to learn more about the person's tastes, style and social connection. This helps them to judge compatibility levels and provide useful conversation material in the same way that adults do. The ritual of Friending friends of friends and other casual acquaintances can lead to consequential face-to-face interaction when young people see one another at school or some social event. In these ways, the custom of Friending can provide the foundations for a future friendship or romance. Importantly, then, these kinds of requests to accept acquaintances as Friends are perceived as *prospective* friendships, with the potential to transform acquaintances into friends. This relates to Haythornthwaite's notion of 'latent ties' (Chapter 1). Communication technologies open up new channels of connection between persons who would not normally communicate in other circumstances. These 'latent ties' are defined as connections that are 'technically possible but not yet activated socially' (Haythornthwaite 2005: 137). The concept of latent ties helps differentiate between various Friending customs on social network sites.

The affordances of social network sites give teenagers the opportunity to develop a new relationship relatively fast by upgrading it to the rank or intensity of friendship or romance. However, several Friend requests from casual acquaintances fail to progress with no further contact involved. This can create confusion about the status of a Friend request. Two people may be Facebook friends yet not talk to one another at school (boyd 2010a). While most teenagers are uncomfortable about deleting people from their Friends lists, some regard Facebook as an effective way to manage friendships in a manner which can be difficult to convey at school. The practice of Facebook Defriending can be precarious, given the lack of consensus about rules of discarding former Friends. In a study by Gershon (2010) on teen-mediated break-ups, she cites an example where one girl noticed she had more than 700 Friends on Facebook and decided to Defriend nearly all except 56 as a way of removing 'clutter' from her Newsfeed. By contrast, another girl who stated that she would never Defriend anyone noticed she had been Defriended. She believed the former friend had a vendetta against her.

The socially unacceptable nature of deleting a 'Friend' that one knows is underlined by the fact that malicious deletions often take place after an argument or break-up. This can lead to social embarrassment if individuals mistakenly delete people they know. Although deleting known individuals from a Friends list can be construed as spiteful, changing an open profile to a closed profile and deleting strangers is seen as normal. Deleting and adding Friends allows teenagers to control access to their profiles and take control of the consequences of their decisions. Given that adolescents tend to link up online with peer groups that they interact with offline, their Friend list choices online impact directly on their everyday, face-to-face connections (boyd 2010a).

Friendship ranking and mediated social drama

Ethnographic studies of teenage girls' friendships in the United Kingdom have confirmed the importance and closeness of young people's friendships (Griffiths 1995; Hey 1997). Sharing, trust, loyalty and keeping secrets mark the closeness of these friendships. Girls often describe their friendships with other girls as 'the most important thing' in their lives. Vivienne Griffiths' (1995) analysis of quarrels between girls suggests that they are often a sign of closeness and intense emotions rather than a sign of shallow friendships as popular stereotypes imply. Griffiths reveals the continuity of relationships and emphasises the ways in which teenagers resist friendship break-ups. Traditionally, friendship connections have been displayed through a variety of symbols and gifts, particularly among pre-teenage girls. These practices decline as children get older but social network sites provide important new ways of continuing public declarations of friendship and of extending it to boys as well as girls.

In online contexts, young users of social network sites can avoid offence by categorising all their contacts as 'Friends'. However, on some sites such as MySpace, an extra feature called 'Top Friends' which used to be called 'Top 8' makes it more complicated by compelling users to declare their most intimate friends or so-called 'bestest friends'. This category was intended to give users the opportunity to exhibit close friendships. However, it generates the kind of controversy that can be avoided on straightforward Friend connections. It confirms young peoples' need for acceptance and affirmation. The Top Friends feature encourages young people to create a friendship hierarchy or friendship ranking by listing up to 24 names on a grid and ordering them from first to last. This generates all sorts of drama as expressed by Anindita, an Indian 17-year-old from Los Angeles:

> People will be like, "Why am I number two? You're number one on my page." I was like, "Well, I can't make everyone number two. That's impossible." Especially with boyfriends and girlfriends, get in a fight like, "Why is she before me? I'm your girlfriend. I should be higher than her." I'm just like, "Okay." I don't really think it's a big deal, the top thing. If you're friends, you shouldn't lose your friendship over that".
>
> (quoted in boyd 2010a: 101)

Many teenagers view the Top Friends feature as proof of the quality of their friendships. It becomes a very public demonstration of teenagers' social standing. Not surprisingly, many teenagers find the social dynamic surrounding Top Friends irritating or distressing. It can undermine confidence and many become obsessed with the process since it forms a key topic of conversation among friends. Sharing is important in the mediation of Top Friends, with teenagers expecting friends named in their top list to reciprocate. The anxieties involved have parallels in offline contexts such as choosing invitations to parties. An example given by boyd is from Jordan, a biracial Mexican-white

15-year-old from Austin, Texas, who was quoted as saying: 'Oh, it's so stressful because if you're in someone else's [Top Friends] then you feel bad if they're not in yours.' Nadine, a white 16-year-old from New Jersey, described this on her MySpace: 'Well, today it's the MySpace Top 8. It's the new dangling carrot for gaining superficial acceptance. Taking someone off your Top 8 is your new passive-aggressive power play when someone pisses you off' (quoted in boyd 2010a: 102).

Pushing friendship ranking into a public domain makes the practice of 'Top Friending' significant, even though it can be altered. Young people can find themselves pressured or intimidated to select, delete or replace individuals as a 'Top Friend'. Teenagers tend to place the person they are dating first, and then order names down from there according to level of intimacy. It is also common practice for some teenagers to place family members first, in the Top 8, either to circumvent tensions with friends or because they regard their family members as close friends. To avert potential arguments, some teenagers avoid using the Top Friends feature entirely or, instead, list musical bands or family members. This mediated positioning of friends is an abstracted practice that leads to tensions and controversies because direct and blunt ranking practices are uncommon in offline interactions. Moreover, adolescents' friendships may fluctuate according to circumstances such as social context: in school, sports teams, leisure and home life. The oscillations and intricacies of everyday life friendships and interactions cannot be reflected accurately on social network site friendship hierarchies such as Top Friends, yet these rankings tend to fix them in an abstracted manner, having offline effects. Through site design, the ranking of Friends renders explicit a practice which usually remains implicit (boyd 2010a: 103–104).

Online friendship rankings such as MySpace and Facebook encourage a *hyper-friendship* experience among adolescents by amplifying the kinds of cliques, popularity ratings and fluctuations in friendships that occur in offline worlds. 'Social drama' is a term used by Ito et al. (2010) to describe the ways that social network sites generate gossip, intrigues and falling outs. Rumours can be spread through gossip, and bullying can take place as part of these social dramas with social media changing the speed, scope and scale of the relations. In my own discussions with A-level students in North East England, a male student mentioned that 'you might sometimes find out that someone held some event, social event like a party and realise you weren't invited'. The group agreed that this was the kind of knowledge that was often hurtful yet would rarely have been an issue in a pre-social media age, since 'ignorance is bliss'. They were also mystified at the way certain individuals generate a cult following as youth cultural gurus on microblogging platforms such as Tumblr. Adolescents use social network sites to display or reshape identities, create narratives about social connections and generate or allay anxieties about reputation and esteem. In these ways, the public networked quality of social media plays a vital role in cultivating teenagers' status and exposing the social struggles and dramas associated with these performances.

Teenagers have to manage personal details in a public sphere and deal with new thresholds and notions of 'privacy' within their intimate relations (Livingstone 2008). In this respect, social media appear contradictory: they create new opportunities for group privacy yet at the same time can undermine personal privacy. The affordances of social media can change the level of visibility of everyday 'social dramas' occurring in school and other favoured teenage settings. Thus, as boyd (2010a) argues, social media forms a major catalyst in teen drama with the technologies making gossip easier to circulate, to go viral. She provides a rich example. Elena, a 16-year-old girl from Armenia who was adopted by a Mormon family in suburban northern California, explained:

> And the thing on a lot of MySpace is it brings a lot of drama. A lot of drama. Because it's like, oh, well, "Jessica said something about you." "Oh, really?" "Yeah, we heard it from this girl, Alicia." So then you click on Jessica and talk about comments that Alicia did and then you go from Alicia to her friends. It's this whole going around. And then I'm like, "I was on Alicia's email last night and she's saying this about you." It just gets really out of control, I think.
>
> (quoted in boyd 2010a: 106)

Friends and comments on people's pages are regarded by many teenagers as symbols of friendliness and mutual support. Others also regard them as markers of social worth, believing that having a substantial range of Friends and comments is proof that they are popular and not marginalised from their peers. A small number of adolescents may use network sites to experiment with their identities to gain self-confidence yet teenagers' online identities tend to be shaped, guided and regulated by the public network of peers who regularly 'check each other out'. Young people can gain information about one another online with ease, so they regularly listen in or 'eavesdrop' on their peers and update themselves on gossip and lives of peers. Ito et al. (2010) refer to ambient virtual co-presence to describe this new form of awareness of each others' lives. This *ambient awareness* can be described as a distracted form of information gathering about other's personal lives, until some detail pops up about one's ex-partner or about someone who is disliked or envied.

The 'News Feed' design feature on Facebook presents updates of the activities undertaken by users' Friends on the site. It intensifies ambient awareness as a dimension of the everyday routines of teenage socialisation. Activities publicised include events such as when two individuals decide to start dating or they break up, when a person places a comment on someone's Wall or uploads new photos. This tool is optional but is viewed as almost compulsory. Most teenagers use it to keep informed about interesting gossip or sensational details and to monitor who is communicating to whom. At one and the same time, the social drama generated by News Feed forms part of the expression and regulation of teenage sociality and sexuality. As teenagers themselves are aware, the downside of the News Feed feature is that 'everybody knows your business' and some even think this viral nature is 'creepy' and similar to 'stalking' (boyd 2010a: 106–107). This tool magnifies the public nature of social network site activity, allowing gossip to go viral at breakneck speed. However, in interviews with teenagers, Ito et al. (2010) found that most rumours proliferate through the more private routes of IM and text messaging. Teenagers can not only communicate with several people at the same time through IM but they can also copy and paste exchanges to distribute information. Text messaging can trigger gossip chains by forwarding messages. Even though these channels are deemed more 'private', information can become 'public' through sharing.

Bullying online

The affordances of social network sites offer many opportunities to offend and intimidate. Computers and mobile phones extend the range of traditional types of bullying. The public and enduring nature of mediated information and its proliferating potential may generate rumours through adolescent gossip and intensify arguments and disputes over status. However, certain studies conclude that Internet-related bullying is not a common experience among teenagers (Wolak, Mitchell, and Finkelhor (2007). Some scholars argue that Internet-related bullying differs in nature from harassment in school (Ybarra et al. 2007). Others have found that young people develop effective strategies to deal with web harassment when confronted by it (Livingstone et al. 2011). Nevertheless, so-called cyberbullying remains a serious issue which has gained extensive media coverage and prompted widespread parental anxieties.

A 15-year-old teenager driven to suicide in July 2011 by online bullies was reported widely in the British press.[1] An inquest confirmed that her name continued to be vilified after her death. It was established that Natasha MacBryde threw herself under a train because she was a victim of Internet 'trolls' who posted a picture of her on a tribute site under the banner 'I caught the train to heaven LOL'. The term 'Internet troll' refers to a person who posts an intentionally insulting, controversial or irreverent message to a newsgroup or in discussion forums in order to cause offence.[2] A video called 'Tasha the Tank Engine' was also removed from YouTube. It was stated that Natasha was bullied by a mixed sex group of ten children who called themselves 'The Ten'. She had received a threatening message through the network site called Formspring a few days before she died. It read 'Youre a f***ing slut hiding under all your makeup. You think you're pretty and that all the guys like you. Start acting nice to people or you will lose everyone.' Natasha had Googled 'the easiest way to jump in front of a train' and 'suicide methods' an hour before her death on February 12.[3] A further tragedy was widely reported in the press after Lady Gaga sang a tribute to 14-year-old Jamey Rodemeyer from Buffalo, New York, who apparently killed himself after sending her a thank-you message on Twitter.[4] He had suffered from homophobic online bullying for more than a year and wrote a blog about the difficulties he experienced at school. Among the anonymous posting was one that said 'JAMIE IS STUPID, GAY, FAT AND UGLY. HE MUST DIE!'.

Parental anxieties have also been triggered by a number of polls on Internet bullying and 'sexting' which is the term used to refer to the sharing of nude photos or videos and other images of a sexual nature. For example, an Associated Press-MTV poll in 2011 drawn from online interviews with 1,355 people aged 14 to 24 nationwide found that more than half of young Americans have experienced taunting, sexting or bullying on social network sites.[5] The survey was part of an MTV campaign called 'A Thin Line' aimed at preventing the spread of digital abuse.[6] A third of young people in the AP-MTV survey said that they had participated in 'sexting'. Despite the risks, sexting is not regarded as a particularly serious issue among many young people. However, half of those who have posted naked photos felt coerced into it, including nearly two-thirds of young women. The AP – MTV poll found that among those young people who were in a relationship, 40 per cent said that their partners had used computers or mobile phones to abuse or manipulate them.

The EU Kids Online survey discovered that bullying online, involving the receipt of malicious or spiteful messages, is the most upsetting risk for European children and teenagers even though it is comparatively infrequent. Among European children who have experienced online bullying, they are more likely to have been bullied on a social network site or by IM than by email, in gaming sites or in chatrooms (Livingstone et al. 2011). The researchers found fewer experiences of online bullying across Europe than the above American surveys: 6 per cent of 9- to 16-year-olds have been sent malicious or upsetting messages online, and 3 per cent admitted sending such messages to others. Over half of European children and adolescents who were sent bullying messages were moderately or very upset. However, the study also found that more bullying takes place offline than online. Online bullying remains difficult to define, despite a wide range of research. This indicates that it is difficult to identify how online bullying differs from other types of bullying. Some incidents are one-offs and others are part of repeated harassment or bullying. Teenagers themselves are unsure about what constitutes cyberbullying (Ito et al. 2010). Many acknowledge that they are unsure whether rumours could be labelled as bullying. The key issue seems to be that when bullying moves online, the technological and social affordances comprising invisible audiences, collapsed contexts and the blurring of public and private (boyd 2011) allow the bullying to escalate in terms of scale, publicity and anguish caused.

Suicides by teenagers that have been associated with online bullying have generated widespread concern in many countries. In response, cyberbullying is being taken seriously by governments who are searching for policy solutions. In March 2011, the US President, Barack Obama, gathered together students, parents and specialists at the White House to address the problem of 'cyberbullying'.[7] In the United Kingdom, the Education Department supports an annual conference to guide schools in tacking the issue. New research on cyberbullying highlights the role of parents in prevention. A number of bodies have been set up to address the problem including, for example in the United Kingdom, the AntiBullying Alliance and in the United States, *Stop Cyberbullying Before it Starts*,[8] a national Crime Prevention Council publication.

Conclusions

As emphasised throughout this book, mediated 'friendship' is being shaped by rules that overlap with yet are distinct from conventional and earlier everyday senses of friendship. However, the distinctive features and qualities of this mediated friendship are being experienced much more acutely by young people. Through the ritual of displaying, selecting and also ranking lists of personal connections to everyone who has access to the profile, social media are transforming the meanings and performance of friendship for teenagers. Most see peer networks as the foundation for their identity formation and associations. Through gossip, flirting, teasing and 'hanging around', social network sites have become a normal part of adolescent life. They enhance teenagers' peer networks by providing young people with the digital tools to be more in tune with and more informed about the lives and interests of their friends and peers. They exchange ideas, share photos, music and other interests and also emotions. These network sites are therefore central to the practices of developing, performing and strengthening friendships and status. However, the public and networked characteristics of online communication shape these everyday practices in new ways. They can both strengthen and break social connections (see Chapter 7).

Thus, social media mirrors or approximates many offline activities that were routine for young people before the age of the Internet. Yet it is also altering the dynamics involved in these social practices. Teenagers clearly use social media to cultivate new friendships, but they tend to cultivate them through existing links, through acquaintances or friends of friends. Teens who search for new friends through social network sites are a minority. Developing online connections is discredited and influenced by adult fears of 'stranger danger' and the strong youth customs that focus on school-oriented sociability. However, some teens seek social approval which is lacking locally. This is exemplified by a new kind of friendship ranking that emerges through social network site engagement which generates a new *hyper-friendship* among the young.

Four sets of issues become apparent within changing meanings and practices of friendship among youth which involve ethical dimensions. First, young people are developing complex skills geared to networked publics about how to articulate and mediate friendships and how to handle mediated drama. Teenagers are realising that new media literacy is *central* to their participation in society (Livingstone 2008). In this sense, youth can be viewed as *polymedia vanguards*: a social group which has had to develop technical and media skills to participate in a range of social media as a fundamental way of managing its relationships. The growing importance of social media means that learning how to administer and cope with networked sociability becomes a vital competence for future college and professional lives where social media skills are deemed necessary.

A second issue relates to the amplified risks and opportunities in presenting the self and socialising. The processes of marking out lists of online Friends make social status and friendship much more explicit and more public for teenagers. Peer negotiation is made more visible and is configured in new ways leading to peer regulation of sociability. Features such as the News Feed exemplify the tendency for youth networks to involve continuous, rolling communication. In these ways, social media are facilitating young peoples' communicative autonomy. Yet by expressing intimacies online, adolescents find themselves exposed to more intensive public monitoring. Teenagers can now display new dimensions of their identities and, at the same time, can have their self-presentations publicly reinterpreted or wrecked by others (boyd 2010a).

A third theme is that, within these wider social and technological changes, young people are collaboratively developing new rules. The circumstances during which codes of behaviour associated with social media use are scrutinised are when intimate relationships end. This issue is addressed in Chapter 7 on dating and breaking up. At the level of interpersonal relations, all young people now have to make ethical decisions all the time about how they use social media. Being the most intense users of social media, young people are compelled to develop an awareness of social behaviour related to these technologies.

A fourth issue is that these new media affordances may be leading to changes in young peoples' relationships with the institutions of family and school. Young people are developing a distinct sense of group identity derived from social media. Yet at the same time, these personalised technologies seem to be amplifying the long-term trend of social and cultural segregation from the adult world. By taking priority over familial ties, social bonds between young people are developing on new terms. Although family and school continue to have a strong influence on the organisation of social media by youth, social media use is leading to a relative separation of parents and teachers from these youth worlds. Social media intensify adolescents' immersion in peer-based status communications and provide them with the tools to negotiate their identities in a setting that is increasingly independent from parents. The issue of child–parent relations is taken up in the following chapter, by looking at how social media correspond with the changing nature of family and home life.

6
Home, Families and New Media

Introduction

Families, households and personal lives are becoming not only increasingly diverse in their forms and practices but also more dispersed through geographical and social mobility. These trends correspond with dramatic changes in the ways that family members communicate with one another through the use of new media (Bengston 2001). Enhanced communication technologies installed in the home and the growing uses of digital technologies have transformed the relationship between homes and the outside world and between individuals who have moved away from their families and home. Factors that influence the adoption and sustained use of communication technologies in the home also impact the cultural and moral values of families and personal lives (Little et al. 2009; Madianou and Miller 2012). Recent research findings have identified some of the beneficial features of new media in fostering and enhancing social and emotional interactions within families, households and personal lives.

The domestic context and the relationships between parents, siblings and extended kin play important roles in structuring individual access to social media and types of use. Even though Internet access is branching out from the home via handheld mobile devices, the domestic environment remains the most likely location of Internet use among children and adolescents, with 87 per cent accessing social digital media from home (Livingstone et al. 2011). To a great extent, the home defines the nature of digital media engagement by setting parameters for technologies of personal communication.

This chapter addresses three interrelated themes that underscore the changing nature of the household and families in relation to social media. First, the presence and positioning of media devices in the home and family negotiations of technology use are examined. Second, family dynamics are focused on to assess how children negotiate privacy, particularly in relation to parental surveillance of children's home-based media use. This includes a discussion of family identities and social media use. A range of issues are highlighted which relate to the influence of parental values and discourses on home-based media cultures. Differences between fathers and mothers in their attitudes and approaches to children's media use are considered. The gap between children's and parents' understanding and skills in using social media becomes apparent. This influences how social media is used to develop and sustain family identities. Third, the uses of social media to mediate familial intimacies among transnational families separated through migration are examined.

The family, home and technologies of communication

Our relationship to domestic space has changed significantly with the arrival of digital media in the sense that the home is being transformed into a key site of multimedia culture (Livingstone 2002). However, modes of engagement with home-based communication technologies are affected by new patterns of migration and a global economic downturn. These trends combine to disturb past traditional meanings of home. Traditional ideas about home in relation to community and 'public' space have been destabilised by the symbolic boundaries being placed around the household as a privatised space (Morley 2000). As examples of this trend, the global economic recession is prompting low-income households either to withdraw into the home for their leisure or to leave their homes in search of employment in other regions of the world.

Ideas of home 'privatisation' gained currency in Western societies from the post-World War II period decade of the 1950s (Williams 1974) with the domestic instatement of television followed by music systems, home movie systems and then digital media technologies. While the growth in home-centeredness did not necessarily occur at the expense of wider patterns of sociability (Allan and Crow 1991), the *idea* of domestic privatisation has been a powerful one in the public imagination (Morley 2008). Perceptions of 'the home' have been shaped by a sense of its physical closure and apparent separation from an 'outside' world. This potent conception of domestic privacy has accelerated and also been complicated recently in relation to ideas about how digital media is domesticated. On the one hand, the home is imagined as a space that we escape *from* with the aid of mobile media gadgets (Spigel 2001). On the other hand, the home is perceived as a venue crammed with more and more media equipment for us to escape *into* for a rich home-centred leisure. Although fewer visitors cross the threshold compared to past centuries, virtual tours of our homes are becoming commonplace. Broadbent (2011) explains that the home may give the impression of being more privatised, yet the house is now rendered more *permeable* to the outside world through digital communications. By means of webcam, Skype, instant messaging (IM), photo and video tours of home on property sale websites, people are regularly opening a digital door to their homes for the outside world to look in, into what is nevertheless conceived of as a profoundly 'intimate space'.

These home-centred digital communication systems are not just facilitating direct conversation with people beyond the home but also opening a view on the home-as-backdrop. As Broadbent observes, social media such as webcams are *immersive* modes of communication in the sense that 'You can access the room from each other, we can move, see what the other does, and sometimes even have dinner together at a distance'.[1] Skype, for example, is used to communicate the physical, home-centred context in which conversations occur: the spaces around the face-to-face dialogues. While communicating, family members and partners are showing each other significant domestic contexts, objects and emotionally relevant mementos via webcam. Thus, the attributes of synchronicity (discussed in Chapters 1 and 2) facilitate highly intimate communication with a small, intimate network of people. And, significantly, this mediated intimacy is signified visually as a physically grounded *domestic* space rather than a *virtual* space. These tendencies indicate that social media are now playing a fundamental role in sustaining and reinforcing the domestic sphere as an intimate sphere which, nonetheless, is being thrust beyond the threshold into a public network.

Decreasing economic resources are crucial in defining the mediated domestic context of 'home'. The reduction in the costs and accessibility of interpersonal technologies coincides with a transnational rise in the cost of living (Madianou and Miller 2012). Broadbent (2011) points out that those who engage in the most intense digitalised communication are often attempting to overcome social difficulties, including households on low incomes, fragmented and 'transnational' families, and citizens with restricted residence permits unable to leave their country. When it is too expensive or problematic to visit one another, an open Skype window linked to family members is a technological solution for geographically fragmented families. This means that the ways people now interact with one another through technology allow the 'home' to be imagined on many different levels. For migrants, technology can bring back the home they left.[2] This highlights the contested nature of 'home'. Traditional meanings of 'home' are being reconceived by the entrance of Skype and other social media in its domain in ways that evoke the former domestication of television technology (see Chambers 2011a; Spigel 2001; Williams 1974).

Home-based social media and family dynamics

Debates about the domestication of information communication technologies (ICTs) from the 1990s have advanced our understanding of the ways that media technologies such as radio and television have been integrated into home and family lives (see Berker et al. 2006; Miller and Slater 2000; Silverstone and Hirsch 1992). Spatial and domestic layout of new media gadgets in the home are major determinants of the type and extent of media use by children and adults. It is also a reminder that personal computers and other new media devices have a materiality (Livingstone 2009b; Miller 2008, 2011). Although social media is increasingly being accessed through mobile devices, young people access most social media and video gaming from their homes. These activities are now largely embedded in family life within the home. The family forms a key context in which children's and adolescents' informal media engagement are shaped and experienced. Constraints in using computer-based media include not only the cost of hardware, Internet connections and levels of media literacy but also the presence and location of the equipment in the home.

In the 1990s, Silverstone, Hirsch and Morley (1992) identified the problems associated with regulating and maintaining family activity boundaries posed by the presence of media gadgets in the home. They found that major decisions are made by parents about what media to allow in the household and what kind of content is accessed. Parental values and cultural discourses about home-based media have a substantial influence on the ways that mediated intimacy is articulated and practiced, particularly by young children. This influence diminishes as children become teenagers and more self-directed in mediating their friendships (Chapter 5). Parental values and discourses are affected by social class, changing parenting styles and commercial imperatives. These factors coincide with and respond to children's media cultures in the negotiation of social media engagement by family members

(Ito et al. 2010; Seiter 1993). Parent–child relationships and ideas of home are being reconfigured by children's growing agency and media literacy (Bovill and Livingstone 2001; Livingstone 2004). With an emphasis on childhood agency, parenting is now viewed as a negotiation between parents and children. 'Reflexive parenting' (Alters 2004) in American families has led to new dynamics in parenting strategies (Lareau 2003). Companionship rather than authoritarian approaches to child socialisation is accentuated (Jamieson 1987, 1998).

If new media devices are placed in children's bedrooms, children usually take control of the equipment and restrict access to others in the household (Holloway and Valentine 2003; Livingstone 2002). Many parents therefore regulate children's use by placing media devices in public spaces, such as hallways, kitchens and lounges, to allow parents to monitor the use of the equipment (Livingstone 2002). This can often be a losing battle for parents since the bedroom has become a major space for adolescents in their use of new media, with portable new media devices becoming more affordable and easier to situate in small spaces. For example, the European Union (EU) Kids Online survey found that 4 per cent of children in Europe aged 9–16 use Internet in their bedrooms (Livingstone et al. 2011). Nowadays bedrooms are more likely to be centrally heated, comfortable and are often treated as *personal* spaces which allow adolescents to gain a sense of control over their media world through privacy beyond parental surveillance (Ito et al. 2010; Livingstone 2009a; Livingstone and Bovill 2001). So if media equipment is installed in the bedroom, children are likely to spend time away from the public spaces in the home and away from the rest of their family. Better-off parents set shared rooms aside for playing games, homework and socialising (Aarsand and Aronsson 2009). Parents worry that bedrooms then become the focal point of children's activities in the home (Livingstone and Bovill 2001). However, many young people do not experience their bedrooms as *private* spaces since parents may enter and leave as they please, with little respect for the personal privacy of their children (Horst 2010a).

Likewise, a sense of invasion of personal space is often felt by adolescents when they have to share a computer with younger siblings. Many young people in a study by Heather Horst (2010a: 157) complained that their siblings went online and pretended to be them by accessing their accounts or using the shared computer to talk to their siblings' friends through social network sites or IM. Young people regularly report that their attempts to gain a sense of privacy and control over their peer-based online communication remain a continuing struggle.

Child–parent negotiations and family identities

Many parents feel pressured to restrict and control their children's use of new media as part of a cultivation of their overall family identity or family reputation (Hoover et al. 2004). In today's domestic media environments, parents take their role as guardians and regulators of their children's use of social media seriously and regard their influence as crucial (Ulicsak and Cranmer 2010). Parents' purchase of new media devices is often motivated by the educational ambitions and desires that they have for their children. Digital hardware and software are bought by parents to enhance children's educational training and are often regarded as an investment in their child's future by enhancing their educational and job prospects (Buckingham 2007; Haddon 2004; Ito et al. 2010; Livingstone 2002; Seiter 2008). New media are also used by parents as incentives to encourage children to perform well in their school work and homework. Children's educational accomplishments are often rewarded by parental purchases of new or upgraded digital media devices as gifts. However, most parents are quite ambivalent about new media's growing significance in the lives of adolescents. Their main fears concern the roles they should play as guardians in shaping their children's engagement with digital media and how this may affect their children's future lives and well-being (Livingstone 2009a).

Parents have to negotiate their way through the waves of media-generated moral panic (Critcher 2008) around digital media content and children's use. In addition to media anxieties about cyberbullying, stories are regularly reported in the news about social media causing children to become aggressive, unsociable, lazy or distracted. Adult anxieties about the mass media having a corrupting effect on children have a long history which dates back to the nineteenth century. Films and television sparked panic in earlier periods followed by current concerns about video gaming, mobile phones and social network sites (Buckingham 2000; Starker 1989; Thorne 2009). Parents and teachers are concerned that child access to media content encourages social contacts beyond the control of parents and teachers, thereby challenging the idea of protected childhood and conventional modes of learning (Thorne 2009). Access to 'adult' content during childhood through television or social media is often thought to undermine childhood as a condition and is viewed as particularly threatening when this content penetrates domestic space.

Parents worry about the time children and adolescents spend online and the possible isolation and alienation they might experience by being 'addicted' to gaming or social network sites. They are also concerned that children will be exploited by aggressive commercial targeting, and by sexually explicit material and violence on the Internet (Alters and Clark 2004; Cassell and Cramer 2007; Clark 2004). For example, in the 'Teaching and Learning with Multimedia' study, it was found that parents are concerned about child predators gaining access to children through sites such as MySpace (Horst 2010a). Some parents experience a loss of control or believe their children have become too dependent on their new media devices and content. Others are concerned about the vast amounts of time their offspring spend communicating with friends through IM, on social network sites or mobile phones (Livingstone 2009a).

However, parents are surprisingly ill-informed about their children's experiences of risk activities associated with social media (see, for example, Ofcom 2009; Ulicsak and Cranmer 2010). The most common risks reported by children are about communicating with new people that they have not met face-to-face, the receipt of sexual messages or of cyberbullying (see Chapter 5). Among those children who have experienced one of these risks, parents are often not aware of this. While the occurrence of such risks involves a minority of children, levels of underestimation among parents are considerable. Among parents whose child had seen sexual images online, 40 per cent were unaware of this. And of those parents whose child had received malicious or upsetting messages online, 56 per cent said that their child had not. Of those parents whose child had received sexual messages, 52 per cent said that their child had not and of those whose child had met with an online contact, 61 per cent said their child had not (Livingstone et al. 2011).

Although they have differing levels of skill in using the equipment, parents indicate that they are eager to find the time to spend with their children through the use of new media. However, the use of this new equipment takes place in a context that can amplify gendered stereotypes about new media technologies, as Horst states:

> The gendered dimensions of spending time together with media – from a kids' perspective, mothers are often described by kids as 'clueless' or 'hopeless' outside the domain of communication technologies and fathers as being the ones who play or tinker with technology alongside their kids – suggest that new media continue to contribute to the production and reproduction of class and gender inequities in American society.
>
> (Horst 2010a: 171)

The EU Kids Online study found that most parents mediate their children's use of social media, with most discussing appropriate Internet use with their children (70 per cent) and remaining nearby while the child is online (58 per cent). However, according to their children, 13 per cent of parents do not engage in any kind of mediation (Livingstone et al. 2011). Parents and children believed that parental mediation was beneficial particularly for younger children aged 9–12. This indicates that social media is becoming an important site for family bonding and intimacy as well as frustration and discord. Over half of the parents address the kinds of issues online that might concern the child and over a third have assisted their child when a problem arose. It was also found that as many as 85 per cent of parents curb children's display of personal information. Half of parents monitor their child's Internet use after they have logged off, and this was the least acceptable strategy for children who preferred positive guidance or the construction of transparent rules (Livingstone et al. 2011).

The EU study found that technical safety tools are not used a great deal by parents, with as few as 28 per cent of parents blocking or filtering websites. However, it also found that most parents (85 per cent) are positive about their role and believe that they can assist their child if they encounter problems that concern them online. Likewise, parents are generally confident in their children's ability to deal with problems online that might bother them (79 per cent). Most parents (73 per cent) are positive that it is unlikely that their child will come upon something that may trouble them in the next six months. Most children receive their advice about safety online from parents (63 per cent), then teachers (58 per cent), then peers (44 per cent). Also, other relatives beyond the immediate family are viewed to be as important as peers in offering advice and support to children on Internet safety. Importantly, then, the home and family are a major forum for the development of children's Internet etiquette. However, for older teenagers and children from lower socioeconomic homes, advice and help from teachers become important.

Digital media is valued for its potential to bring families together, as addressed below, yet it is also seen as capable of disrupting children's school and family life. Parents try to deal with the potentially disruptive features of new media by restricting their children's access to gaming or social media until homework and chores are completed, or they set time limits on daily use. Among parents who regulate their children's media use, many admit a lack of knowledge of digital media and fear it (Horst 2010a). Some parents set up accounts on MySpace and Facebook online in order to view their children's accounts. In response, children say they make their pages private. As Horst recounts, 'Many kids reference similar "horror stories" of parents' breaking into their sites, pages, and profiles, acts that teenagers view as invasive and embarrassing' (Horst 2010a: 189). Parents are motivated by the desire to protect their children's well-being rather than wanting to hassle them. But children tend to perceive these practices as violations of privacy and trust in the same way as eavesdropping conversations or prying into personal diaries. Children tend to regard online 'snooping' as a practice prompted by lack of knowledge and lack of courtesy. However, a significant minority share their online conversations with parents by informing them of their MySpace passwords (Horst 2010a: 198). Nevertheless, most families disclose that privacy and control issues are controversial. Teenagers report that they are keen to protect their privacy and independence in using new media.

Distinctive gender patterns have been found in the parental disciplining of children's media use in the US study by Horst (2010a). In nuclear and extended families, mothers tend to bear responsibility for 'upholding the morality of the family'. Mothers tend to sustain and preserve the routines and patterns of activities of the household and find themselves in charge of structuring and monitoring their children's use of time, that is, when they can and can't watch TV, go online or play video games. This pattern does not occur within single-parent families if the father is the main child carer. Fathers are generally more indulgent when it comes to video-game playing and spending playing time with their children (Horst 2010a). This reflects fathers' more playful and light-hearted approach to digital media in the home, which can lead to negative portrayals of mothers as harassing, interfering regulators or as 'incompetent' or both (Horst 2010a: 174). While mothers, in particular, have a sense of duty to monitor their children's' use of media, they are often hindered by their children's defiance and their own lack of technical proficiency and the undermining of their regulations by members of the family.

Parental anxieties about children's access to social media differ according to social class, geographical region and cultural background as well as gender. Many parents emphasise the need to convey to their children the value of the computer for education rather than social media entertainment. This is not surprising in poorer and working-class homes where the financial burden of purchasing computers is high. In these circumstances, it is tempting to value the device much more for its educational purposes. Christo Sims (2010) found that some home-schooled rural children often accessed friends on websites such as Bebo in the presence of their parents. In middle and upper class families, some parents prevented their children from accessing MySpace in response to anxieties about child predators online. Others in these socioeconomic categories believed it was essential for children to explore the media technology but monitored their children's use by placing computers and laptops in public spaces in the home. Moreover, they took advice from parenting organisations that offer guidelines such as no more than an hour of television a day (Horst 2010a; Sims 2010).

Despite many examples of family tensions about children's use of social media, studies demonstrate that parents are keen to share media use with their children and that new media is used to bind families together (Horst 2010a; Livingstone et al. 2011; Nikken et al. 2007; Ulicsak and Cranmer 2010; Wellman et al. 2008). Parents are drawing on their children's enthusiasm for new media to bond as a family around particular kinds of interests (Horst 2010a). Parent–child collaborative play is now viewed as an important mediating strategy for parents (Nikken et al. 2007). Playing video games together and children helping their parents negotiate their way round the Internet and equipment are all ways in which families bond (Aarsand and Aronsson 2009; Chambers 2011b; Ulicsak and Cranmer 2010). Nevertheless, parents feel compelled to make contracts with their children about when and where they can use the Internet and play video and computer games, such as at weekends or after completion of school homework (Livingstone 2007).

Children often teach parents how to Skype, upload pictures from their camera to email or download music onto digital media players. Horst (2010a: 168) refers to an upwardly mobile middle-class family who explained their use of social media to engage in family-centred activities. They described the creation of a family website that included photographs, descriptions of family vacations (their 'trip log') and information about major family events including birthdays, anniversaries, graduations and religious events for their three children. Interestingly, Horst recorded that the family members developed a strategy of 'egalitarian expertise' in using the digital media so that they could all engage fully with the media objects in creating the videos and websites. In another example by Horst (2010a: 169), parents, especially fathers, tended to take the lead in collaborative media processes whether they were the most competent or not. The increase in media equipment in the home offered children and parents new contexts in which to discover and delve into these devices. Visual digital media is also used for the writing of the family history through the use of photos, collages and by sending them to family members abroad (Madianou and Miller 2012). In these ways, family intimacies are strengthened.

Transnational families and digital media

Recent research shows that a rising number of recent immigrants sustain strong contact with their extended families back home through ICTs (Falicov 2007: 157). The polymediated nature of today's digital media engagement is demonstrated by the multiple uses of these technologies by 'transnational families'. Dispersed families with strong ties and few resources are maintaining and strengthening connections through online media such as email and Skyping. Technologies such as voice-over-Internet services, IM and webcams are cheap or even free. Families also go online to get news or to download music from home. Videos of family-oriented ceremonies such as graduations, weddings, funerals are regularly disseminated to family members living abroad (Horst 2006, 2010a; Panagakos and Horst 2006; Wilding 2006). Families with higher resources tend to use Skype and webcams to sustain online conversations (Horst 2010a).

Moreover, cheap international phone calls through prepaid calling cards have helped to maintain family and personal relationships with intimates back home (Ito and Okabe 2005; Vertovec 2004). Letters involve days or weeks of delay between interactions, but cheap calling cards allow families to maintain constant contact (Wilding 2006). Digital media have also reduced the financial costs for migrants who formerly spent large amounts on collect calls (Horst 2006). Cheap telecommunications enhance migrant parents' engagement in the lives of their spouses and children. They can offer support and encouragement, and participate in their children's educational and emotional development while being involved in the decision-making routine in the household back home (Horst 2006: 149).

Migrants are among the most advanced users of communications technology. For example, Broadbent (2011) refers to a family of immigrant workers from Kosovo who live in Switzerland and have installed a large computer screen in their lounge. Nearly every morning they breakfast with their grandmother back in Kosovo via a webcam. Indeed, Broadbent argues that migrants emerge as some of the 'most aggressive' adopters of new communication tools. In a Spanish family who live in Switzerland, the daughter often conducts her homework with her aunt who lives in Spain over a free Skype video link. The sense of immediacy offered by conversational media is viewed as an ideal quality for families that communicate across great geographical distances.

Research undertaken in Australia, Canada and Europe also demonstrates that rates of computer and Internet access and use tend to be higher among international migrants than among those who are native born (Chiswick and Miller 2005). The differences are greatest between native born and immigrants from China, India, Indonesia, Germany, Korea and the Philippines by an average of 27 per cent. Immigrants whose first language is not English are online 30 hours or more per month compared to the native born. Similarly, use of email among immigrants is higher, as is the use of Internet to keep in contact with family and friends according to Madianou and Miller (2012). They refer to Statistics Canada (2008) which indicates that the need to communicate with family and friends abroad and the relative accessibility in terms of the cost of Internet as a method of communication explains the key differences in use between native born Canadians and recent immigrants to Canada. Research on uses of cell phones by Jamaican families in Jamaica indicates that ICTs help them obtain a more comprehensive knowledge of migration and its implications (Horst 2006). Communication technologies such as videoconferencing have had a major influence for Salvadorians living in Washington DC (Benítez 2006). Despite the geographical distance, the combination of visual and audio communication brings families and friends together to celebrate group occasions and give a stronger sense of occasion to the interaction. This kind of bonding can form an important aspect of the sustaining of family ties. In these circumstances, ICTs are powerful communication channels for emotional expression and intimacy (Panagakos and Horst 2006).

With the range of applications now available through the Internet, migrants are also able to record their lives abroad through online photo albums which they can share with families back home by uploading and sharing images. Raelene Wilding (2006) refers to 'connected relationships' whereby distant members of a family can have an impression of closeness and immediacy through communication technologies. These connected relationships may change the distinction between 'absence and presence' and offer a feeling of being at home away from home (Wilding 2006: 132). Unlike the kind of communication afforded by letter writing, which delivers old news, email allows migrants to become absorbed and engaged in the immediate daily routines of their families. Wilding emphasises the importance for migrants of 'shared time' with their families through email contact (Wilding 2006: 133). Websites have the capacity to combine different kinds of information such as letters, images, music. They can function as a link between migrants and source communities which are signified as a 'cyber village' through which encounters and emotions can be exchanged (Benítez 2006). When family members are ill, ageing or in a state of crisis, ICTs can be regarded as inadequate modes of communication. Raelene Wilding (2006) points out that the kin most likely to need support, such as the elderly and the infirm, are least likely to understand how to use new communication tools. She also found that email is often used to evade or challenge traditional communication channels and hierarchies of decision-making among families, in which elders conventionally take the lead. Children's proficient use of the Internet can underscore the generation gap by giving them access to information that older family members no longer benefit from (Benítez 2006). Importantly, then, young peoples' new skills can radically impact on the traditional power relations in kinship groups and change the social ranking of members (Mansour Tall 2004).

ICTs are also helping migrants to preserve their cultural identities in important new ways by generating a feeling of connection with family and friends. As Hamel (2009) argues, explaining the movement of people as a westernising tendency belies the complexities of the cross-cultural impacts and hybridisation effects that ICT contact has on cultures around the world. However, the problems of the digital divide are often exposed as the virtual network expands, given that those who are not part of the network culture are marginalised by their lack of access and unable to relate their experiences as migrants to those who might be able to care for and support them (Mitra 2001). Governments can play a vital role in facilitating digital exchanges between migrants and their families to encourage diasporas to invest in their communities back home as exemplified by the governments of India, China and Korea (Saxenian 2006; UNDP 2001: 93).

Transnational parenting and new media

Most studies of new media and migration have examined issues of identity and integration. However, in an important ethnographic study of the use of communication technologies by migrant Filipinos to keep in touch with their children back home, Mirca Madianou and Daniel Miller (2012) address the key question of sociality and intimacy in a transnational framework. The escalation of global migration, coupled with the feminisation of migration, has generated a new 'transnational family' characterised by a woman from the global south who migrates for employment to the global north and who leaves behind her children. This leads to a new category of transnational motherhood (Hondagneu-Sotelo and Avila 1997) which entails the management of the relationship through long-distance communication. Madianou and Miller studied this form of distant mothering by interviewing migrant mothers in the United Kingdom and also their children left behind in the Philippines. Their study makes a major contribution to the understanding of digital media, distant love and mediated relationships. As mentioned in Chapter 2, Madianou and Miller developed the concept of polymedia to underscore the ways that multiple mediums are combined to maintain intimate and other forms of contact.

As over 10 per cent of the population of the Philippines works abroad and the majority of the migrant workers are women with children left behind, 'distant mothering' has become commonplace. Over 10 million Filipino children are reported to be left behind. The generation of migrants that first came to the United Kingdom in the 1970s and 1980s relied mainly on the letter and the cassette tape. The adoption of the mobile phone, the Internet and related digital technologies among Filipinos both at home and abroad transformed familial communication, particularly for those who experienced prolonged separation (Pertierra et al. 2002). Migrants distinguish between the media technologies in terms of the differences in the kinds of sentiments they feel they can express in the process of communicating with their children (Madianou and Miller 2012). Mothers use the technology to justify their decision to work abroad, arguing that it will be easier to keep in touch. Yet the opportunities for continual communication can generate conflict between parents and children. For older children, continuous communication can feel invasive and unwelcome.

It is only recently that migrant mothers have been able to use mobile phones and stop relying on high-cost and difficult–to-access landlines to engage in voice-based communication with their families. Some used the voice application facilitated by voice over Internet Protocol (VOIP) communication such as Skype through the computer. But for some families, this was not possible since they lived in an area without Internet connections. Voice-based communication is preferred for its dialogical qualities: its immediacy and spontaneity was more satisfying. The quality of the voice can convey much emotion, even without visual cues. Although mobile devices are liked for the qualities of 'reachability', privacy and spontaneity, it was often viewed as intrusive by children of migrants, especially teenagers who felt they were being checked on by their absent mothers.

Mothers went to great lengths to ensure they acquired IT skills through classes, but they preferred to communicate with their children using synchronous voice-based communication. Yet children preferred email precisely for the same reasons that mothers preferred not to use this medium. Children often find phone calls invasive and distracting. While young people in the United Kingdom and the United States rarely use email as a formal medium, emails are preferred by Filipina children of transnational families because it affords them autonomy: to reply at a time of their own choice and compose the reply in advance. Thus, the low level of interactivity of email and its lack of synchronicity were its appealing qualities for children. Madianou and Miller (2012) use Gershon's (2010) concept of 'media ideologies' to describe the differences in attitudes to the communication technologies by users. Media ideologies encompass a set of beliefs about social media technologies that participants draw on to guide them and to describe and justify the ways they use the various media forms (see Chapter 1). Children's preference for email rather than the phone to take control of communication may suggest that their own media ideologies clash with those of their parents.

IM is more prominent than email or texting in transnational communication, particularly when combined with webcam. Its affordances of interactivity and simultaneity are appealing. However, as Madianou and Miller explain, it requires real-time co-presence, with each participant having to sit at the computer. It is therefore often combined with the leaving of messages to be read later. Both types of communication are possible on social network sites as they have their own IM facility. IM shares the same affordances as email and texting and can be used to affirm a relationship. It can be used for imparting information and detailed instructions. So mothers use it to help their children with homework. However, time-zone differences and shift work can prevent synchronicity. Mothers may wake in the night to communicate with their children through IM. Users can see which of their friends or relatives are online through the use of the status facility of IM, but some children choose to be 'invisible' so that they are not accessible (Madianou and Miller 2012: 113).

Social network sites enable a different type of bonding. The medium enhances ties among diaspora groups oriented more towards their own community than the host community (Kotimo 2011). It allows a low-level ambient awareness among a scattered network and also generates a wider exchange across relatives rather than just dyadic relationships (McKay 2010). However, social network sites were used more by the children than parents among transnational families. In the Philippines, the refusal of a request by a friend is unthinkable (Madianou and Miller 2012: 114). The main usage by young Filipinos is with peers from school and college, reflecting social patterns in the United States. However, significantly, their social network sites were also used to maintain contact with relatives overseas. They are used for posting photos that allow an individual to keep in contact with diaspora family, through shared awareness of social events, holidays and other activities.

Social network site use strengthened transnational parent–child relationships since those mothers who were users discovered that Friendster, Multiply and Facebook were extremely useful for gaining information about the circumstances of their children's lives. They could explore their children's profiles to find out about their friendship ties, the parties they attended and so on. Madianou and Miller (2012) found that one mother obtained her 10- and 12-year-old sons' passwords to check their account regularly. She regarded this as acceptable, as an absent mother. One 55-year-old woman was reunited with her godson in the Philippines, who found her on her social network site, and they began communicating with one another. Many migrant mothers started using social network sites after being invited to do so by their adult children. However, children of migrant mothers are often unsure about the benefits of this kind of connection. One daughter might use it to develop a best-friend relationship with her mother while a son may be troubled by the Friending of his mother because it leads to revelations about his life. However, others used social network sites in a benign way. One son uploaded photos of his kids for his mother and the mother would reciprocate by sending photos of her weekend break. Social network sites can expose the speed with which children are maturing and the children may feel ambivalent about their parents seeing this.

In some situations such as among adult children, the overlap between friendship and kinship is viewed as normal and acceptable and can develop the relationship between grandparents and grandchildren. However, among teenage children the connection may seem intrusive. The quality of the pre-existing relationship and the blurring of the boundaries between public and private on social network sites can exacerbate the relationship. As significant others, mothers become part of this 'invisible audience' described by boyd (2010: 48) when they unintentionally come across profiles of their children's friends (Madianou and Miller 2012: 115). A way to circumvent the problems of the blurring of the public and private by social network sites is to have more than one site.

In the Philippines, blogging is mainly used by children and not their mothers (Madianou and Miller 2012). College-educated young adults share with their friends a common sense of ambivalence about or anger with their immediate family. Webcam combined with forms of VOIP such as Skype has risen in popularity in countries such as Philippines. For mothers of very young children left behind, being able to see a face transforms the sense of being in touch. It sustains the kind of kin relationship, such as between grandparents and small children, that could not have existed before. It also assists other familial practices such as helping children with homework (Madianou and Miller 2012: 118). The researchers note the disappointments that can be felt as well as the joy, with experiences of grandparental carers dressing the children up for the webcam session only to find that the children show no interest in their distant parents. Moreover, webcams can give the illusion of co-presence and a reminder of separation. The webcam often motivates individuals to gain media literacy, particularly grandparents who wish to see their grandchildren. As mentioned, webcam has the quality of being able to appear like a family gathering since it is synchronous and dialogic and allows relatives to see the children growing up.

Conclusions

This chapter demonstrates that affective relations are shaped and facilitated not only by digital media of exchange and communication but also by the materiality and social interactions that comprise 'home' and 'family'. Parents and young people are negotiating, creating and changing the meanings and perceptions of family identity through social media. Recent research highlights the ways in which the home is structured along a public–private axis (Allan and Crow 1989) which forms and is formed by the encounters and experiences in this context. Today, the dynamic interplay between the public and private shaped by mediated intimacy in the family home now extends from the lay-out of the home to the lay-out of online networking beyond the home. The complications and diversity of home life are overlaid by the complications and diversity of personal and family media technology use by household members. Thus, the level of privacy of children's spaces becomes a key issue, with bedrooms often seen by children as a place of escape and the communal areas often viewed as a space of surveillance. How these public–private boundaries are managed between adults and children through their engagement with social media has implications for young people's freedom and choice of personal communities and for adults in the supervision of children and the management of the potential risk associated with social media.

As well as factors of social class, ethnic identities and rural/urban differences, participation in new media is determined by parenting styles which, in turn, influence parents' values and ideals about new media technologies and children's need to be protected or gain experience and independence. Parenting styles shape children's styles of media participation. A key factor influencing all families is that parents are anxious about the risks of social media use for children, including the effects of excessive social media use on their education and well-being. Parental actions and decisions about regulation are prompted by anxieties about the correspondence between ownership of computers and education, about their own lack of experience and understanding of new media and how far their children are capable of exercising their own judgement. Conversely, parents can be surprisingly ignorant of its potential and often lack the skills to participate in social media use with their children. This can lead to frustrations for both parents and children and may also impede the potential of using social media to cultivate family intimacies and identities.

The chapter indicates that parents use a variety of different strategies to regulate children's use of social media. Both cooperative and inflexible parent–child dynamics structure the meanings and practices of social media use. New media can be a site of tension and discord for parents and children and also between siblings. The issues are about access and control and the extent of regulation and restrictions placed on young people's control of the technology. Children are often exasperated by parents who seem inexperienced, ignorant or inept in their use of social media. Conversely, in some families, parents and children collaborate in developing cross-generational interaction and family identities through social media production and help to advance the skills and confidence of their children.

Research on the ways in which social media are being used by families geographically separated by migration shows how social media mediate emotional family interactions. Madianou and Miller argue that the wide choice of social media can thereby allow the mother–child relations among transnational families to move towards a *pure relationship*, in the sense described by Giddens (1991). By negotiating the type of medium to be used and finding ways of managing the relationship through choice of mediums, children can gain a sense of equality as they grow older. For mothers, the sense of immediacy offered by synchronised conversational media is viewed as the best way for families across great geographical distances to communicate. For the child, an asynchronous medium may be preferred in order to gain a sense of control over the communication. By this means, it can become a more equal relationship, one of friendship in which traditional external criteria have been weakened. The paradox of the parent–child relationship is of being in a 'friendship media' relationship, a relationship that grows through mediated interactions.

However, as mentioned in earlier chapters, the ability to choose the medium according to the circumstances amounts to a significant transformation in the moral framework of personal communication. The multiplication and convergence of communication technologies offers more options so that the act of deciding the medium through which to communicate increasingly involves *social* and *moral* questions rather than just technical or economic considerations (Madianou and Miller 2012). This moral dimension is explored further in the following chapter which focuses not only on the choices available to flirt, date and sustain romances online but also on the communicative choices made, in particular by young people, about how to convey to partners that a relationship has come to an end.

7
Digital Dating and Romance

Introduction

Communication channels such as social network sites, instant messaging (IM) and texting are generating new dating rules and conventions. This indicates that the affordances of digital communication technologies are capable of managing complex emotions. Displaying information about one's relationship status has become a regular feature of social network profiles among adults as well as teenagers. Sites such as Facebook ask participants to state their relationship status, as *'single'*, *'in a relationship'*, *'engaged'*, *'married'*, *'it's complicated'*, *'in an open relationship'* or *'widowed'*. The relationship categories on Facebook are difficult to handle not only for those in failing relationships but also for new ones. As Gershon states, 'Facebook official' status 'has come to stand in for exclusivity' (Gershon 2010: 83). Many people are uncomfortable about displaying their relationship status, so they leave it blank or, for example among adolescents, they might play jokes (such as selecting 'in a relationship with' a friend's dog).

Digital dating can be viewed as an example of a late modern solution to the challenges of embarking on relationships. The customs associated with online dating seem to correspond effectively with the idea of a 'plastic sexuality' within the trend towards elective intimacy. Giddens (1992) argues that the increasing emphasis on individual autonomy has generated greater diversity in intimacy and sexual behaviour. Relationships are more freely chosen and more equal. For Giddens (1992) sexuality is decentred, thereby highlighting the fluid and changeable nature of all modes of intimacy (see Chapter 3). Today's 'plastic sexuality' is distinguished from the modernist notion of 'fixed sexuality' which is preset by social norms that govern normal/committed and perverse/promiscuous. By contrast, plastic sexuality is unfettered by traditional gender roles and recognition of individual erotic needs. As part of the late modern characteristics of intimacy – based on pleasure and freedom from constraints – plastic sexuality represents individual identity and radical sexual choices. However, the notion of abundant choice in deciding one's sexual identity and activities and intimate lifestyle can generate anxieties about how to initiate and manage relationships. Dating is now framed by high expectations of infinite choice in partners yet also by anxieties about being excluded or left behind. Technologically mediated dating seems to offer a perfect solution by providing a sense of personal autonomy and control.

While digital romance is now commonplace, the risks associated with disclosure can be high, particularly for young people. Tensions can be intensified in response to the reduced social signals that lead to uncertainties and misunderstandings, and mediation can also accelerate idealisation and love. Participants of social media seem unable to agree on emergent dating rules and conventions, particularly among adolescents and especially when it comes to the break-up of relationships (Gershon 2010). The lack of consensus among young people about the most considerate way to end a relationship with an online dimension raises major questions about the management of intimacy in the digital age in terms of social media etiquette, agency, privacy and publicity, and vulnerability.

This chapter examines some of the key uses and features of social media and dating forums to identify the ways in which 'intimacy' is being negotiated and reconfigured in an online context. The first section addresses young people's use of social media for their dating practices. In the second section, online dating among adults is explored, first by focusing on social network site engagement and then dating forums. As the previous chapters indicate, most online friendships and intimacies have prior offline contexts, and most connections initiated online do not transform into face-to-face relationships. Nonetheless, as Baym (2010: 124) points out, many people have formed at least one lasting close bond online. While online romances are routinely established through social network sites between individuals who knew of each other offline, dating forums differ since they are designed for individuals to connect with complete strangers. Dating sites such as *Match.com* and *e-Harmony* have been created specifically to introduce strangers with similar interests. These websites are distinctive in comprising a major way in which online connections migrate to offline meetings. Like social network sites, online dating provides one of the most heightened contexts for a reflexive engagement in the project of self-identity within the processes of individualisation. These practices are analysed in terms of some of the key contradictions produced for intimate ties.

Teenage romance online

In Western cultures, adolescence is a phase of life in which romantic and sexual lives are exposed to public scrutiny. As Chapter 5 indicates, online friendships usually correspond with offline associations, but social media also offer young people the tools to overcome traditional barriers in forming romantic associations. Courtship customs are less formal than they were up to the mid-twentieth century (Bogle 2008). By the 1970s and 1980s, formal dating was on the decline (Modell 1989: 291). The terms used in the 1950s such as *courtship* and *dating* have been replaced by 'an item', 'going out with someone' (Miller and Benson 1999: 106) or 'hanging out' (Ito et al. 2010). Yet recent ethnographic research on teens' use of social media in the United States indicates that the rituals are as intricate and as significant as in more formal past times (Gershon 2010; Pascoe 2010). Contemporary romance relationships among adolescents tend to be more spontaneous, casual and brief and yet they are often more complicated and intense (Brown 1999: 310). These intimate connections are also intrinsically *social*, despite their apparent emphasis on privacy and their exclusiveness (Brown 1999). This social and public dimension is amplified through social network site use (Lenhart and Madden 2007).

Digital interaction performs a key role in starting casual relationships and in developing the initial stages of serious relationships. Teenagers use IM, text messages and social network messaging. They often make use of texts and images from established website collections of traditional images such as Photobucket, indicating that youth organise their romantic attachments within a dominant discourse of love (boyd 2010; Gershon 2010). Multiple channels of communication provide adolescents with the tools to build on casual meetings or present themselves to an acquaintance whom they have met in passing through a mutual friend. Those who develop a romantic interest in someone find it less intimidating to flirt on a social network site such as Facebook than face-to-face. Many teenagers begin dating after exchanging flirtatious messages online. The usual vulnerabilities associated with dating can be managed more effectively online through a 'controlled casualness' (Sims

2007). A pattern has been identified whereby teenagers meet in person, flirt online and then date (Pascoe 2010).

Teenagers' relationships tend to advance through distinctive stages (Sims 2010). At the start of a relationship when they are finding out about each other, written communication is likely to be used through text messaging and IM or on social network sites. Sending text messages is regarded as low stakes and often 'had the right level of informality for starting to flirt with someone' (Gershon 2010: 23). It offers a slower, more thoughtful and controlled way of exploring and building the intimate connection. Social network sites become more significant as the relationship develops. Paradoxically, social network sites provide a way of carefully contriving 'spontaneous' and 'casual' interaction. If the connection becomes more serious, then the interaction extends to include phone calls and face-to-face communication. Evidence also suggests that certain kinds of social media match certain kinds of associations or stages in the relationship (Pascoe 2010). The stability of the relationship may be expressed through the rearrangement of the Friends ranking by displaying photos and changing the display of formal relationship status. By this stage, the relationship might be called 'Facebook official'. The strength of the association may be expressed by sharing passwords, posting bulletins and changing headlines. For those relationships that break up, former partners usually revise their self-representations by changing their public self-displays. Pascoe (2010) describes this as a 'digital housecleaning' – reminiscent of the ritual disposal of photos and other memorabilia associated with a break-up.

Social network sites can be effective tools for gaining an impression about someone that a person may have a romantic interest in (boyd 2007; see Chapter 4). Some refer to this initial research as 'Facebook stalking', as a tool for discovering more about someone they are interested in, then for flirting and getting to know the person better (Bogle 2008; Pascoe 2007). Placing Wall posts on the site is considered an informal way of communicating when involving a love interest (boyd 2007). Mediated flirting is part of the process of moving cautiously, implying an interest in each other and enquiring about their feelings in what appears to be a controlled and casual way. Messages can be carefully constructed to sound casual yet also informative. They can easily be dismissed without humiliation if feelings are not reciprocated. Much more informal linguistic tones are now being used in this kind of online communication to emphasise spontaneity and informality (Baron 2008). Saving face through a contrived casualness is especially important if the communication takes place in the public settings of users' Walls.

Meeting strangers online is generally regarded by teenagers as bizarre and risky. A prior face-to-face meeting, however casual, can confirm the authenticity of the person. As online identities can be validated through online and offline checks, an increasingly common approach is to engage in online introductions through shared friends online, with offline friendship networks being relied on as verifications and checks (Pascoe 2010). Yet young people do express a fear that the offline person does not live up to the online expectations, confirming the 'hyperpersonal effect' described by Walther (1996; returned to below). It signifies that online intimacy might be intensified and not reflect the offline personae. Nevertheless, among adolescents who find themselves marginalised by their peers in an offline world, which may be the case for gay and lesbian teenagers, social media communication allows them the flexibility to meet other people with shared interests (Holloway and Valentine 2003; Maczewski 2002; Osgerby 2004). As many gay and lesbian teenagers find dating difficult, social media becomes a key form of communication which can give them an opportunity to circumvent the problems of being ostracised in the search for partners. Social network sites allow them to network with the kind of people that are difficult to meet in physical environments. It can offer them a sense of control and privacy against the judgemental reactions of parents and peers (Gray 2009; Hillier and Harrison 2007).

Given the flexibility of digital media, young dating couples now have high expectations of continuous availability, connection online and reciprocity in their online exchanges. They may make several phone calls, texts or IMs each day (Baron 2008; Gershon 2010). This increased contact defines the quality of the relationship and distinguishes it from other kinds of connections (Pascoe 2010). Social media also allow teenagers to sustain romantic associations that parents may not sanction or which are maintained over geographical distances. Signs of affection are exchanged through digital messages to maintain the relationship. Regular mobile phone and social network site check-ins are expected by partners to avoid misunderstandings about their actions and to account for their whereabouts in order to maintain trust in the relationship. In these ways, the ever-present technology can free them up from parental monitoring and yet can chain them to their partners.

Declaring the romantic attachment on social network sites to one's networked publics as well as partner is an important practice. Tokens of affection, posting pictures and recording the starting date of the relationship form public declarations of the seriousness of the relationship.

Through default relationship options on Facebook, young people have also found ways to insert details and shared meanings in describing their intimacy and to indicate to others in their public networks that they are spoken for. Intimate decisions about 'going official' and broadcasting their relationship status online is usually decided by the couples together offline (Sims 2007). Pasco (2010: 131) refers to a student at the University of California, Berkeley, interviewed by Megan Finn who exemplified how these misunderstandings can arise:

> Yeah, I have friends [who] have confirmed they have gone official with their boyfriends through Facebook, which is ridiculous. I have known people that are dating and they'll get a request "so and so said that you are their girlfriend." They pushed the button and they are like, "Oh my God, we're official."

(Finn, Freshquest[1])

The relationship status, along with all social network profiles, becomes a major digitalised public expression of teenagers' relationships and its quality. Some young people have disagreements about the public statements if one partner does not place their boyfriend/girlfriend in the top ranking of their Friends list. Posting 'couple' pictures on one's social network profile is also a form of relationship maintenance. These practices ensure that each partner agrees on their status and is willing to publicise it. However, all this information means that, for those who are inclined to 'Facebook stalk' their significant others, the site can be an infuriatingly comprehensive database of photos and public conversations.

Mediated break-ups

Although social media are used as essential tools for developing a romantic interest, young people consider them to be wholly inappropriate for ending a relationship. Yet these technologies are now so integrated into intimate relationships among the young that any medium can be chosen to end a relationship, in addition to face-to-face communication. Individuals who display their intimacy publicly also perform their break-up very publicly (boyd 2010a, 2010b; Pascoe 2010). By publicising their relationship and their break-up, ex-partners are looking for validation and support from their peers (boyd 2010a, 2010b). In an ethnographic study on dating, Gershon (2010) asked 72 undergraduate students in the United States to describe 'bad' break-ups. She was interested in finding out how people use a technology intrinsically designed for *social connection* in ways for which it was clearly not designed: *breaking up* a relationship. The most widespread break-up problem was the lack of appropriateness of certain mediums used to end a relationship. A range of moral dilemmas are thrown up by the choice of medium and its appropriateness for the kind of message being conveyed (Gershon 2010). If a person uses a cell phone to text their partner to say that they want to break up, does that constitute a break-up or is it just a suggestion within a longer process? If a couple break up, should they change their Facebook status to 'single' immediately or should they tell their best friends about it first so that they won't simply find out on their Facebook News Feeds? While texting was regarded as the appropriate level of informality for starting to flirt with someone, this level of casualness was considered to be far too informal for a break-up (Gershon 2010). Ending a relationship by sending a text message was considered cruel because it closes down communication too abruptly.

Significantly, Gershon (2010) found that there is little shared consensus among students about how to use sites such as Facebook. Some students respond to break-ups by displaying their relationship problems on their Facebook profile and by changing their *In a relationship with* status to *It's complicated* and ultimately *single*. Some respond by eliminating their relationship status after a break-up, and others deal with the challenge by linking their relationship status to the profile of a platonic friend. A small number of students would even deactivate their Facebook account. The profiles of partners often contain evidence of the acrimony associated with some break-ups. Site users can promptly eliminate an intimate relationship throughout their profiles by deleting photos and written references to ex-partners and removing them from their Friend list. While one ex-partner may publicly convey their grieving or anger on their profile, the other ex-partner might now be linked intimately to another person's profile, moving on from the old partner very publicly.

Most of Gershon's interviewees believed that face-to-face conversations were the best medium for break-ups because people want an adequate explanation as to why the break-up is occurring. Break-ups communicated through IM were more uncommon and strongly disapproved of because the conversation could be ended without any warning. However, one interviewee said she favoured breaking up by IM because 'if they get upset, you can just sign off, and okay, it's done ... if I am absolutely certain about the break-up, then it's instant messaging'

(Gershon 2010: 30). Gershon suggests that this notion of *appropriateness* corresponds with each person's media ideology: their own media values. Media ideologies comprise the framework of values and attitudes about social media technologies that influence the decisions made by participants in using the range of media technologies (see Chapter 2). Having an awareness of these ideologies provides an understanding of the norms that shape the way the technology is to be used and how other people's uses of the technology are judged and defined as appropriate or inappropriate.

Gershon reminds us that it took a long time and much effort on the part of institutions involved in earlier communication technologies such as the telephone to standardise people's uses of the technology. In terms of social media, the extensive educational work deals with intellectual property rights and privacy issues rather than on netiquette. As yet, shared expectations about how to manage the social dilemmas associated with using new communicative technologies are not matched by shared practices, and this renders break-ups more confusing and upsetting (Gershon 2010: 198–199). Social software relies on the power of users to stretch the boundaries and bend the rules so that establishing netiquette becomes problematic. It could close off creative uses of online social networking.

As part of the formation of media ideologies, students are negotiating idioms of practice including the management of second-order information such as News Feed: 'the information that can guide you into understanding how particular words and statements should be interpreted' (Gershon 2010: 18). Echoing Marshall McLuhan's (1964) dictum, Gershon concludes that the medium is part of the message. The way an individual chooses to announce to their partner that they want to break up can deeply affect the reception of the message – whether it is face-to-face or by phone call, email, text message, instant message or Facebook Wall post. The media ideologies of the receiver will also frame the interpretation of the message. Gershon draws on the notion of *remediation* advanced by Bolter and Grusin (1999), reminding us that people's use of newer media needs to be understood in the context of their use of old media. In this respect, Gershon provides a new perspective, arguing that the moment when interpersonal communication is most fraught is the moment when the socially constructed nature and newness of the medium is exposed and when questions around customs of use are raised. This highlights the moral dimension of social media use in a polymediated environment. The choice of medium has significant moral implications in a context where the technology has been socialised, that is, when it has become *embedded* in everyday interpersonal communication.

An important related issue raised by Gershon (2010) is that these new digital media channels may be encouraging college-age love affairs to become more conventional. She argues that Facebook is implicitly conservative in terms of its *sexual* morality. Its relationship categories imply that monogamy is the ideal, even for young people. It encourages couples to fix themselves to one another's profiles as a way of curbing and confining what might be more fluid interconnections between young people. Gershon detected a general desire among youth to have these social media somehow governed by strict etiquette so that they become more accountable to peers. She poses and answers her own important question, 'Why does it matter if you break up by text message, by Facebook, or face-to-face? It matters because people are social analysts of their own lives' (Gershon 2010: 201). When someone's personal life is being conducted in public, every word and gesture can be open to criticism.

Jealousy and stalking

The moral dilemmas associated with the choice of medium can extend way beyond the break-up stage since couples usually continue to occupy intersecting networked publics after a break-up. They can retain ex-partners as friends and receive automatic updates or monitor their activities and channels of communication. A white 19-year-old from suburban northern California remarked:

> Monitoring one's ex on a social network site is one thing that you shouldn't do but everyone does. You can go check all their stuff. Like you look at their Facebook, you look at their MySpace, you see if they take off the photos of you, you see if they changed their relationship status to something, you see if they've got a new person writing on their wall. Like you become a stalker, and a highly efficient stalker. Because all the information is already there at once. You don't have to ask your friends or her friends if she's seeing someone new. Like you know. And then they want you to know.
>
> (Documented by Sims, Rural and Urban Youth[2] project in Pascoe 2010: 137)

Some ex-partners communicate their feelings to their exs indirectly by changing their relationship status on Facebook to 'in a relationship', even though they are not involved with anyone, to ensure that the ex-partner does not raise hopes of getting back together again. Teens develop the skills and experience to communicate passively through their online profiles or through mediators. Young people thereby preserve indirect forms of communication after ending a relationship.

Jealousy and stalking are not peculiar to youth, but most studies on this topic focus on youth and imply that these problems apply more centrally to them. For example, Muise, Christofides and Desmarais (2009) conducted an online survey of 308 college students in the United States and found that the more time students spend on Facebook, the more likely they are to suffer from Facebook-related jealousy. They argue that this effect may be the outcome of a 'feedback loop': by using Facebook individuals are too frequently exposed to confusing details about their ex-partner that they may not otherwise have access to, and this new information provokes further Facebook use, fuelling further jealousy. Some respondents described their escalating use of Facebook as 'addictive'.

'Facebook rage' described as 'fuelling a vicious cycle of surveillance' has been publicised through reports in the press. For instance, a headline in the *Daily Mail* stated 'Facebook Rage as social networking sites fuel jealousy and stalking partners online'.[3] Similarly, social media technology can facilitate dating abuse. As mentioned in Chapter 5, among young people who were in a relationship, 40 per cent said that their partners had used computers or mobile phones to abuse or manipulate them (AP-MTV Digital Abuse Study 2009).[4] The Digital Abuse Study (2009) also reported that nearly 3 in 10 young people said that their partner has checked up on them online several times per day or read their text messages without permission. Fourteen percent said that they had received more abusive behaviour from their partners, involving name-calling and malicious messages via Internet or cellphone.

Since digital media offers high monitoring potential to users, they can easily be used in ways that may be defined as emotional control or abuse. The opportunities for young people to monitor each others' romances and break-ups online are exacerbated by the custom of sharing passwords with romantic partners which can signify intimacy yet also be a potential invasion of privacy. Also, the habit of regularly checking one another's' profiles may complicate matters if a break-up ensues (boyd 2007). Some partners change their passwords regularly to retain control. Pascoe found that it was usually girlfriends who wanted to share passwords, in order to feel a sense of control in the relationship (Pascoe 2010). This may be related to gendered power inequalities in teenage heterosexual relationships in general with girls compelled to find ways to manage their relationships (Hillier et al. 1999; Hird and Jackson 2001; Jackson 1998). Elaborate changes are sometimes made by individuals to protect their digital footprints, to prevent partners from searching histories, phone numbers, names on mobile phones, texts or site information that might offend the partner. When teenagers' phone bills are paid for by parents, they tend to conform to parents' rules about mobile phone use. But for girls who let boyfriends pay for their mobile phone bills, the privacy of social media use is likely to be compromised, often by trading parental control for boyfriend control (Pascoe 2010).

The monitoring affordances of new media provide a way for teenagers to manage potential anxieties in a relationship. Yet many are negotiating intimate ties for the first time and often in a public domain. As Pascoe (2010: 145) states, 'New media allow teens to manage their vulnerability; permit them to have intensely emotional, vulnerable conversations; and render them potentially susceptible to the forwarding of information about them and vulnerable to those who wish to take advantage of them.'

Adults dating online

A growing number of online adults who date are conducting their relationship homework online. Search engines, email, IM and social network sites are all used to connect with a romantic partner. Some of the most comprehensive, detailed research on patterns of online dating comes from the United States. Although there are bound to be cultural specificities, the data provides informed clues of possible trends across Western nations. According to research by the Pew Internet and American Life Project, one in five users of MySpace and Facebook admit using the websites to flirt (Lenhart 2009). Eleven per cent of *all* American Internet-using adults stated that they have used an online dating website or other site in order to meet people online according to a Pew study (Madden and Lenhart 2006). And among single people, 74 per cent report that they have used the Internet in at least one way to facilitate dating and romance. Over a third of them (37 per cent) go to an online dating website (Madden and Lenhart 2006). These people are referred to as 'online daters'. Online daters tend to be younger and are more likely to be employed. The youngest cohort aged 18–29 is the largest group of online daters, with 18 per cent of all online adults in that age group visiting a dating site. However, 11 per cent of online adults aged 30– 49 have ventured to dating sites, and 6 per cent of those aged 50–64 and a mere 3 per cent of those aged 65 and older have tried dating sites. Online daters are more likely to be employed than non-daters, but they also tend to be earning lower incomes. This may be explained by the younger age of online daters. The Pew study found no statistically significant differences in online dating use across race and ethnicity categories or education levels.

Nowadays, Internet users are more likely to search online for details about the person they are dating or in a relationship with. One in six (16 per cent) Internet users search online to find information about the relationship status of someone they know (Madden and Smith 2010). Among adult Internet users, younger groups aged between 18 and 29 tend to be the most motivated to search for romantic interests online and relationship status information. Nearly one in three of these young adult users (29 per cent) seek out details about people they are dating or in a relationship with, compared with just 6 per cent of users aged between 50 and 64 (Madden and Smith 2010). Interestingly, online men are as likely as online women to seek out details about those they are dating or in a relationship with. There are no differences among racial and ethnic groups in this respect and only significant differences among the highest and lowest socioeconomic groups. Social network site users are four times more likely than non-users to go online to seek out information about their romantic partners (28 per cent vs 7 per cent) (Madden and Smith 2010). It seems, then, that the rise in popularity in researching romantic partners is widespread across social groups and across digital mediums.

Amongst the 37 per cent of Americans who said they had gone to a dating website, 7 per cent were currently seeking romantic partners. Among online daters, 43 per cent had been on dates with people they met through the sites and 17 per cent of them had entered long-term relationships or married their online dating partners. Three per cent of Internet users who are married or in long-term committed relationships say they met their partners online. Among those who have been to online dating forums, 52 per cent stated they had mainly positive experiences. Nevertheless, a substantial proportion of 29 per cent report mostly negative experiences. The younger the Internet user, the more likely he or she is to rate the services favourably. Around 15 per cent of those in the Pew survey of the general public stated that they know of someone who has been in a long-term relationship or married someone they met online. Twice as many know someone who has at least experimented in online dating.

Despite the growth in popularity of dating sites, most Internet users (66 per cent) claim that online dating is dangerous because personal information is placed on the Internet while 25 per cent do not consider online dating dangerous (Madden and Lenhart 2006). Among those most wary of the risks are women Internet users, older users and people who have lower levels of income or education. Those who have actually used the services tend to be more positive with 43 per cent believing that it entails risk. Fifty two per cent do not regard the activity as dangerous. Some 57 per cent of Internet users agree that a many people who use online dating lie about their marital status, 18 per cent disagree and 25 per cent say they do not know. People with lower levels of income or education are more likely than the average Internet user to suspect that people lie (Madden and Lenhart 2006).

Online dating tends to be steeped in practices that confirm conventional romance and sexual practices (DeMasi 2006). Yet research findings by the Pew Centre indicate that online daters are inclined to identify with more liberal social attitudes, compared with all Americans or all Internet users (Madden and Lenhart 2006). Users of dating websites are more likely to be supporters of gay marriage and see themselves as 'someone who likes to try new things'. They are less likely to be religious or to believe in traditional gender roles for men and women.

Online dating forums

Dating websites are one of the key contexts in which online initiated connections are likely to transfer to offline meetings. Most profit-making dating sites such as *eHarmony*, *OKCupid* and *Match.com* have been designed with the intention of offering individuals the opportunity to make contact with complete strangers who may have shared interests. These dating forums are often regarded as a labour-saving device in search for a partner (DeMasi 2006). The idea is that with busier working lives and the growing accessibility of the Internet, it becomes an increasingly attractive option to meet strangers online rather than through traditional community, leisure or work-based links. Many sites are tailored to specific age groups as well as sexual orientation. So online dating allows users to identify individuals who share their interests by scrutinising the profile of the type of person being searched for, before making first contact.

In the context of online dating and flirting, narratives of intimacy form key elements of the presentation of self. Online self-presentation becomes a central dimension of partner searching. Findings indicate that most people exaggerate their attributes, with 81 per cent of people misrepresenting their height, weight or age in their profiles (Toma and Hancock 2012). Daters lie to meet the expectations of their imagined audiences. However, people tend to limit themselves to small lies since they may eventually meet in person. Profiles often describe an idealised self, one with qualities they intend to develop, such as 'I scuba dive'. Giddens refers to contemporary therapeutic discourses which foster the project of self-identity within a culture of self-reflexivity and self-fulfilment. Through these personal narratives, individuals shape their identities, manage their intimate relationships and judge the merits of them.

Self-help books on intimacy and sexuality in couple relationships have expanded to encompass the theme of Internet dating, a genre which turns out to be eminently suited to this kind of therapeutic theme. These books act as guides to help people navigate safely through the 'perilous' landscape of cyber-dating, as indicated by their titles such as *Dating and Sex on the Internet: Exclusive Advice for Guys from a Woman* by Cherry Bomb (2010); *Eighty-Eight Dates: The Perilous Joys of Internet Dating* by Rachel Goodchild (2010); *The Golden Rules of Online Dating, 6 Crucial Rules to Finding the Perfect Online Date* by Shu-Ching Hsu (2011) and *The Perils of Cyber-Dating: Confessions of a Hopeful Romantic Looking for Love Online* by Julie Spira. These kinds of books range in focus from the personal 'rules of netiquette' to providing advice on how to avoid the 'perils of cyber-dating'. Interestingly, such texts contribute to the configuration of online dating etiquette. How to avoid unscrupulous contacts is a major theme which highlights the pitfalls associated with digital dating. Often laced with a selection of real-life horror stories that readers should avoid, this theme is dealt with in such books to highlight the risk associated with attempts to initiate online contact with complete strangers. For example, *Eighty-Eight Dates: The Perilous Joys of Internet Dating* is described as

> a 'fun collection' of anecdotes and advice for anyone interested in what it's really like to date online. The book includes: how to create a personal profile; selecting your image and choosing a photo; what you should be looking for; making the first connection; taking it further; etiquette and personal safety; coping with disasters; taking the next step.

Although online dating is hailed as the hallmark of a plastic sexuality and elective intimacy, dating websites tend to offer a narrow representation of intimate relationships that accentuate love, romance and monogamy. Conventional gender and sexual identity categories are likely to be used, thereby excluding more novel identity constructions. These sites promote traditional ideals of intimacy not only among heterosexual users but also among gay, lesbian, bisexual and transgender (GLBT) users (DeMasi 2006). Also, many dating forums have been designed exclusively for blacks, Latinos, Asians as well as GLBT users. The visual graphics that structure dating forums often display stereotypical images of love and romance and emphasise that the site is designed for the 'serious' and 'discerning' client. These forums tend to structure the search for intimate partners within a consumer market model. They evoke a shopping experience for partner selection (DeMasi 2006). Paid-up members are offered extensive consumer choices but within the confines of existing gender and sexuality identities. However, significant variations do occur with a growing number of sites offering opportunities to transcend conventional sexual classifications.

The Internet has also become established as a tool for arranged marriages online among immigrants to the West from India (Adams and Ghose 2003). Popular matrimonial websites in the United States integrate domestic and international marriage markets. They are also used by families in India searching for eligible men and women in the United States, Canada and the United Kingdom and other countries as well as India. In India, *Shaadi.com* boasts that it is the largest matrimonial website in the world. Matrimonial websites range from conservative, family-directed markets to unorthodox self-directed markets that have more in common with Western matchmaking sites. Family-directed matrimonial sites often contain a small photograph of prospective partners. They consistently include detailed information about caste, religion, ethnicity, education and employment, indicating the emphasis placed on these features for a marriage rather than on physical appearance. Yet colour of skin is also regularly highlighted as an issue. If a daughter has lighter, 'wheatish' coloured skin, attention may be drawn to this feature as a status symbol. One site, www.matrimonialonline. net lists hundreds of 'caste' options, underlining the importance of this factor in partner selection. Matrimonial websites can serve a significant role in situations where socialising with the marriage partner is forbidden before parental consent or if the social customs for arranging marriage have been disturbed by migration. The practice of online arranged marriages as an aspect of dating forums indicates not only the technological affordances of this medium but also some of the most conservative features of online intimacy.

Disembodied dating

Even though there are general concerns voiced about the risks involved in using dating sites, the percentage of users mentioned above demonstrate the huge importance and widespread nature of social media in the search for a partner. This raises wider questions about the ways in which the self as a physical being is presented and promoted online in the context of sexual intimacy. Most work on intimacy has focused on 'embodied intimacy' (Gabb 2008: 81). However, given the virtual framework of online romance and sexual expression, online dating implies a disembodied state of intimacy. Yet the sexed body comprises a critical component in the construction and management of subjectivity (Turner 1996). In a sense, site profiles comprise presentations of a bodily self, whether real or invented, and therefore presuppose some kind of bodily awareness. In the case of online dating, while the body has often been an 'absent presence' (Shilling 1993) bodily awareness is paramount. On dating sites, the body may be the inducement and potential reward as part of an erotic package. For example, the importance of body image on sexual interpersonal communication has been widely documented (Cash et al. 2004; Wiederman 2000). In her work on disclosing intimacies, Jamieson (1998) highlights the distinction between intimacies of the self and intimacies of the body: 'although the completeness of intimacy of the self may be enhanced by bodily intimacy' (1998: 1). How is the lack of a bodily presence in online dating managed? How is the embodied being represented and as appealing, as a potential reward in online environments?

While most studies focus on representations of the body either in virtual or physical space, there is little research on the ways in which these spaces are negotiated and how online and offline interactions *intersect* in the context of dating website encounters. The use of photographs has accelerated the popularity in dating sites. Despite the virtual nature of online dating, material bodies have a central significance not only for dating forums but also for social network site communication. For instance, Siibak (2010) undertook a study of the ways in which boys and young men present themselves on dating websites. In terms of the management of identity, Siibak found that photos constitute an important additional impression management tool for young men. These images are used to visually portray different versions of masculinity and confirm the use of photos for identity 'performances' on sites. Young men mostly pose alone in order to emphasise their looks and appear as willing sexual or romantic objects. Visual youthfulness becomes a vital dimension of sexual attractiveness.

In a study of self-presentations on dating sites, Toma and Hancock (2012) found that bodily self-embellishment was rife among older people. On average, women's profile photos were a year and a half out of date. Men's were on average six months old. Photoblog is also being used by young people as part of the development of identity. Adolescents in regions such as Chile use photoblogs such as Fotolog to receive social validation, gain social control and to maintain social relationships, which are regarded as important functions of self-disclosure during adolescence (Donoso and Ribbens 2010). Rate is the most popular online social network site for young Estonians, with more than hundreds of thousands of active users, which contains profile images for visual self-presentation (Siibak 2010).

Despite the apparent incorporeal nature of online intimacy, the body is *hyper- present*. In addition to verbal cues, the visual display of bodies comprises a major form of pleasure and fascination within date searching. It forms a key feature of social experiences and understandings of self and other. Through the presentation of photographic images, the body performs a vital role as a symbol of sexual desire, orientation and status – both as a potential 'gift' and assertion of sexual standing. For instance, in an ethnographic study of Internet sex and pornographic self-display in Hong Kong culture, Katrien Jacobs (2010) found that a particular sex and dating site was used as massive social network for sexual self-display using photographic images. Notions and standards of sexiness are being established in online mode, with imaging strategies adopted by users for the playful adoption of commonplace notions of sexiness as 'cybertypes'. These online behaviours are being interpreted as central features of changing sexual culture (Jacobs 2010).

Importantly, then, dating forums and social network sites entail a virtual yet *hyper-embodied* intimacy. Physical as well as emotional expressions of intimacy can be communicated online through a number of sophisticated visual and textual cues. Understanding the codes of communication involved and performing the necessary shifts between public and private personas (Goffman 1959) become a major component of online dating. The movement of relationships on dating forums to offline contexts is implied or made explicit. For example, the site studied by Jacobs (2010) encouraged members to migrate offline by finding real-life partners for sex, ranging from casual sex affairs between singles, swinging couples or extra-marital affairs between 'aba' (attached but available) individuals and their lovers. In terms of the personal control of risk in meeting strangers or casual acquaintances, the Internet can offer a sense of safety in exploring through bodily boundaries. The risks may come later, during embodied encounters.

The 'hyperpersonal effect'

Several studies support the claim that friendships which began offline tend to be more stable and enduring than those initiated online. How does this tendency relate to the practice of online dating? The limited range of cues may be relevant, particularly at the early stages of online communication (Choi 2006: 181). Research by Choi found that partners who first met online spent less time with one another and engaged in fewer shared activities. Cross-sex friendships that develop in a face-to-face context tend to be slightly *more* developed than those developed online (Chan and Cheng 2004; Mesch and Talmud 2006). Mesch and Talmud (2006) suggest that online intimacy might appear less developed because they are newer and less advanced.

While few longitudinal studies have yet been conducted, preliminary findings suggest that differences between online and offline relationships in terms of quality and intensity of friendships increase in the first year but then tend to diminish (Chan and Cheng 2004). Online relationships are likely to be more hesitant in early stages then grow and become more like offline ones. McKenna et al. (2002) found that online relationships which lasted over two years compared favourably with offline relationships. They found that 71 per cent of romantic relationships and 75 per cent of all relationships begun online were still going. Most had grown closer and stronger. Importantly, the speed at which people disclose may differ between online and offline contexts (Baym 2010: 128). As a relationship develops online, both partners tend to add other media in a predictable pattern of 'media multiplexity' (Haythornthwaite 2005). Online partners often begin with public discussion then add private one-to-one interaction via messaging, email or chat. The telephone may then be included and then a meeting in person arranged (McKenna et al. 2002).

Although the majority of connections initiated online do not transform into intimate relationships, Baym (2010) suggests that we have a tendency to exaggerate the appeal of people we meet online. She refers to a process of 'early idealisation' which can occur when people meet one another online. With limited identifying signs, individuals often seem to be attracted to each other more than they might if they had met in person. Referred to as 'hyperpersonal communication' (Walther 1996), this phenomenon was first recorded in experiments that compared clusters of students who worked together on projects in person or remotely via text-based online discussion.

Walther (1996) suggests three reasons why we might be attracted, early on, to the people we meet online more than those we meet offline. In online impression formation, the lack of clues offers wider scope for imagining the other. We may seem more appealing to others because the limited cues we use give us more control over our messages and allow us to be more selective in disclosing information about ourselves. Walther (1996) suggests that hyperpersonal communication may result from a tighter focus on message production in a context where other distracting cues are absent. One of the major affordances of asynchronous media is the possibility of revising and editing written message (Baym 2010). Baym also suggests that the anticipation of hearing from the online contact and of finally meeting them is also significant in heightening the attraction. She surmises that this 'hyperpersonal effect' of heightened intimacy may be peculiar to online contexts, in a way that might not translate seamlessly into offline relationships (Baym 2010: 127).

Conclusions

Transformations in romance ideology in late modern Western contexts correspond with an elaborated understanding of sexuality, greater tolerance of diverse forms of sexual expression and a stress on individual agency as the drivers of personal life. This is the context in which online dating is set. The fluidity and choice apparently offered by online dating fits in neatly with today's new ethos of elective intimacy. Processes of individualisation which produce a greater reflexive engagement in the project of self-identity are exemplified in the context of online dating where individuals become self-reflexive in their presentation of self (Mead 1934). Yet even in the context of mediated love, conventional romance remains a strong ideal that propels the discourse and sets parameters on desires and practices of intimacy. While social network site intimacies signify choice, fluidity and plastic intimacy, their design and use indicate a surprisingly conventional culture of intimacy.

This chapter demonstrates that social media offer a new and dynamic setting for young people's romantic practices which have become central to their lives. Ito et al. (2010) argue that the current use of new media by young people may well be a unique moment in the recent history of teen dating practices. Through their design, social network sites promote overt, open and often candid communication about their intimate relationships. By publicising details about themselves and gaining access to each others' personal information, new media technology is reconfiguring teenagers' notions of 'privacy' and 'publicity', of concepts of 'personal' and 'intimate'. It offers the communicative tools for building on casual meetings and for initiating new relationships. Digital media enable young people to track ex-partners, future relationships and provide them with easy access to peer-based interactions in general. The technology mediates the introduction and conclusion of relationships. Among teenagers, online relationships are usually formed with offline acquaintances.

However, the very technology that offers the opportunity to *control* their emotional disclosures has the potential to render youth more susceptible to risk. While teenagers have found online spaces in which they can meet people, flirt, form and end relationships away from parental surveillance, they find themselves exposed to the scrutiny of their friends and peers. Adolescents' experiences confirm the struggle to establish a set of norms to shape the use of social media in relation to intimate relationships. Starting a relationship is less intimidating since a range of social media allows young people to manage their vulnerability. The controlled casualness of mediated dialogues afforded on social media is a form of emotion management and a way to control vulnerability. The apparent flexibility and choice involved in online dating corresponds with the new kind of casual intimacy being generated today.

However, this fluidity and choice is all too fragile when a break-up happens. The challenge for today's youth is coping with the public nature of mediated break-ups. Students agreed that text message and Facebook break-ups are morally wrong. When breaking up, their social network sites play a key role by displaying the event. This means that teenagers' dating practices and intimate relationships occur in the context of their networked publics (Ito et al. 2010). By sharing networked publics, adolescents can follow and monitor ex-partners' activities and check their relationship status online after the conclusion of intimacy. This high level of intimate publicity provides the means for teenagers to retaliate for emotional injury and convey their anger to ex-partners.

Taken as a whole, the growth and popularity in online dating may be interpreted either negatively or positively. Within a positive account, online dating can be perceived as a self-directed activity that offers greater choice and control for those searching for a partner yet also as a sign of a fragmented and superficial society, exacerbated by a 'long hours' culture and lack of meaningful contexts for people to meet beyond the frantic urban club scene. It may exemplify the social dilemmas of the 'cash rich and time poor' as a key feature of modern urban culture and the atomised nature of interaction in urban environments. The solution is to go online, to search for partners. Online dating may be approached as an important channel for the search for and re-enactment of traditional romance in difficult circumstances.

Conversely, while online romance confirms the late modern ethos of agency, it also suggests that 'romance' is not a spontaneous, authentic and passionate process but something necessarily calculated, stage-managed and premeditated. The practices and meanings of meeting partners and sustaining intimate relationships are being rethought. They are being reconfigured as both contingent and engineered. Drawing on Foucault (1991), we can say that the government of the self is now taking place across several social media platforms. Neo-liberalist ideologies of personal transformation are being articulated online as part of the range of discourses of 'personhood'. Self-presentation on dating forums and social network sites is a particularly useful context for what Paul Du Gay has called 'entrepreneurial individualism' or an enterprise of the self (Du Gay 1996: 157). The reflexive neo-liberal subject must use a self-monitoring gaze to engage in a continual virtual renewal of the self. As part of the process of regulating and continually updating the mediated self, digital dating can be viewed as a major project of presenting and projecting a personal biography.

8
Virtual Communities and Online Social Capital

Introduction

Social network sites are said to have the potential to create virtual communities. In this respect, the medium's particular affordances and patterns of engagement have been viewed both optimistically and pessimistically. On the one hand, online social networks have been described as 'virtual communities' to highlight their socially beneficial qualities and as an indicator of renewed 'community'. The rise of digital media has therefore generated hope about the recovery of community in an electronic form through social network sites such as Facebook and Twitter. On the other hand, negative claims have been made that heavy social network site users are more likely to be socially isolated than occasional users and that new technology leads to a breakdown of traditional community. This negative account views online networking as a sign of a fragmentation of identities and the disintegration of community. This chapter addresses debates about the qualities of remote and face-to-face interaction, the relationship between the two and how the societal disadvantages and benefits of these connections have been described and assessed. It explores the ways that these online associations are thought to affect social cohesion, participation and the generation of social capital. The concept of 'community', 'virtual community' and 'social capital' is therefore examined in relation to the idea of the 'personal' and 'network' to consider the role of social network sites in fostering social cohesion online.

The first section looks at the way 'community' has been used to describe the nature of online personal connections. It begins by examining the debates triggered by the term 'virtual communities' about whether social network sites promote sociability or community fragmentation. Some notable scholars claim that these new structures of personal communication may be replacing traditional communities and connections in a networked society. Hence the second section considers whether social network site connections generate social benefits by assessing a range of empirical studies of 'online social capital'. Whether social interaction on social network sites enhance or complicate community belonging and also whether they enhance individual or social well-being are issues investigated in this chapter.

The community, the personal and the network

As the previous chapters indicate, today's social media have prompted increased public interest in the concept of 'friendship' as a relationship that embodies personal choice and agency. Similarly, the idea of 'community' is a prevailing idiom linked to debates about online connections and new social ties which carries positive meanings. The community metaphor has a powerful influence on the way we think about the nature of sociality on the Internet today. It is used by social network sites themselves to articulate and enhance their ethos of social connectivity as socially valuable. For example, Myspace.com refers to the process of *connecting* as a 'community'. In a recent internal search of social network sites, Malcolm Parks (2011: 106) found 317,000 references to 'community'. However, arguments about a renewal or crisis of community in the age of social media indicate that, like 'friendship', the concept of 'community' is particularly malleable and unstable. The question is: 'How useful is it for understanding the social benefits of social network site ties?'

The notion of 'community' as a positive form of online connectivity was evoked in the 1990s by the rise of online discussion groups and other social venues. This idea of community corresponded with growing aspirations for interpersonal democratisation and the extension of friendship to include more flexible relationships. The term 'community' was brought into play in earlier online networks through the use of the phrase 'virtual communities'. Even though the concept contains affective and historical deficiencies, 'community' continues to influence popular ideas and meanings of today's mediated networks. Considerations about community or community-like experiences endure within academic debates about contemporary mediated networks (e.g. Chua 2009; Fogel and Nehmad 2008; Sohn 2008; for a review, see Fernback 2007; Jankowski 2002). For example, Kate Raynes-Goldie and Fono (2005) found that individuals were motivated to Friend one another on

LiveJournal because, among other values, Friendship stood for 'online community'. Similarly, Jan Fernback (2007) confirms that individuals interviewed about their online social activity generate meanings about community through social interaction. Tufekci (2008: 547) refers to social network site participants observing one another engaging in activities of connectivity 'in an interlocked dance of community formation'. Yet Parks (2011) contends that social network sites are not 'communities' in any particular sense. They act as social settings through which various communities have the *potential* to be formed.

The term 'community' has strong nostalgic connotations, traditionally generating feelings of friendliness, trust and belonging within past debates about social ties. Scholars such as Tönnies (1957) argued that urbanisation, industrialisation and rapid social and geographical mobility have undermined traditional cohesive and supportive communities once linked by immediate ties of kin and locality. The sharing of a geographical space is perceived as a principal marker of traditional community in these early sociological writings. Respect for the group, reciprocity between members and group self-sufficiency within specified physical boundaries are among the positive ideals that represent traditional notions of integrated communities. Present-day deliberations about the changing meanings of 'community' amongst academics, politicians and policy makers coincide with concerns that modernity has undermined traditional communities. The positive values of being culturally embedded in a physical space have been set against pessimistic ideas of rootlessness, social isolation and individualism in contemporary urban societies (Bauman 2001; Putnam 2000).

Putnam (2000) argues that the kinds of non-political, voluntary organisations that are vital for civil society are declining. Public anxieties about a decline of community and civic culture have been articulated in relation to a rise in anti-social behaviour and a decline of commitment and reciprocal responsibilities. The concept of 'social capital' has been advanced as a way of identifying the shortcomings associated with a lack of community ties and a way of engaging with and measuring the benefits of such ties. In *Bowling Alone*, Putnam details the severe decline of social capital in the United States from the 1960s to 1990s defined by declining participation in voluntary associations, clubs and societies including attendance at public meetings, club or organisation membership, membership of parent–teacher associations (Putnam 2000). For Putnam, this process points to a weakening of civil society. He blames media technologies: first television, then the Internet as causes of the deterioration of traditional ties of social solidarity.

A critique of this view of community decline was made by scholars who studied 'virtual communities' to explain emergent online networks of social relationships. Online networks were described as 'community' ties with shared values and attitudes rather than shared proximity (Baym 1997; Hampton and Wellman 2003; Rheingold 1993; Wellman and Guila 1999). For example, Howard Rheingold spoke of networks on the Internet as 'virtual communities', describing them as 'webs of personal relationships in cyberspace' (Rheingold 1993: 5). Although these pre-Web 2.0 online connections sometimes progressed to face-to-face encounters, the main focus was on initiating and sustaining online connections. By drawing on psychological language or characteristics of sociality, more generalised ideas of community emerged: as a culture, set of values and interpersonal attitudes (Anderson 1991; Calhoun 1980). Proximity was not centrally relevant. This earlier notion of virtual communities is distinguishable from today's Facebook connectivity which is founded on a social network arrangement that initially brought together self-selecting individuals from institutional and geographical settings such as universities and colleges. Unlike virtual communities of earlier times, these networked individuals used their real names as a default and conformed to a set of norms and identifiable profile fields (Ellison et al. 2011b).

Thus, while 'virtual community' describes online networks that display the psychological and cultural qualities of strong community with little or no physical proximity (Willson 2006), today's social network sites are largely used to connect people with current or former geographical ties. As the previous chapters show, what makes today's social network site associations so interesting is not only the strong emphasis on informal, intimate and sociable affiliations but also the clear linkage between offline and online connections as a cultural framework for these connections. The question is whether or not traditional community ties have been recovered in a new setting by enhancing the cultural bonding and integration of disparate individuals through online networks. Are close, face-to-face, geographically based, affective communities that were apparently threatened during modernity being recuperated in new ways online? Is it accurate to call the social ties on social network sites 'communities'?

As the previous chapters show, social network site use has clearly been incorporated into and embedded in everyday life. Online network engagement is not only highly significant for the young. It has also been integrated into family life and become a central mediator in the rituals of starting and ending relationships. For many users, then, social network site engagement is not a liminal or marginal experience. It can form a major, structuring part of people's 'real' lives. However, modes of interaction developed through social network site engagement can vary widely to encompass either 'thick' ties of family, kinship, friendship and neighbourhood or 'thin' ties of acquaintanceship (Granovetter1973; see Chapter 1).

Individualised patterns of connection

Although there are problems in employing the 'community' narrative in an online context, common themes in the literature on community can be identified to see if they have a presence on social network sites. The idea of a 'personal community' as a more self-selected and more individuated source of support (Wellman 1979: 1211, 1993: 433) was developed from the 1960s onwards and extended in sociological discussions. However, for Wellman (2002), the community metaphor is inappropriate because individuals in the same household can be members of different personal networks. Computer-communication networks evolve towards loosely structured, interpersonal networking, rather than tight, bounded groups. Wellman states, 'The broadly-embracing collectivity, nurturing and controlling, has become a fragmented, variegated and personalized social network' (2002: 2). Thus, the concept of 'networked individualism' challenges the idea of a collectivism or group activism initiated in online interactions. For Wellman, computer-mediated communication is not a symbolic online community of firm social ties and commitment.

The idea of a more individualised, personalised community has been linked to the notion of personal ties encompassing associations of friendship and represented as 'hidden solidarities' (Pahl 2005: 629; also see Chapter 3). Importantly, these emphases are supported by studies of family, kinship, social movements and community life in Britain which have challenged the disjunction between 'community' and 'individualism'. Drawing on Durkheim's concept of solidarity, Graham Crow and colleagues (2002) highlight individualised patterns of connectedness in their research into neighbour relations in the South of England. Most respondents had strong neighbourly connections and were likely to identify neighbours in their street as friends or best friends. However, the study suggests that modern social bonds do not arise from a conscience collective but, rather, through differentiation and individuation.

This and other contemporary neighbourhood studies indicate that 'community' no longer refers to traditional supportive networks as they become more individualised (Crow et al. 2002; Morgan 2005; Pahl

2005). These studies highlight much more *personal* ways of engaging with social groups, as freely chosen activities (Crow et al. 2002). First, individuals have to resolve conflicting responsibilities and expectations. Second, social relationships are no longer tied to particular physical locations (Pahl 2005). These approaches complement the perspectives outlined in early chapters concerning the weakening of traditional social boundaries which uphold intimacy as a *private* and *personal* activity through reactions to work pressures, new family and intimate experiences and a broad collapse of public and private boundaries (Jamieson 1998). While the term 'personal community' emphasises the significance of chosen ties in the context of family and friends, as described in Chapter 3, 'personal community' implies that a personal commitment can achieve collective outcomes: that is, as a source of social capital and resource for public policy.

Research by Jennifer Wilkinson (2010) suggests that personal community and new solidarities that include friendship ties may offer the possibilities of more public and more collective forms of expression. As she emphasises, the term 'personal community' relies on the integration of two seemingly incongruent sociological principles: 'community' and 'individualism'. On the one hand, the concept of community has been linked with accounts of belonging, local solidarities, social commitment and public and collective interests. On the other hand, individualism encompasses notions of self-actualisation, individual achievement, identity and personal autonomy. This apparent contradiction raises questions about whether individualism has the capacity for realising collective outcomes (Wilkinson 2010). Research on personal communities has addressed this problem by approaching friendship as a *resource*: as social capital with public value. Spencer and Pahl (2006) suggest that personal communities can be used to achieve collective consequences. It does not necessarily occur through a collective forum, but instead through casual, private, informal social support.

In the case of social network site engagement, the question is whether collective interests can be achieved on social network sites through individualistic expressions and pursuits of self-fulfilment. Can personal communities online create a new kind of friendship that combines intimacy and civility in the public domain? While the concept of 'personal community' foregrounds the personalised and individuated nature of social network ties, the term 'network public culture' (boyd 2007, 2011; see Chapter 3) to describe online interactions takes this notion a step further. It does so by explaining the significance of personal cultures being extended into public realms, mediated through digital technology. This helps to advance an understanding of how personal networks, or 'personal communities' (Spencer and Pahl 2006), are translated into and articulated as public networks in online settings. Importantly, these networks are not simply 'virtual'.

These networked publics may be approached as *'personalised* networked publics' in order to highlight individual endeavours to gain personal control over online networks while emphasising the public nature of social network site interactions and the new risks and affordances involved. While the notion of 'personal' on social network sites describes autonomous, individualised modes of sociability, 'network' foregrounds shared contexts and understandings without the misleading connotations of 'community' which implies social commitment and collective action. Yet the question is whether social network site ties can create *new* solidarities. Is some kind of public participation taking place through personal relationships, as inferred in the concept of 'personal communities'?

Social network sites as 'communities'?

In a study of MySpace in the United States to detect whether social network sites operate as 'communities', Parks (2011: 108) identifies factors that could be used to measure online community engagement: the ability to engage in collective action, information sharing, shared rituals and social regulation, a sense of belonging and attachment, and a self-awareness of being a community. He contends that the concept of 'virtual community' can be drawn on to explain social network sites in the sense that the sites provide the technological and social affordances for pursuing online 'communities'. The designers and promoters of social network sites are right to emphasise the relational and communal potential of these sites. For example, MySpace offers easy access to diverse groups of people, a variety of options for users to focus on and communicate their personal interests, and is organised in such a way as to foster communication and relational links among members. Yet what is striking is the limited nature of this kind of 'community' engagement. Parks argues that the 'building blocks of community' happen far less frequently than usually thought. Thus, he concludes that virtual communities are uncommon on MySpace: 'That is, the portion of users who are active enough, express themselves in individuating ways often enough, and who interact with others frequently enough to generate the higher-order characteristics of community is quite small' (Parks 2011: 116).

However, Parks also found that a small number of highly engaged users *do* exhibit features of community. Between 15 and 25 per cent of members of MySpace met the minimum requirements for the formation of virtual communities by being active enough, having established a clear identity and having forged enough social ties. He undertook detailed case analyses of several of these highly engaged users, revealing that active users essentially have networks comprised of local, geographically shared connections. Intriguingly, the biggest difference between these engaged users and less engaged users is that the former draw more extensively on pre-existing offline networks, especially their local networks. He cites one case of a 20-year-old man who had completed high school in Texas with 79 listed Friends. Of the 67 Friends who gave their location information, 66 per cent lived within 10–15 miles of the user. In another case of a 17-year-old high school student in a town in suburb of Dallas who had 105 Friends, all those who gave location details (76 per cent) lived in the same town. This indicates that those with rich offline connections who transfer them to MySpace are more likely to become active users and to have strong online connections. The study suggests that geographical proximity and pre-existing *offline* contacts are highly significant for sustaining *online* communities. Parks states, 'Importantly, these findings imply that virtual communities are not so virtual after all.' He goes on to say that ' . . . it may be more accurate to say that virtual communities are often simply the online extension of geographically situated offline communities' (2011: 120). These outcomes concur with other research findings: that individuals who use social network sites learn more about people they have observed or already met in offline settings and are likely to feel *more connected* to their offline networks (Ellison et al. 2009).

A further defining feature of community is the self-awareness of being a 'community' and the ritualised sharing of information. While patterns of interaction are observable in the public areas of social network sites, there is confusion about the role and importance of a 'public commons' (Parks 2011; Sohns 2008) in the life of these networks if we approach them as 'communities'. The positive attitudes of community cohesion fostered in public areas seem to depend on *private* associations among members of communities rather than, or as well as, conduct in public space. Parks (2011) suggests that interlinked private networks such as the dispersed networks on social network sites may actually *replace* notions of the public forum. Rates of participation may well be higher in these scattered networks than in the shared public zones of these sites. Thus, the potential of collective action expected from traditional communities is present but not extensive on social network sites. This confirms the much more personal nature of connections, thereby echoing key features of the recent British kinship, neighbourhood and community studies mentioned above. Nevertheless, the idea of a personalised networked public remains a useful one in the context of mediated network ties. This term emphasises the personal control yet also the problem or challenges associated with the *public* nature of the interaction. Although these individualised networks are usually highly personalised networks articulated in public spaces, they typically have geographical significance.

In the following sections, the issue of social capital is addressed to explore the potential social benefits of social network ties.

Online social capital

Informal and varied intimate bonds are now acknowledged by policy makers to be key social resources within wider social support networks as part of 'social capital'. The term 'social capital' describes social practices that enhance cooperation between individuals for mutual benefit. The concept is utilised in social policy as a value with which to measure the 'productivity' of community networks including neighbourhood ties, participation in clubs and voluntary associations (Putnam 2000). In this way, social capital is employed to explain the benefits obtainable from relations and interactions between people through their social networks. The question is whether small or wider circles of micro-social worlds are now the most solid and enduring forms of social capital in contemporary society and whether they flourish in mediated networks.

The term 'social capital' has its roots in the work of Bourdieu (1985) and Coleman (1988), and has been advanced by Putnam (1995) and Lin (2001). The concept was conceived by Bourdieu as a combination of actual or latent resources associated with a stable network of 'institutionalized relationships of mutual acquaintances and recognition'. These networks involve key resources such as access to useful information, emotional help and exposure to varied cultural beliefs. Social capital tends to be approached as an asset, like financial or human capital, which is encompassed within the associations between individuals and is gauged either individually or at the level of the group (Ellison et al. 2011b). Explanations of social capital take into account the role of social structure, social norms, mutual support, trust, flow of information and solidarity. The term 'social capital' is now being employed by scholars to understand the parallels and differences between resources generated offline and online. Online networks have been approached as 'online capital' and also referred to as sociotechnical capital (Resnik 2001; Wellman and Guila 1999; Williams 2006).

Leading researchers of online social capital such as Ellison, Steinfeld and Lampe (2006) are asking whether social network sites encourage members to engage in activities that help build and maintain social capital. Does this form of online interaction provide the social benefits of access to resources and practical solidarity? And if so, is an inability or reluctance to engage in online social interaction a serious drawback to a person by hindering their accumulation of social capital? While there is continuing media speculation that online interactions impede the development of relationships by discouraging people from participating in the 'real world', many studies have found that users of sites such as Facebook are the least likely to be socially isolated (e.g. Hampton et al. 2011). Yet studies of online social capital face a persistent problem that the term 'social capital' is difficult to measure (Ellison et al. 2011b: 889). Nonetheless, the body of work that explores online social capital has uncovered some distinctive opportunities and affordances offered by social network sites. So far, this collection of research is largely composed of quantitative, survey-based studies which provide important clues about emerging social trends.

Putnam (2000) distinguished between two forms of social capital: bonding and bridging capital. Bonding social capital refers to the benefits gained from 'strong ties': close, personal, intimate relationships in which support is exchanged in relationships with very close friends or family members. This can include emotional or physical support or other more tangible benefits such as financial loans. Bridging social capital refers to the forms of 'weak ties' described by Granovetter (1973): loose, non-emotional connections that mainly exchange information. Bridging social capital therefore identifies the advantages generated by casual acquaintances and weak connections. These acquaintances can also result in positive effects such as new information from remote, weak connections and access to other people's belief systems. Social network sites seem to be well placed to offer social benefits from weak ties even though early research was pessimistic.

Early research indicated that the Internet causes seclusion and alienation which then has a detrimental effect on social capital. It was initially thought that individual's social networks and well-being were reduced (Kraut et al. 1998). However, a second study found not only that these outcomes fade over time but also that those individuals with robust support ties gained more benefits than those with weaker ties

(Kraut et al. 2002a). It was claimed that because the type of people who use the Internet are highly sociable to start with, the technology does not necessarily enhance sociability. But it was also argued that time spent using the Internet reduces the time available for face-to-face interactions.

Further early research came to conclusions that differed from both of the above findings by suggesting that the Internet should, instead, be regarded as a supplement to other social connections. A study by Hampton and Wellman (2003) discovered that the Internet did not substitute other kinds of communication such as telephone or face-to-face contact. Instead, it was used when other means were not accessible. However, a study by Wellman et al. (2001) found that the Internet did not affect amounts of use of other types of communication and that it complemented participation in political and other organisations. One of the most fascinating outcomes to emerge was that Internet users were found to be more connected to their offline networks than non-users. This was denoted by the better information they had about neighbours and improved interaction they had with them (Hampton and Wellman 2003). Thus, this range of early research suggested that the Internet did not *change* social capital. Instead, it functioned as an additional enhancing facility if used in combination with other kinds of contact (Quan Haase and Wellman 2004).

Studies have also found that social network sites may not necessarily increase the number of *strong* ties that people have. However, there is evidence that this technology may support the formation and maintenance of *weak* ties, thereby increasing the bridging social capital of its users (Donath and Boyd 2004). Following Granovetter (1983), who argues that a substantial network of weak ties provides benefits derived from wider access to more and varied information, researchers found that social network users can use their large number of Friends as acquaintances to help them find employment or information. The value of bridging social capital is exemplified by the discovery that individuals whose social ties include a broad variation of occupations tend to gain more help in circumstances such as searching for jobs or acquiring health information (Boase et al. 2006). Thus, social network sites seem to facilitate the creation of social networks by reducing the financial and temporal costs of communicating which, in turn, involves social capital benefits. This is because the medium makes it easier to communicate with and keep up-to-date with hundreds or even thousands of 'Friends'.

Three distinctive sets of online behaviour that enhance social capital have been identified by Ellison et al. (2009) in a study of Facebook use among college students in the United States: first, *initiating* behaviour which assessed the use of Facebook to meet strangers or make new friends; second, *maintaining* existing close ties; third, *information-seeking*, learning more about people with whom the user had an offline connection. The least common use of the social network site was for *initiating* contacts. By contrast, the practice of *maintaining* was the most frequent activity, thereby supporting earlier findings that Facebook is commonly used to link up with existing or latent ties than to meet strangers. However, the only significant predictor of bridging and bonding social capital was *information-seeking*, which is discussed in further detail below in relation to online trust. Facebook members who used the site to find out information about latent ties, rather than to engage in random 'friend collecting', were more likely to accumulate social capital from their use of the site.

Ellison et al. (2011a) argue that students who are Facebook users are likely to gain from a widened social network by bridging with other networks and being exposed to new, different ideas and information. At the same time, they may also expand their bonding capital by having supplementary modes of communication for sustaining close friends (Ellison et al. 2011b). Importantly, social network sites are said to facilitate the potential to turn latent ties into weak or strong ties (Hayworthwaite 2005: 137). However, given that Facebook is not normally used to connect with strangers, Ellison et al. (2011b) suggest that users may be less receptive to these advances. Nevertheless, some social network sites facilitate the interaction of 'friends of friends' which offers users access to an even more diverse set of weak ties. It provides individuals with beneficial skills on how to handle, speak to and deal with the conflicting opinions represented by others, which may generate social capital effects (Burt 2009). So far, then, the overall evidence suggests that the Internet offers opportunities for individuals to increase their bridging social capital by providing more possibilities for interaction with people beyond their close network. Social network sites are able to act as 'social supernets' by expanding the number of weak ties a user can maintain (Donath 2007; Donath and boyd 2004).

However, these online opportunities may exacerbate existing offline social inequalities. Evidence suggests that the aim of Facebook CEO Mark Zuckerberg is to organise the site to become even more personalised and humanised in order to encourage users to treat their circle of friends, family and weaker ties such as colleagues and peers as their main source of information when searching for a doctor, plumber or a best buy product, rather than doing a Google search, for example

(Fenton 2012). Through this process, online networks tend to intensify and expand the exchange of like-minded people. As Fenton (2012) points out, this process of online social capital may actually sustain social inequalities through zones of exclusion configured by class, race and gender. These online inequalities are likely to echo offline informal networks established through 'who you know'.

Online trust

The effectiveness of sharing information online is not only dependent on who you know but also on levels of trust. Giddens (1991) argues that, in response to the fragmentation of traditional community relations and the uncertainties they trigger, trust has become indispensable to sociality in the late modern era. This seems to be confirmed within approaches to social capital as trust has been identified as one of the core features of social capital (Patulny 2005). So, how is trust defined and how does it feature and work within networks? Two kinds of trust have been identified in relation to social capital: generalised trust and particularised trust (Uslaner 1999a, 1999b). Generalised trust is related to faith in strangers. It refers to emotional-normative trust and is linked negatively to information because it involves an altruistic, moral trust rather than rational calculation (Patulny 2005: 3). Particularised trust is rational trust linked positively to information (Patulny 2005). However, Mary Holmes (2010) argues that in present-day society trust is often based mainly on emotions. Since individuals do not usually have the knowledge required to make a fully rational decision, they often have to rely on feelings about things and activities or on an aesthetic: a liking for a person, persons or thing (Holmes 2010: 149). This notion of emotional trust appears to correspond with the motivation to trust others in online contexts.

Recent studies of Internet connections indicate surprisingly high levels of trust among users and that degrees of online interaction are positively related to generalised trust (Best and Krueger 2006). Similarly, the findings of a study by the US Pew Research Centre suggest that social network site users are more trusting and more sociable than non-users (Hampton et al. 2011). Over two thousand American adults were interviewed in the Pew study about their use or non-use of social network sites. It was found that social network site users usually have a wider circle of close friends, are more trusting and receive more social support than their non-networked counterparts. Facebook users are likely to receive 50 per cent more social support, emotional support and companionship. Indeed, high users of social network sites are more than three times more likely than non-Internet users to feel that most people can be trusted (Hampton et al. 2011). Interestingly, the survey was conducted during the US elections in 2010. As well as having more close ties they have also been identified as more politically engaged than those who are not network site users.

A survey on trust by Dwyer et al. (2007) also found that online trust involves a willingness to share information, with trust and usage goals affecting what people are willing to share on sites. Facebook users expressed greater trust in Facebook than MySpace users did in MySpace and were therefore more willing to share information on the site. Significantly, the extent of a person's social network site use and their level of trust seem to be a predictor of bonding capital (Tufekci 2008). This is also confirmed in a study of Facebook by Meredith Morris et al. (2010) who found that trust is a significant factor in users' decisions to ask questions through the site. Facebook users tend to trust responses from Friends more than from strangers and prefer asking questions on Facebook rather than search engines, indicating that Zuckerberg's vision is being enacted. This technique of information gathering was preferred by users because it provided additional opportunities to connect socially with their network.

In a study by Vitak and Ellison (2012), participants described a further benefit in relation to their Facebook Friend network: the fact that there was a pre-existing relationship in place. For instance, when 'Monique' needed advice on what medicine to prescribe for her daughter, she said she preferred posting the question on Facebook rather than using a search engine:

> ... because a lot of people deal with similar things. So especially with kids, they know exactly what to give a child and what not to. When you Google it, they just give you a list of medicines. You don't know if the medicine works or not. You talk to somebody else who has a child and know that they gave it to their child.
>
> (quoted in Vitak and Ellison 2012: 11)

Vitak and Ellison explain that the authenticity and shared experience involved in gaining information from a known connection prevailed over the less personal information that Monique would have received from a Google search. And this sentiment was echoed by other participants in their study. Evidence suggests then that more personalised the advice, the more highly valued it is and the more likely to be regarded as trustworthy. Thus, the 'generalised trust' related to faith in strangers (Uslaner 1999a, 1999b) described above does not appear to be a common feature of social network site trust in this study. However, Vitak and Ellison point out that there may be disadvantages to this process of obtaining information since, following Granovetter (1973), network composition is likely to be too homogenous and dense, made up of intimate and wider friendship ties of like-minded people, rather than more diverse networks linked to wider information. And they also point out that:

> While having a smaller network on the site may diminish users' ability to access new information and ideas, users may be purposefully limiting Friend connections due to privacy concerns, constituting another barrier to using Facebook for information needs.
>
> (Vitak and Ellison 2012: 11)

They illustrate this through the case of another participant, 'Nancy', who was conscious of this problem as she kept a low Friend count (30), rarely made disclosures through the site and described herself as 'a very private person'. When asked whether her unwillingness to share personal information online restricted the value of the site to her, she stated, 'Yes, definitely. I don't get as much out of Facebook as I think a lot of people that I know do.' As Vitak and Ellison (2012: 12) put it, 'For Nancy, the risks associated with sharing personal information on Facebook outweighed the potential benefits to sharing information through the site, even when her potential audience was limited to close friends.'

While Vitak and Ellison found that participants identified both benefits *and* constraints in using Facebook for information-seeking purposes as a key form of bridging social capital, they also discovered a significant difference between weak and strong ties in this process of trusting others online. They state that some participants doubted the authenticity of support provided only through the site precisely because it was so easy to post a short comment or 'like' a post. They suggest that Facebook may be better positioned to act as a facilitator of support through *other* channels, particularly for those who have these concerns. They draw on Haythornthwaite's (2005) idea of media multiplexity to explain that close ties interact through a wider range of channels. Although Facebook may offer an excellent channel through which weak ties can offer support, *strong ties* are more likely to be activated to post information on Facebook as a way of initiating communication through a more private channel, for instance a phone call or face-to-face meeting (Vitak and Ellison 2012: 13). Trust is usually approached as a process that develops over time, as 'incremental trust building' (Gilbert et al. 2010). However, in the case of social network sites, it seems that trust relies heavily on bonding capital and, hence, that emotional trust is being exercised based on knowing and liking a person. And, importantly, this medium is being used in combination with other social media, in a polymediated environment. Yet Vitak and Ellison's findings suggest that we can tentatively describe this emotional trust as strategic since it is used as a way of opening up further interaction with 'significant others' initiated through this digital connection.

People searching and reconnecting

Studies of proximity have, for some time, indicated that proximity between two individuals increases the chances that a relationship will form (Verbrugge 1977). Thus, a way of approaching the relationship between Facebook use and social capital is by taking into account the relationship between physical proximity and relationship development. Friendships are regularly formed according to where a person lives, works, attends school or spends leisure time, given that there are more prospects for communication (Kraut et al. 2002b) and because proximity decreases the effort required to initiate a relationship (Kraut et al. 2002b). Ellison et al. (2011b) argue that Facebook use extends these proximity-based social processes in two ways. First, it allows those who formed a relationship through physical proximity, and then lost that proximity, to maintain or regain the relationship. High school students moving to college, people moving jobs or family moving are examples of this. Second, Facebook can reinforce relationships formed through proximity that would be too fleeting to survive otherwise. They give the example of two students who meet through class who may connect for the duration of the class due to forced proximity. When that proximity is removed, the relationship may not survive the rise in the cost of maintaining the tie. However, Facebook makes it easier to keep what they call 'lightweight contact' with each other even when the benefits of proximity are no longer available.

Thus, one of the most significant strategies in social network sites use is to connect with people from the past. In a longitudinal American study that compared activity between 2006 and 2009, Madden and Smith (2010) found that users of social network sites are much more likely than non-users to search for information about others in their present or past lives. Users are more likely to search for information about people with whom they have lost touch than non-users: 64 per cent of social network site users have searched for information about someone from their past, compared with 30 per cent of non-users. They are also more likely to be younger Internet users, college graduates, parents, broadband users and wireless users. Young people lose touch with past friends fairly early on in their lives through progression to college or work in new geographical surroundings. Likewise, young adults who become parents are juggling major life changes of cohabiting or marriage and bringing up children. These groups are finding that social network sites form a useful, fast medium for recovering past friendships that were lost after moving into a long-term relationship and moving in together. Social network sites are, then, playing a central role in reshaping intimacy and friendship as *mediated intimacy* by facilitating the recovery of past personal connections. Since we live in an age where geographical mobility is on the increase, reconnecting with past friends is becoming an important feature of our lives and of online personal communities.

The practice of searching for information about others is clearly not restricted, then, to checking up the details of new, current or former partners in the context of dating. In terms of family relationships and the maintaining of personal communities of family and friends, it is significant that Internet users are becoming much more inquisitive about their relatives in an online context. Thirty per cent of users have searched for information about their family members online. And, of course, this is even extended to the popularity in using online family history websites which provide services in undertaking searches for family trees. Madden and Smith (2010) also observed that new connections encourage new searches with 19 per cent of site users having searched for information about someone they just met or were about to meet for the first time. The search for social network profiles and photos has increased significantly over time. In the age of social media, a Facebook profile is likely to receive more traffic than a resume or biography on an employer's website. Over time, 'people searchers' are gradually more likely to search for social network profiles than to seek information about someone's professional activities or interests. Again, men are more likely than women to initiate this kind of search (41 per cent of men compared with 31 per cent of women). People who have a college degree or reside in higher income households are also more likely than those with lower levels of education or income to seek out this kind of information (Madden and Smith 2010).

On the other side of the coin, people seem to be managing their social contacts more selectively. Over half of social network site users have 'unfriended' contacts from their networks (56 per cent), by deleting individuals from their friends list, if the numbers of contacts become excessive or certain contacts are no longer wanted. Just over a third alters the information posted about them by others and a third removes their name from photos labelled to identify them. Over half have prevented people from observing updates. Young adults are the most practiced in this type of social network organisation. Madden and Smith (2010) found that of users aged 18–29, 64 per cent have removed individuals from their network or friends list. This compares with 52 per cent of the 30–49 age group and only 41 per cent of older users between 50 and 64. Although deleting 'Friends' from one's network is now common practice, some participants prefer to tune people out rather than to defriend in order to avoid offence. Certain features can be used to filter out people from a person's site, such as the 'hide' function on Facebook which excludes selected individuals from friends' updates on the News Feed. Madden and Smith (2010) found that as many as 41 per cent of users have filtered updates posted by some of their friends. While those aged 18–49 are the most likely to filter updates in this way, only a third of those aged 50–64 are likely to do so.

Conclusions

Like the concept of 'friendship', the notion of 'community' has had a commanding influence on the meanings and values associated with mediated social networks by presenting a language of social cohesion and optimism. The continuing appeal of the discourse of 'community' is exemplified by the employment of the term by social network sites themselves to describe their attributes and capabilities for networking. The idea has been combined with that of 'friendship' by these sites to generate positive connotations of sociality. Both concepts express powerful ideals. However, while 'friendship' conveys buoyant notions of choice and compatibility, it also contains potentially anti-social elements of individualism and self-absorption which generates concerns among communitarian scholars. The term 'community', on the other hand, expresses the less risky and much more stable features of solidarity, commitment and collective action.

Overall, social network sites such as Facebook are well designed to foster social interaction because they have the ability to perform the three major tasks that support relationships offered by other mediums such as cell phones and email but all in one package (Ellison et al. 2011b). First, social network sites allow individuals to identify those with *shared interests*, for example through Groups or searchable profile fields. Second, they enable *self-expression* through the profile, providing numerous chances to share information about cultural tastes, friendship networks, political views and other dimensions of the self. Third, social network sites offer multiple opportunities for *public and private communication* which can be broadcast and yet targeted and may be lightweight and yet more substantive (Ellison et al. 2011b).

The range of studies of online social capital implies that users who are able and inclined to participate in certain social network site activities are more predisposed to gain social capital benefits. Research on social capital demonstrates that social network sites provide technological affordances that not only enhance bonding capital but can also foster weak ties known as bridging capital. Thus, public spaces are being stretched out to allow individuals to embrace and benefit from the kinds of social ties that would be difficult to sustain offline. Strong, close, intimate ties described as bonding social capital rely on media multiplexity (Hayworthwaite 2005). Close friends, families and intimates are likely to make use of numerous, varied methods of contact including face-to-face interaction, texting, phoning and Internet. This is in contrast to the way weak ties tend to be maintained since these are likely to rely on one, asynchronous method (Ellison et al. 2011b).

The question is whether the kinds of personal narratives expressed on social network sites can be fused with more public or communal aims of civil engagement and collective action. By way of an answer, this chapter has highlighted the individuated, personalised nature of social network ties in relation to debates about the way 'community' has been used to describe online connections. I argue that the term 'network public culture' coined by boyd (2007) helps to elucidate the importance of personal cultures being extended into and mediated through public realms. The networks do not exhibit features of virtual 'community' in the conventional sense. They are, instead, *personalised* public networks that correspond so closely with the physical or institutional spaces that people inhabit, including the recovery of past links based on proximity, that notions of virtuality may be misleading. Nevertheless, the transformation of 'personal communities' into personalised networks in public contexts through mass self-communication (Castells 2009), as exemplified by the 2011 UK riots (see Chapter 2), the 2008 Obama presidential campaign in the United States and the 'Arab Spring' of 2011 indicates the potential for a shift from personal to collective interaction. As such, this process can be approached as a latent resource in the context of both social capital (Bourdieu 1985) and media multiplexity (Hayworthwaite 2005) which has significant consequences for the nature of sociality. Although beyond the compass of this book, this points to the evolving potential for a *personal* register to be used to generate complex political support (Papacharissi 2010).

Overall, the series of studies about online social capital suggests several trends in the context of mediated intimacies and wider online friendships. First, a significant predictor of social capital is the use of social network sites to trace and find out about people with whom some kind of offline connection has been previously established. A second, related trend is that sites such as Facebook increase bridging capital by enabling individuals to sustain larger sets of weak ties. Social network sites perform as 'social supernets' by expanding the number of weak ties a user can maintain (Donath 2007; Donath and boyd 2004). These sites allow individuals to transform ephemeral connections into lasting ones (Ellison et al. 20011b). Facebook profiles can also overcome some of the obstacles that get in the way of initial interaction by creating common ground.

A third trend within these mediated networks is a stretching of the scope of available information sources. A network of casual acquaintances *and* close friends is well tailored for supporting impromptu advice-seeking (Ellison et al. 2011b). Larger diverse networks with a mix of strong and weak ties are more likely to consist of a wide range of individuals who share a peripheral connection but can also serve as resources for new information. A fourth, related feature is that studies are uncovering high levels of trust among site users. Yet findings suggest that trust is a predictor of bonding capital. This kind of online trust could be defined as a *strategic, emotional* trust since it seems to rely on close ties rather than connecting with strangers, and it is often treated as a channel for generating further interaction with significant others. However, Fenton (2012) warns that online social capital may uphold social inequalities through modes of social exclusion based on class, race and gender which are likely to reflect offline informal networks.

Thus, in answer to the question about whether online personal communities resolve the contradictions surrounding the pursuit of *personal* concerns in a *public* context, the evidence suggests that most activity on these sites tends to be of a personalised nature. Importantly, however, they offer the technical affordances and the social possibilities for making the kinds of connections envisaged by 'virtual communities' and to enhance the social capital that lies within them.

9
Mediated Intimacies

Introduction

The employment of the term 'friend' to describe *all* social connections on social network sites is not a coincidence. A strong social drive already existed before the era of social media to identify new kinds of interpersonal relationships based on choice, agency and equality. This impetus corresponds with a particular set of tendencies involving changing interpersonal relationships during late modernity. Chapter 3 addressed the significance of the individualisation thesis advanced by late modern theory which implies a democratisation of intimacy, characterised by diversity and flexibility in emotional intimacy. Importantly, this process of detraditionalisation paves the way for a more fluid and transient notion of intimate connections, beyond the family to incorporate friendship and to acknowledge the social significance of looser, more flexible ties. The intention of this book has been to develop a theory of mediated intimacy in order to contribute to an understanding of the changes in today's personal relationships in the context of social media. The task in this final chapter is threefold. The first is to draw together the key issues raised in previous chapters in order to identify and confirm the key features of digitally *mediated intimacies*. Focusing on the mediation of close and loose associations among youth, adults and families, we have seen that the concept of 'friendship' emerges as a powerful tool in shaping contemporary meanings of social connectivity. How and why this ideal binds together all mediated connections as personalised networks in articulating digitally framed relationships is addressed.

The second objective is to examine the ramifications of mediated intimacies by focusing on the characteristics and organisation of the *mediated self* in late modernity. It asks what kind of self is being constructed and presented, particularly in the context of social network sites. The technological affordances of social media comprise social choices that can be approached as processes of governmentality. Neoliberal discourses of agency and choice are highlighted to explain today's project of the self in the context of networked publics. How individuals present online selves and gain a sense of autonomy within new, flexible modes of sociability is examined.

The third objective is to consider the commercial framework in which mediated networks such as Facebook are embedded, and what the effects might be on the nature of interpersonal relationships. A number of tentative observations are made which indicate that the mediation of intimacies through commercially structured communication technologies has implications for the nature of personal ties online. In conclusion, I suggest that we have entered an era in which 'friendship' becomes both a potent exemplar of individuality and personal choice and a global marketing tool to influence our personal tastes and patterns of consumption.

Mediated intimacies

A range of more fluid personal relationships has become central in providing intimacy and companionship in an individualising world, and these relationships have become pivotal to people's core values. The idea of an autonomous intimacy signifies the emancipatory potential of *all* relationships. It sets the scene for the rise of an elective intimacy. Intimacy is now defined as a means of expression and affective fulfilment (Plummer 2003). Within this thesis of a democratisation of interpersonal relationships, the late modern concept of 'friendship' seems to echo Aristotle's (1955) philosophy: friendship is not simply a more inclusive relational paradigm. It is also conceptualised as an ideal relationship: entered into voluntarily and marked out as egalitarian by emphasising positive attributes of respect, mutual disclosure and companionship. This approach offsets the pessimistic tones of those academic and public discourses that advance the idea of a crisis in personal relationships and community.

Marked out and celebrated as a valued relationship in late modern society, friendship also has important strategic attributes. It becomes a social marker of equality and reciprocity. Changing patterns of intimacy that value and privilege friendship exemplify not only a democratisation of relationships but also a repersonalisation of relationships through aspirations to make them more meaningful, to extend their positive attributes and to use them to explore one's multifaceted identities and desires. The structure and dynamics of online relationships correspond with these ideals. In an age of 'networked intimacy', love, friendship and moral values have become renewed sites of an engagement with 'the other'. However, importantly, face-to-face and phone interactions are not being replaced by instant messaging and social network site use. Rather, among all social groups and particularly among teenagers, interpersonal communication is stretching outwards from face-to-face interaction to embrace a wide range of multiple communication technologies.

While all social ties are mediated in some way or another, in the digital age mediated intimacies emerge to encompass distinctive features which I have identified in earlier chapters. I shall foreground each of these intersecting features in turn, first by identifying the ways in which mediated intimacies are technologically and socially structured and then by identifying the type and content of relationships being supported through these structural tendencies. First, the structural elements of mediated intimacies comprise the following interrelated elements:

- highly *personalised channels* of communication;
- a *personalised network public*;
- specific *technological affordances*;
- a diverse *polymediated* environment;
- a *re-socialisation* of media.

Second, these structural elements support the following types and content of interaction as key features of mediated intimacy:

- connections articulated through a *'friendship'* discourse. This includes a *ritualisation of friendship* and the rise of a *hyper-friendship*;
- the rise of a *personalised public discourse*;
- expressed through an *informal register*;
- the *staging and management of identity*;
- the accumulation of distinctive *social benefits* of *connectivity*;
- the evocation of a sense of personal *choice* and individual *control*, including the rise of a *mediated pure relationship*;
- an accent on the *moral questions* associated with choice of medium for conducting relationships.

I shall elaborate on each of these elements of mediated intimacy in turn. Mediated relationships are articulated and negotiated through highly *personalised channels* of communication which, at the same time, can be highly public. The research outlined in previous chapters confirms that although social media platforms such as social network sites provide the technological tools to sustain extensive weak ties, they are mainly used to maintain relationships among a relatively small number of contacts and in conjunction with other personal media channels. Greater possibilities for intimate contacts online are now being offered, leading to a reappropriation of social networking within a *personalised network public* which implies the personal choice and individual control involved in the type and content of mediated intimacies. While social media are capable of connecting large groups in local and global networks, and certainly do so in times of social crisis and rapid social change (see Chapter 2), they are more frequently used to make connections between a close circle of friends and family.

Mediated intimacies also operate within relational media structures in a diverse media environment, a *polymedia* environment in which several mediums are likely to be used regularly to keep in contact with intimates and selected according to the circumstances and emotional register required (Madianou and Miller 2012). The more intimate the relationship, the more media platforms are involved in supporting the interaction. Social media draw on specific *technological affordances*, that is, attributes and opportunities offered by the particular mediums. These affordances include persistence, replicability, scalability and searchability (boyd 2011). Mediation brings together the technological and the emotional (Madianou and Miller 2012: 2142) in the sense that the technological affordances lend themselves to a particular emotional register or mode of articulation. Thus, the medium itself and the combination of mediums in which it is used is a powerful indicator of the degree of intimacy involved and being expressed. Mediated intimacies thereby entail a *re-socialisation of media*. The reciprocal attributes of social media technologies shape social interactions as personal exchanges.

In terms of the type and content of relationships, today's mediated intimacies are being approached and categorised largely as *friendships*. Social network sites compel us to categorise our network connections as Friends however strong or weak the ties and whether they comprise family members, friends, friends-of-friends, work-related contacts or acquaintances. Hence, what makes social network sites unique is not that they allow individuals to meet strangers, but rather that they enable users to publicise their personal connections (boyd 2007). These mediated relationships are articulated as informal by drawing on an *informal register.* Thus, a discourse of casualness and spontaneity typically frames the interactions particularly on social network sites. Yet the informal tone that characterises these online intimacies can nevertheless support more intense, more complicated and more problematic interactions: they can be banal, passionate or disruptive. Informality evokes the use of a particular vocabulary of emotions and feelings associated with disclosing intimacy (Jamieson 1998), and with jocular familiarity which invokes equality.

These mediated friendships are performed within a *personalised public discourse* which implies a focus on self-identity, personal as opposed to political details and objectives, and involves an increasing permeability of public and private. This is related to the creation of a *personal networked public* (boyd 2011) which brings together the notion of a 'networked individual' linked into 'networked publics'. These personal networked publics are made up of personal communities or 'micro-social worlds' (Pahl and Spencer 2004) and organised by networked technologies around media audiences, texts, emotional exchanges and the sharing of cultural artefacts such as family photos, video clips, jokes and homilies.

The informality being expressed in interpersonal communication also coincides, paradoxically, with a *ritualisation of friendship* as a feature of mediated intimacies. Despite being set within an informal and personalised discourse, friendship ritualisation refers to the practice of publicly proclaiming friendship through the publicisation of our lists of contacts. This practice amounts to a new ritual of social connection. Friendship ranking, popular among the young, which involves the listing of one's top friends in a ranked order, is part of this practice, indicating a new process and category of what we might call *hyper-friendship*. Hyper-friendship indicates an increasing dependence on the process of selecting and grading online Friends according to status for the construction of self-identity, rather than solely emotional and reciprocal factors associated with family and companionships. Thus, by having the potential to operate as personalised networked publics, social network sites involve the *staging and management of identity* through self-presentation. The process of self-presentation is configured by imagined audiences and marks a contemporary mode of self-reflexivity or 'regime of the self'. The mediation of this staged self is the topic of the following section.

Mediated intimacies take place within networked publics that generate distinctive *social benefits* of increased sociability through the extension and development of weak ties. This has been highlighted by research outlined in Chapter 8 regarding online social capital. Social network sites are playing a central role in reshaping intimacy by facilitating the revival of past connections. This practice of retrieving lost personal ties is indicative of the age we live in, exemplifying the fallout from the geographically and socially transient nature of late modern life. In this respect, informal communication technologies such as social network sites are perfect tools for reigniting past ties, for mending the fractures that ensue in our life trajectories.

The diverse technologies of social media seem to contain democratising features in the sense that these personalised mechanisms of communication apparently offer immense *choice and personal control* in fostering mediate intimacies. Several options are now available in the selection of a medium appropriate to the receiver and subject matter of the message. The technological affordances of social media match aspirations towards the *pure relationship* by allowing a sense of control over the relationship, uncluttered by power and privilege. As Madianou and Miller (2012) argue, the polymediated context of today's personal communication technologies offers opportunities to evoke the impression of a pure relationship, particularly during times of great change involving geographical mobility and the social upheaval experienced by transnational families. Being able to conduct and maintain intimacy at a distance is a great comfort in times of discord. However, this choice of medium increasingly involves moral issues in addition to technical and financial matters. The re-socialisation of media as interactive and reciprocal reflects the fact that mediated intimacies entail *moral questions* about choice of use (Gershon 2010; Madianou and Miller 2012). The technological attributes offer users extensive opportunities to upset, demoralise and humiliate intimates, former intimates and weaker associates, particularly in the case of relationship break-ups and online bullying. Choice of medium entails a moral act to be judged and reflected upon because the individual and combined use of communication medium conveys the level of intimacy.

Thus, in terms of personal control and choice, mediated intimacies are increasingly being governed by sets of conventions or tacit rules to organise the moral dimension of communication. The technologies of texting, social network sites and tweeting can offer a sense of personal control to manage the kinds of vulnerabilities involved in making a more emotionally intense connection. Indeed, the more personalised and varied the interaction becomes, the more we attempt to control our interactions since all interactions entail potential interdependence and therefore potential emotional and social risks (Baym 2010: 129;

Broadbent 2010). New media offer young people opportunities to manage their sense of emotional risk in the context of dating, as shown in Chapter 7. However, at the same time, these norms are much more than just online protocols or 'netiquette'. Referred to by Gershon as 'media ideologies', they comprise beliefs about how the various mediums should be used and, significantly, they vary from person to person thereby demonstrating the nascent qualities of social media. Thus, while social media offer the possibility of selective sociability, through increased choice and agency, they also highlight issues of accountability.

Social media such as social network sites are, then, eminently suited to new modes of friendship as casual, transient and playful yet also as intense, passionate and enduring. Conventional and new meanings of friendship are performing side by side in this new digital space.

The mediated self

A key feature of mediated intimacies is the *staging and management of identity* in online contexts. This digital epoch accentuates the project of the self and the prevailing question: 'who am I'? How people present the self, as a reflexive subject, and gain a sense of control in these networked publics becomes a central issue. Producing and networking online content is becoming an essential process for managing one's identity, lifestyle and social connections. The online presentation of self involves the kind of symbolic interaction described by Mead and Goffman and has evolved into a form of self-display to articulate friendship links and serve as an identity marker for profile owners. This self-management of online identities is becoming increasingly elaborate and involves the juggling of complex, multidimensional relationships. As part of this process, adults and teenagers are negotiating 'Friends' to stage their identities (Livingstone 2008). The project of the online self is, then, being cultivated through three levels of generalised others (Mead 1934): as imagined audiences (boyd 2006a), more specific 'generalised others' and named 'significant others' (Holdsworth and Morgan 2007). The accent on individualism foregrounds the idea that the individual is constantly subjected to pressures and constraints from *beyond* the self.

Ideas about the prospects for increased social cohesion associated with the technical affordances of social network sites chime with powerful sentiments of personal autonomy. Individuals are expected to cultivate their self-presentations and shape their demeanour according to socially acceptable standards while always articulating the construction and performance of identity as freely chosen. However, at the same time as offering personal choices, these networks require meticulous and conscientious management of the self as modes of governmentality and self-regulation within uncertain and risky public contexts. In this respect, as indicated in Chapter 4, social network sites have evolved into significant sites of self-regulation compatible with neo-liberal discourses of agency and choice. Hence, the neo-liberal subject comprises an individual who constantly needs to reinvent him- or herself (Rose 1999).

Certain key demands are made of the individual that are specific to these new, simultaneously personalised and public technologies. While Mead and Goffman's symbolic interactionism confirms the underlying interactive nature of the construction of self in an online as well as offline context, Foucault helps foreground self-government: the way in which subjectivity is self-regulated. In his exploration of a genealogy of subjectification, Nikolas Rose (1996) highlights the issue of 'our relation to ourselves', in the reflexive mode which allows us to understand the way that identity or subjectivity is being shaped through online self-presentation as a form of self-regulation. Following Foucault (1991), Rose (1999) argues that neo-liberalism entails a mode of governmentality that functions across several social spheres and conceptualises individuals as the entrepreneurs of their own lives (Rose 1999). As mentioned in Chapter 7, online self-presentation in these contexts can be viewed as a process of 'entrepreneurial individualism' or an enterprise of the self (Du Gay 1996: 157). In particular, social network sites and online dating forums offer the perfect environments for the continual *updating of the self* involved in today's self-presentations. Through online self-presentation, the self has become the object of a regime of subjectification.

Neo-liberalist ideologies of personal transformation are now being articulated through online publicity. The self functions as a regulatory ideal on social network sites as part of our projects of life planning and conducting relations with one another. In this way, the online presentation of self becomes a technique of self-regulation. Online self-presentation comprises a virtual renewal of the self. The network site individual profile is presented as a personal source of power yet requires constant monitoring, surveillance and remodelling. Individuals now have to build their own personal brand by emphasising their qualities and learning how to 'sell' them by launching a 'personal visibility campaign' (Peters 1997: 83). This trend demonstrates a shift towards a self-policing, a self-monitoring gaze in the reflexive neo-liberal subject. Thus, an unmediated subject is rendered a fragmented subject. The mediated self in a public network represents a new form of citizenship.

Social network sites are shaping our conduct in desired directions by driving us towards public discourses of 'the personal' through declarations and categorisations of our relationships, likes and dislikes and so on. Alice Marwick (2005b: 12) goes so far as to suggest that they expose 'identity, self-presentation and relational ties, with the result of removing value and signification from the network'. Social media compel us to experience ourselves as autonomous beings with personal command over the technologies. Rose refers to a 'passional ethic' which obliges the person to disclose themselves in terms of a particular vocabulary of emotions and feelings (Rose 1996: 141). While Foucault talked of the hierarchical observations of institutions such as prisons, schools and the asylum as technologies, we can talk of the technologies of social media techniques such as the practice of confession and self-disclosure as ways of drawing the person into a range of schemes of self-scrutiny, self-disclosure, self-analysis and self-nurturing. We are simultaneously facilitated and governed by the organisation of social network sites within a technological field.

Social network sites now form a key dimension of the self-regulation of personal biographies through the use of certain vocabularies and accounts of the self online. As Rose (1996: 143) states, the modern subject has been required to identify and expose his or her subjectivity, so that there is nothing privileged about 'private life'. Within new technologies of the conduct of self, '...the person is presumed to be an active agent, wishing to exercise informed, autonomous and secular responsibility in relation to his or her own destiny' (Rose 1996: 145). While the 'personal' is heralded by conferring agency and control on the individual, it is reconfigured and compromised through a personalised public network culture. Drawing on Rose's ideas, we can say that social network sites authenticate and endorse the idea of the autonomous subject. And this brings us to the problem of the commercial context of social network sites such as Facebook.

The commercial framework of personal relationships

In this book, I have argued against moral panics about the social anxieties associated with a crisis about interpersonal and community relationships and for a more considered and comprehensive study of the contours of a new, mediated set of intimacies. However, I wish to end on a more circumspect note by addressing the implications of a Western and globalised social media structured largely by commercial imperatives. Realising the predominantly personalised nature of communication between individuals on social network sites and the commercial potential of this medium, big business is propelling a fundamental transformation of the Web. It is therefore worth considering the impact of these processes on the nature of mediated intimacies. The question is whether mediated intimacies and related looser ties are being moulded by commercial agendas and if so, does it matter?

The status of Facebook as an online directory for a vast share of the world's population (including their names, images, personal interests, wishes, likes and dislikes) allows this leading social media company to generate profits from the use of members' personal details by customising advertisements and segmenting audiences (Castells 2009). At the time of writing, when its shares were floated on the stock market amid speculation about future profits, Facebook was accumulating $5.11 of revenue per user.[1] Our online activities leave digital tracks which can be followed and analysed in order to be sold to advertisers to support what Fuchs (2009) calls 'deep commodification'. And Facebook boasts that it has 3.2 billion Likes and Comments per day.[2] Although the implications have yet to be clarified in marketing terms, this practice is not a sideshow. Through a new form of social marketing which involves targeted advertising, a commercial agenda has become *embedded* in our online conversations. By clicking on the 'Like' symbol so that particular brand names are ostensibly adopted as 'friends', advertisers are attempting to encourage users to endorse their brands in the context of mediated intimacies and friendships. In this way, brands receive free exposure on users' profiles in the form of a recommendation. Promotional messages figuring an ordinary customer can be sent by marketers to the friends of that customer. They disclose an individual's browsing patterns and buying practices, and include implied product endorsements (McGerevan 2009).

The process of 'Liking' is now being adopted by young people in presenting themselves through status updates. For example, teenagers are posting 'cool' or mad pictures of themselves or personal announcements and inviting others in their network to endorse and 'Like' the message in the way advertisers do. If few Friends respond or if the performance is ignored, the invitation to 'Like' the user is hastily removed. Product endorsement and self-endorsement are colliding with one another and blurring through the use of similar codes. New relations between consumer goods and services and self-presentation are, then, emerging in the context of sites such as Facebook. Through self-presentation and the embedding of product endorsements, these commercial practices evoke a particular model of the user. The repertoires of personhood presupposed by social network sites are interrelated with technologies of marketing and the shaping of consumption. Marwick (2005b) argues that by encouraging people to express their identities through entertainment products such as music, films, books and television programmes, applications on social network sites manage the user primarily as a consumer rather than a citizen.

A significant and enduring myth about social network sites is that these technologies have been created by those who use them. Together with the use of benign terms such as 'Friend' and 'community' and an appealing sense of agency associated with them, this illusion evokes an egalitarian framework. Yet, as Mark Andrejevic (2011) suggests, the concept of 'friendship' is being colonised by the potential of economic investment returns, within the commercial context of social networking. He points out that the prospect of social network sites being governed by a marketing logic has been anticipated by the title of an investment note on social networking put out by Lehman Brothers – 'How Much Are your Friends Worth?' (Foley 2007) – and by the Facebook application 'Friends for Sale' which invites participants to 'Buy people and make them your pets! Make money as a shrewd pet investor or as a hot commodity' (Facebook 2009a, quoted in Andrejevic 2011: 85).

Market researchers are currently exploring ways to tap into and influence the active opinions, ad-clicks and web usage patterns of 'power users' in order to influence the tastes and consumption patterns of mediated friendship networks. Site users with high connection numbers who can act as 'social supernets' by expanding their weak ties (Donath 2007; Donath and boyd 2004) have been identified in market research as 'influentials'. Initially, the 'linear cascade' model or 'word-of-mouth' model (Goldenberg et al. 2001) attempted to predict how users in a network influence network neighbours when adopting a new behaviour through 'viral growth'. More recently, Wilson et al. (2009) identified a core set of 'power users' or well-connected users of Facebook, finding that half of all interactions are made by the 10 per cent most well-connected users. However, the idea that the most efficient and influential 'spreaders' in a social network are inevitably the best connected people has since been disputed (Kitsak et al. 2010). Some marketing theories are moving away from the notion of 'influentials', convinced that small linked groups of friends are now more significant in spreading information and trends (Adams 2011).

As connection patterns among friends and intimates on social networks confirm that individuals move in small circles and trust relatively few people, market research is further focusing on trust among small friendship networks. Findings suggest that individuals tend to source information informally through trusted personal networks. Thus, Paul Adams (2011), Global Brand Experience Manager at Facebook and formerly leader of Google's social research team working on Google+, recommends that marketers target small, connected groups of friends rather than highly influential individuals. Corporate actors are now realising the highly personalised nature of much communication and exploring the commercial possibilities of this trend. Accordingly, researchers like Adams (2011) predict that studies of social network sites and measures of closeness and trust will increase over the next few years, with a shift from a focus on 'public influentials' to influential personal friends (see, for example, Farmer 2009). Commenting on the marketing/commercial possibilities that can be generated from knowledge about social networks, Adams' advice to advertisers and marketers is:

> If we want ideas to spread, if we want people to evangelize our brand and for their messages to spread, we need to focus on everyday people, and understand how their groups of friends are connected. This is where marketers will start to focus their attention in the next year or two. This is our opportunity. Many connected groups of friends.
>
> (Adams 2011)

However, of significance is the recent US research finding that most adults do not want Internet marketers to tailor advertising to their interests, particularly when it entails online data collection and monitoring (Turow et al. 2009). Issues of commercialisation, privacy and trust are, then, likely to be at the forefront of concerns about the kinds of structures influencing the context of mediated intimacies.

With online relationships increasingly being framed by market principles, the question is 'what codes of knowledge support these commercial ideals and to what ethical rationalities are they connected?' Social network site companies face the dilemma of juggling these commercial prospects with the apparently contradictory issues of privacy and trust. These companies must ensure that they do not destroy the sense of reliance and discretion perceived and valued by users or attract regulatory inspection. The practice of supplying large corporations with wide-ranging data for online marketing, business promotion and the study of personal ties is being viewed by many as an anti-democratic trend that leads to a mode of civic privatism (Fenton 2012).

It seems that within the arena of the 'personal', the concept of 'friendship' presented in today's digital epoch entails a clash of values. It becomes a site of tension in the context of social media. Aristotelian attributes of egalitarianism, respect and mutual disclosure appear to be in conflict with commercial and strategic notions of networking for product marketing and promotion of self. Trust and morality in the context of commercial impulses are being highlighted alongside questions about the moral imperatives associated with the re-socialisation of media. Thus, the moral dimensions of mediated intimacies and networked friendships not only involve codes of behaviour about personal responsibilities to avert offence and power abuse within interpersonal communication but also involve social media marketing ethics. In an era when agency and personal autonomy are revered, users of social media are increasingly concerned to ensure they protect their control over the technology to avoid becoming brand carriers. Future moral and ethical debates about the protection of mediated intimacies and wider social ties need to address the nature of commercial power as well as state regulation during crises such as the 2011 riots (Chapter 2). However, since the polymedia environment that supports today's mediated intimacies fosters more flexible, complex and multifaceted modes of communication, friends and wider personal networks may find novel ways to circumvent the negative features of commercial forces. Media multiplicity coupled with a stronger public and collective awareness of social media ethics may generate the technical and social opportunities for individuals to keep a step ahead in sustaining their mediated personal networks.

Notes

1 Introduction

1. Facebook Inc. Amendment No. 4 to Registration statement on Forms S-1 as filed with the Securities and Exchange Commission 23 April 2012, p.1, available at: http://www.sec.gov/Archives/edgar/data/1326801/0001193125 12175673/d287954ds1a.htm (accessed 29 May 2012).
2. See Facebook Inc. Amendment No. 4 to Registration statement on Forms S-1 as filed with the Securities and Exchange Commission 23 April 2012, ibid.
3. *Sunday Times* (2007) 'Generation Shock Finds Liberty Online', 25 February, available at: http://www.timesonline.co.uk/tol/news/uk/article1433751.ece (accessed 30 January 2008).
4. Keith Watson (2011) 'Mark Zuckerberg: Inside Facebook was a Fascinating Peak into His World', *Metro*, 5 December 2011, available at: http://www.metro.co.uk/tv/reviews/883673-mark-zuckerberg-inside-facebook-was-a-fascinating-peek-into-his-world, (accessed 23 July 2012).
5. Quoted in Facebook Inc. Amendment No. 4 to Registration statement on Forms S-1 as filed with the Securities and Exchange Commission 23 April 2012, p. 1.
6. However, Broadbent (2011) is referring more specifically to the way that social media devices tend to be used regularly in the context of paid work for making personal calls.
7. Also see, for example, the special issue of the *Journal of Computer-Mediated Communication*, 2007 edited by boyd and Ellison (2007) devoted to the analysis of various dimensions of social network sites.
8. 'Most Facebook friends are false friends', by David Derbyshire, *Mail Online*, 14 September 2007.

2 Technologically Mediated Personal Relationships

1. Broadbent, S. (2007), quoted in 'Home Truths about telecoms, Technology and society: Anthropologists investigate the use of communications technology and reach some surprising conclusions', Technology Quarter Q2, *The Economist*, available at: http://www.economist.com/node/9249302 (accessed 22 February 2012).
2. Ibid.
3. Ibid.
4. See, for example, *International Journal of Communication* (IJoC) which has published a special feature section, 'The Arab Spring and the Role of ICTs', Volume 5, 2011.
5. Last.fm is an Internet radio site used for streaming music, with 40 million active users across 200 countries.

4　Self-Presentation Online

1. 'Facebook remark teenager is fired', *BBC News* online, 2009, available at: http://news.bbc.co.uk/1/hi/england/essex/7914415.stm (accessed 17 December 2011).
2. Ibid.
3. Hayden Smith (2011) 'Apple fires employee over iPhone Facebook rants', *Metro*, 30 November 2011, available at: http://www.metro.co.uk/tech/883333-apple-sacks-worker-for-ranting-about-iphone-on-facebook (accessed 19 March 2012).
4. Ibid.
5. Quoted in Clive Thompson (2008) 'Brave New World of Digital Intimacy', *New York Times* magazine, 5 September 2008, available at: http://www.nytimes.com/2008/09/07/magazine/07awareness-t.html?pagewanted=all (accessed 22 March 2012).

5　Social Media and Teenage Friendships

1. See, for example, Andy Dolan (2011) 'Coroner Slams 'vile' school bullies who taunted suicide girl, 15, in death', *Mail Online*, 22 July 2011 available at: http://www.dailymail.co.uk/news/article-2017330/Natasha-MacBryde-Coroner-slams-bullies-taunt-suicide-girl-15-death.html (accessed 5 February 2012); and Andrew Parker (2011) 'Suicide Girls' Dad Slams Web Sickos', *The Sun*, 23 February 2011, available at: http://www.thesun.co.uk/sol/homepage/news/3427677/Suicide-girl-Natasha-MacBrydes-dad-slams-web-sickos.html (accessed 5 February 2012).
2. See, for example, definitions for relatively new terms being used for actions on social network sites at sites such as *Urban dictionary*, available at: http://www.urbandictionary.com/define.php?term=troll (accessed 5 February 2012).
3. Quoted in article in *The Sun* by Andrew Parker (2011) op.cit.
4. See, for example, Rachel Quigley (2011) 'What do I have to do for people to listen? Boy, 14 kills himself after gay taunts and thanks Lady Gaga in his final post', *Daily Mail*, 21 September 2011, available at: http://www.dailymail.co.uk/news/article-2039801/Bullied-gay-teen-Jamey-Rodemeyer-commits-suicide-Thanks-Lady-Gaga-post.html (accessed 11 July 2012).
5. Richard Hartley-Parkinson (2011) 'More than half of young Americans have been subjected to taunting or bullying on social network sites', *Mail Online*, 27 September 2011, available at: http://www.dailymail.co.uk/news/article-2042373/More-half-youths-subjected-taunting-bullying-social-network-sites.html
6. 'A Thin Line' (2009) AP-MTV Digital Abuse Study, available at: http://www.athinline.org/MTV-AP_Digital_Abuse_Study_Executive_Summary.pdf (accessed 5 February 2012).
7. Stacy A. Anderson (2011) 'Poll: Young people say "digital abuse" pervasive', *USA Today*, available at http://usatoday30.usatoday.com/news/health/wellness/teen-ya/story/2011-09-27/Poll-Young-people-say-digital-abuse-pervasive/50566460/1 (accessed 28 December 2012).

8. Stop Cyberbullying Before it Starts, National Crime Prevent Council, available at: http://www.ncpc.org/resources/files/pdf/bullying/cyberbullying.pdf, (accessed 27 May 2010).

6   Home, Families and New Media

1. Stefana Broadbent quoted from BBC World Service, the Forum, 8 January 2012.
2. Ibid. Knowing that a record one billion people worldwide are now on the move, the poet Ruth Padel has suggested that 'in many ways, "home" is not a stable concept; instead it is something people are always searching for', also quoted from BBC World Service, the Forum, 8 January 2012.

7   Digital Dating and Romance

1. Interviewed by Megan Finn, PhD student at UC Berkeley School of Information, as part of the Fresh Quest Project. Details of the Fresh Quest project are available at: http://groups.sims.berkeley.edu/ikids/freshquest/ (accessed 16 July 2012). The project forms part of a series of studies conducted within *Digital Youth Research* at the University of Southern California and University of California, Berkeley, and funded by the MacArthur Foundation. These studies have formed part of the publication by Ito et al. (2010). Details of the research are available at: http://digitalyouth.ischool.berkeley.edu/ (accessed 16 July 2012).
2. Christo Sims' research within The Rural and Urban Youth Project also forms part of a series of studies conducted within *Digital Youth Research* at the University of Southern California and University of California, Berkeley, and funded by the MacArthur Foundation. See footnote above for details.
3. 'Facebook Rage as social networking sites fuel jealousy and stalking partners online' by Caroline Grant, *Daily Mail*, 9 July 2009, available at: http://www.dailymail.co.uk/sciencetech/article-1205018/Facebook-Rage-social-networking-sites-fuel-jealousy-stalking-partners-online.html
4. AP-MTV Digital Abuse Study (2009) 'A Thin Line', available at: http://www.athinline.org/MTV-AP_Digital_Abuse_Study_Executive_Summary.pdf (accessed 5 February 2012).

9   Mediated Intimacies

1. Facebook Inc. Amendment No. 4 to Registration statement on Forms S-1 as filed with the Securities and Exchange Commission 23 April 2012, op.cit.
2. See Facebook Inc. Amendment No. 4 to Registration statement on Forms S-1 as filed with the Securities and Exchange Commission, ibid.

Bibliography

Aarsand, P.A. and Aronsson, K. (2009) 'Gaming and Territorial Negotiations in Family Life', *Childhood* 16: 497–517.

Adams, P. (2011) *Grouped: How Small Groups of Friends Are the Key to Influence on the Social Web*. Berkeley, CA: New Riders Press.

Adams, P.C. and Ghose, R. (2003) 'India:com: The Construction of a Space Between', *Progress in Human Geography* 27(4): 414–437.

Adams, R. and Allan, G. (1998) *Placing Friendship in Context*. Cambridge: Cambridge University Press.

Allan, G. (1979) *A Sociology of Friendship and Kinship*. London: Allen and Unwin.

Allan, G. (1998) 'Friendship, Sociology and Social Structure', *Journal of Social and Personal Relationships* 15(5): 685–702.

Allan, G. (2008) 'Flexibility, Friendship and Family', *Personal Relationships* 15(1): 1–16.

Allan, G. and Crow, G. (1989) *Home and Family: Creating the Domestic Sphere*. Basingstoke: Palgrave Macmillan.

Allan, G. and Crow, G. (1991) 'Privatization, Home-Centredness and Leisure', *Leisure Studies* 10(1): 19–33.

Alters, D.F. (2004) 'The Family in U.S. History and Culture', in Hoover S.M., Clark L.S., and Alters, D. (eds.), *Media, Home, and Family*. New York: Routledge, pp. 51–68.

Alters, D.F. and Clark, L.S. (2004) 'Introduction', in Hoover, S.M., Clark, L.S., and Alters, D. (eds.), *Media, Home and Family*. New York: Routledge, pp. 3–18.

Altman, D. (1982) *The Homosexualization of America, the Americanization of the Homosexual*. New York: St. Martin's Press.

Altman, I. and Taylor, D.A. (1973) *Social Penetration: The Development of Interpersonal Relationships*. New York: Holt, Rinehart and Winston.

Andersen, W. (1997) *The Future of the Self: Inventing the Postmodern Person*. New York: Penguin Putnam.

Anderson, B. (1991) *Imagined Communities, Reflections on the Origins and Spread of Nationalism*. London: Verso.

Anderson, B. (2000) *Doing the Dirty Work: The Global Politics of Domestic Labour*. New York: Zed Books.

Anderson, B. (2006) *Imagined communities: Reflections on the Origin and Spread of Nationalism* (new ed.). New York: Verso.

Andrejevic, M. (2011) 'Social Network Exploitation', in Papacharissi, Z. (ed.), *A Networked Self: Identity, Community and Culture on Social Network Sites*. London: Routledge, pp. 82–102.

AP-MTV Digital Abuse Study (2009) *A Thin Line*. Available at: http://www.athinline.org/MTV-AP_Digital_Abuse_Study_Executive_Summary.pdf (accessed 5 February 2012).

Aristotle (1955) *The Ethics of Aristotle: The Nichomachean Ethics*, trans. Thomson, J.A.K. Harmonsdsowrth: Penguin, Book 9, pp. 1169 a23–b11.

Baron, N. (2008) *Always On: Language in an Online and Mobile World*. Oxford: Oxford University Press.

Bauman, Z. (2000) *Liquid Modernity*. Cambridge: Polity Press.

Bauman, Z. (2001) *The Individualized Society*. Cambridge: Polity Press.

Bauman, Z. (2003) *Liquid Love: On the Frailty of Human Bonds*. Polity Press, Cambridge.

Bauman, Z. (2007) *Consuming Life*. Cambridge: Polity Press.

Bacigalupe, G. and Lambe, S. (2011) 'Virtualizing Intimacy: Information Communication Technologies and Transnational Families', *Therapy, Family Process* 50(1). Available at: http://www.familyprocess.org/Data/featured_articles/107_bacilambe.pdf (accessed 16 June 2012).

Bakan, A. and Stasiulis, D. (1997) *Not One of the Family: Foreign Domestic Workers in Canada*. Toronto: University of Toronto Press.

Bakardjieva, M. (2005) *Internet Society: The Internet in Everyday Life*. London: Sage.

Baker, S.A. (2011) 'The Mediated Crowd: New Social Media and New Forms of Rioting', *Sociological Research Online* 16(4): 21. Available at: http://www.socresonline.org.uk/16/4/21.html (accessed 15 August 2012).

Baldassar, L., Wilding, R., and Baldock, C. (2007) 'Long-Distance Caregiving: Transnational Families and the Provision of Care', in Paoletti, I. (ed.), *Transnational Families and the Provision of Aged Care*. New York: Nova Science, pp. 201–227.

Barendregt, B. (2008) 'Sex, Cannibals, and the Language of Cool: Indonesian tales of the phone and modernity', *The Information Society* 24(3): 160–170.

Baron, N.S. (2008) *Always On: Language in an Online and Mobile World*. Oxford: Oxford University Press.

Bawin-Legros, B. (2004) 'Intimacy and the New Sentimental Order', *Current Sociology* 52(2): 241–250.

Baym, N. (2010) *Personal Connections in the Digital Age*. Cambridge: Polity Press.

Baym, N.K. and Ledbetter, A. (2009) 'Tunes That Bind? Predicting Friendship Strength in a Music-Based Social Network', *Information, Community and Society* 12(3): 408–427.

Baym, N., Zhang, Y.B., Kunkel, A., Lin, M., and Ledbetter, A. (2007) 'Relational Quality and Media Use', *New Media and Society* 9(5): 735–752.

Baym, N., Zhang, Y.B., and Lin, M.C. (2004) 'Social Interaction Across Media: Interpersonal Communication on the Internet, Face-to-Face, and Telephone', *New Media & Society* 6: 41–60.

Beck-Gernsheim, E. (1999) 'On the Way to a Post-Familial Family,' in Featherstone, M. (ed.), *Love and Eroticism*. London: Routledge, pp. 53–70.

Beck, U. and Beck-Gernsheim, E. (1995) *The Normal Chaos of Love*. Oxford: Polity Press.

Beck, U. and Beck-Gernsheim, E. (2002) *Individualization: Institutionalized Individualism and its Social and Political Consequences*. London: Sage.

Benco, D. (2011) 'Weak Links, Alcatel-lucent Techzine blog archive', 3 January 2011. Available at: http://www2.alcatel-lucent.com/blogs/techzine/2011/weak-links/ (accessed 20 July 2011).

Bengston, V.L. (2001) 'Beyond the Nuclear Family: The Increasing Importance of Multi-Generational Bonds', *Journal of Marriage and the Family* 63: 1–16.

Benítez, J.L. (2006) 'Transnational Dimensions of the Digital Divide among Salvadoran Immigrants in the Washington DC Metropolitan Area', *Global Networks* 6(2): 181–199.

Berger, C.R. and Calabrese, R.J. (1975) 'Some Exploration in Initial Interaction and Beyond: Toward a Developmental Theory of Communication', *Human Communication Research* 1: 99–112.

Berker, T., Hartmann, M., Punie, Y., and Ward, K.J. (eds.) (2006) *The Domestication of Media Technology*. Maidenhead: Open University.

Berlant, L. and Warner, M. (2000) 'Sex in Public', in Berlant, L. (ed.), *Intimacy*. Chicago: University of Chicago Press, pp. 311–330.

Best, S.J. and Krueger, B.S. (2006) 'Online Interactions and Social Capital Distinguishing Between New and Existing Ties', *Social Science Computer Review* 24(4): 395–410.

Bettie, J. (2003) *Women without Class: Girls, Race, and Identity*. Berkeley, CA and Los Angeles, CA: University of California Press.

Binder, J., Howes, A., and Sutcliffe, A. (2009) 'The problem of conflicting social spheres: Effects of network structure on experienced tension in social network sites'. *Paper presented at Computer Human Interaction 2009*, Boston, MA.

Blau, M. and Fingerman, K.L. (2009) *Consequential Strangers: The Power of People Who Don't Seem to Matter ... But Really Do*. New York: W. W. Norton & Company. Available at: http://www.consequentialstrangers.com/about/

Boase, J., Horrigan, J.B., Wellman, B., and Rainie, L. (2006) 'The strength of Internet ties. Pew Internet and American Life Project'. Available at: http://www.pewinternet.org/pdfs/PIP_Internet_ties.pdf (accessed 20 May 2006).

Bogle, K. (2008) *Hooking up: Sex, Dating and relationships on Campus*. New York: New York University Press.

Bohnert, D. and Ross, W.H. (2010) 'The Influence of Social Networking Web Sites on the Evaluation of Job Candidates', *Cyberpsychology, Behavior, and Social Networking* 13(3): 341–347.

Bolter, J. and Grusin, R. (1999) *Remediation: Understanding New Media*. Cambridge: The MIT Press.

Boneva, B.S., Quinn, A., Kraut, R.E., Kiesler, S., and Shklovski, I. (2006) 'Teenage communication in the instant messaging era', in Kraut, R., Brynin, M., and Kiesler, S. (eds.), *Computers, Phones, and the Internet: Domesticating Information Technology*. New York: Oxford University Press, pp. 201–218.

Bomb, C. (2010) *Dating and Sex on the Internet: Exclusive Advice for Guys from a Woman* [Kindle Edition]. Amazon Media EU S.à r.l.

Bourdieu, P. (1985) 'The Forms of Capital', in Richardson, J.G. (ed.), *Handbook of Theory and Research For The Sociology Of Education*. New York: Greenwood, pp. 241–258.

Bourdieu, P. (1986) *Distinction: A Social Critique of the Judgement of Taste*. London: Routledge.

Bovill, M. and Livingstone, S. (2001) *Children and their Changing Media Environment: A European Comparative Study*. Mahwah, NJ: L. Erlbaum Associates.

boyd, d. (2006) 'Friends, Friendsters, and Top 8: Writing Community into Being on Social Network Sites', *First Monday*, Volume 11, Number 12–14 December 2006. Available at: http://firstmonday.org/htbin/cgiwrap/bin/ojs/index.php/fm/article/viewArticle/1418/1336 (accessed 17 July 2012).

boyd, d. (2007) 'Why Youth (Heart) 'Social Network Sites: The Role of Networked Publics in Teenage Social Life', in Buckingham, D. (ed.), *Youth, Identity, and Digital Media*, John, D. and Catherine, T. MacArthur Foundation Series on Digital media and Learning. Cambridge, MA: The MIT Press, pp. 119–142.

boyd, d. (2008) 'Taken Out of Context: American Teen Sociality in Networked Publics', Ph.D. dissertation, University of California, Berkeley, CA. Available at: http://www.danah.org/papers/TakenOutOfContext.pdf (accessed 27 September 2011).

boyd, d. (2010a) 'Friendship', in Ito, M., Baumer, S., Bittanti, M., boyd, d., Cody, R., Herr-Stephenson, B., Horst, H.A., Lange, P.G., Mahendran, D., Martinez, K.Z., Pascoe, C.J., Perkel, D., Robinson, L., Sims, C., and Tripp, L. (eds.), *Hanging Out, Messing Around, and Geeking Out: Kids Living and Learning with New Media*. Cambridge, MA: MIT Press, pp. 79–116.

boyd, d. (2010b) 'Box 3.1 The public nature of mediated breakups' in Ito, M., Baumer, S., Bittanti, M., Boyd, D., Cody, R., Herr-Stevenson, B., Horst, H.A., Lange, P.G., Martinez, K.Z., Pasko, C.J., Perkel, D., Robinson, L.S., Sims, C., and Tripp, L. (eds.), *Hanging Out, Messing Around, Geeking Out: Kids Living and Learning with New Media*. Cambridge, MA: The MIT Press, pp. 133–134.

boyd, d. (2011) 'Social Network Sites as Networked Publics: Affordances, Dynamics, and Implications', in Papacharissi, Z. (ed.), *A Networked Self: Identity, Community, and Culture on Social Network Sites*. New York: Routledge, pp. 39–58.

boyd, d. and Ellison, N. (2007) 'Social Network Sites: Definition, History and Scholarship', *Journal of Computer-Mediated Communication* 13(1): 210–230. Available at: http://onlinelibrary.wiley.com/doi/10.1111/j.1083-6101.2007.00393.x/full (accessed 4 April 2012).

boyd, d., Hargittai, E., Schultz, J., and Palfrey, J. (2011) 'Why Parents Help Their Children Lie to Facebook About Age: Unintended Consequences of the Children's Online Privacy Protection Act', *First Monday*, Volume 16, Number 11–7 November 2011. Available at: http://www.uic.edu/htbin/cgiwrap/bin/ojs/index.php/fm/rt/printerFriendly/3850/3075#tab7 (accessed 20 August 2012).

boyd, d. and Heer, J. (2006) 'Profiles as Conversation: Networked Identity Performance on Friendster', *Proceedings of the Hawaii International Conference on System Sciences (HICSS-39)*, Persistent Conversation Track. Kauai, HI: IEEE Computer Society. January 4–7, 2006.

Briggs, D. (ed.) (2012) *The English Riots of 2011: A Summer of Discontent*. Hampshire: Waterside Press.

Broadbent, S. (2009) 'Interview "How the Internet Enables Intimacy"'. Available at: http://www.ted.com/talks/stefana_broadbent_how_the_Internet_enables_intimacy.html (2 November 2009).

Broadbent, S. (2011) *L'intimite' au Travail*. Paris: Fyp editions.

Brown, B.B. (1999) ' "You're Going out with Who?" Peer Group Influences on Adolescent Romantic Relationships', in Furman, W., Brown, B.B., and Feiring, C. (eds.), *The Development of Romantic Relationships in Adolescence*. Cambridge: Cambridge University Press, pp. 291–329.

Buckingham, D. (2000) *After the Death of Childhood: Growing Up in the Age of Electronic Media*. Cambridge: Polity Press.

Buckingham, D. (ed.) (2006) *Youth, Identity and Digital Media. John D. and Catherine T. MacArthur Foundation Series on Digital Media and Learning*. Cambridge, MA: The MIT Press.

Buckingham, D. (2007) *Beyond Technology: Children's Learning in the Age of Digital Media*. Cambridge: Polity Press.

Budgeon, S. and Roseneil, S. (2004) 'Editors' Introduction: Beyond the Conventional Family', *Current Sociology* 52: 127.

Buffardi, L.E. and Campbell, K.W. (2008) 'Narcissism and Social Networking Web Sites', *Personality and Social Psychology Bulletin* 34(10): 1303–1314.

Burr, J. (2009) 'Exploring Reflective Subjectivity through the Construction of the "Ethical Other" in Interview Transcripts', *Sociology* 43(2): 323–339.

Burt, R.S. (2009) *Neighbor Networks: Competitive Advantage Local and Personal*. Oxford: Oxford University Press.

Calhoun, C.J. (1980) 'Community: Towards a Variable Conceptualisation for Comparative Research', *Social History* 5: 105–129.

Calhourne, C. (1991) Imagined Communities and Indirect Relationships: Large Scale integration and the Transformation of Everyday Life', in Bourdieu, P. and Coleman, J.S. (eds.), *Social Theory for a Changing Society*. Boulder, CO: Westview Press and New York: Russell Sage Foundation, pp. 95–120.

Carpenter, C.J. (2012) 'Narcissism on Facebook: Self-Promotional and Anti-Social Behavior', *Personality and Individual Differences* 52(4): 482–486.

Carr, Austin (2011) 'Facebook Booting "20,000" Underage Users Per Day: Reaction to Growing Privacy Concerns?' *Fast Company* (22 March). Available at: http://www.fastcompany.com/1741875/facebook-booting-20000-underage-users-per-day-reaction-to-growing-privacy-concerns (accessed 5 February 2012).

Cash, T. et al. (2004) 'Body Image in an Interpersonal Context: Adult Attachment, Fear of Intimacy, and Social Anxiety', *Journal of Social & Clinical Psychology* 23(1): 89–103.

Cassell, J. and Cramer, M. (2007) 'High Tech or High Risk? Moral Panics about Girls Online', in MacPherson T. The John D., and Catherine T. MacArthur *Digital Youth, Innovation, and the Unexpected*, Foundation Series on Digital Media and Learning. Cambridge, MA: The MIT Press, pp. 53–75.

Castells, M. (1996) *The Rise of the Network Society*. Oxford: Blackwell.

Castells, M. (1997) *The Power of Identity*. Oxford: Blackwell.

Castells, M. (2009) *Communication Power*. Oxford: Oxford University Press.

Castells, M., Ferandez-Ardevol, M., Qiu, J.L., and Sey, A. (2006) *Mobile Communication and Society: A Global Perspective*. Cambridge, MA: MIT Press.

Chambers, D. (2006) *New Social Ties: Contemporary Connections in a Fragmented Society*. Basingstoke: Palgrave Macmillan.

Chambers, D. (2011b) ' "Wii Play as Family": The Rise in Family-Centred Video Gaming', *Leisure Studies* 31(1): 69–82.

Chambers, D. (2011a) 'The Material form of the Television Set', *Media History* 17(4): 359–376.

Chan, D.K.S. and Cheng, G.H.L. (2004) 'A Comparison of Offline and Online Friendship Qualities at Different Stages of Relationship Development', *Journal of Social and Personal Relationships* 21(3): 305–320.

Chen, Y., Chien, S., Wu, J., and Tsai, P. (2011) 'Impact of Signals and Experience on Trust and Trusting Behaviur', *CyberPsychology, Behavior and Social Network Sites* 13(950): 539–546.

Chen, W. and Wellman, B. (2005) 'Minding the Cyber-Gap: The Internet and Social Inequality', in Romeo, M. and Margolis, E. (eds.), *The Blackwell Companion to Social Inequalities*. London: Blackwell, pp. 523–545.

Chen, Y.F. and Katz, J.E. (2009) Extending family to school life: college students' use of the mobile phone. *International Journal of Human Computer Studies* 67(2): 179–191.

Chiswick, B.R., Lee, Y.L., and Miller, P.W. (2005) 'A Longitudinal Analysis of Immigrant Occupational Mobility: A Test of the Immigrant Assimilation Hypothesis', *International Migration Review* 39(2): 332–353.

Choi, J.H. (2006) 'Living in *Cyworld*: Contextualising Cy-Ties in South Korea', in Bruns, A. and Jacobs, J. (eds.), *Use of Blogs (Digital Formations)*. New York: Peter Lang, pp. 173–186.

Chouliaraki, L. (2006) *The Spectatorship of Suffering*. London: Sage.

Chua, C.E.H. (2009) 'Why Do Virtual Communities Regulate Speech'?, *Communication Monographs* 76(2): 234–261.

Chun, H., Kwak, H., Eom, Y.H., Ahn, Y.-Y., Moon, S., and Jeong, H. (2008) Comparison of online social relations in volume vs interaction: a case study of Cyworld. In *Proc. of Internet Measurement Conference*, Vouliagmeni, Greece, 2008.

Clark, L.S. (2004) 'Being Distinctive in a Mediated Environment: The Ahmeds and the Paytons', in Hoover, S.M., Clark, L.S., and Alters, D. (eds.), *Media, Home and Family*. New York: Routledge, pp. 79–102.

Cook, D.T. (2008) 'The Missing Child in Consumption Theory', *Journal of Consumer Culture* 8: 219–243.

Coleman, J.S. (1988) 'Social Capital in the Creation of Human Capital', *American Journal of Sociology* 94(Supplement): S95–S120.

Consumer Reports (2011) 'CR Survey: 7.5 million Facebook Users are Under the Age of 13, Violating the Site's Terms', *Press release* (10 May). Available at: http://pressroom.consumerreports.org/pressroom/2011/05/cr-survey-75-million-facebook-users-are-under-the-age-of-13-violating-the-sites-terms-.html (accessed 5 February 2012).

Constable, N. (2007) *Maid to Order in Hong Kong. Stories of Migrant Workers*, 2nd edn. Ithaca, NY: Cornell University Press.

Côté, J. (2000) *Arrested Adulthood: The Changing Nature of Maturity and Identity*. New York: New York University Press.

Couldry, N. (2008) 'Mediatization or Mediation: Alternative Understandings of the Emergent Space of Digital Storytelling', *New Media and Society* 10(3): 373–391.

Crawford, M. and Popp, D. (2003) Sexual Double Standards: A Review and Methodological Critique of Two Decades of Research. *Journal of Sex Research* 40: 13–26.

Critcher, C. (2008) 'Making Waves: Historical Aspects of Public Debates about Children and Mass Media', in Drotner, K. and Livingstone, S. (eds.), *The International Handbook of Children, Media and Culture*. London: Sage, pp. 91–104.

Crow, G. (2002) *Social Solidarities: Theories, Identities and Social Change*. Buckingham: Open University Press.

Crow, G., Allan, G., and Summers, M. (2002) 'Neither Busybodies nor Nobodies: Managing Proximity and Distance in Neighbourly Relations', *Sociology* 36(1): 127–145.

Cummings, H.M. and Vandewater, E.A. (2007) Relation of Adolescent Video Game Play to Time Spent in Other Activities. *Archives of Pediatrics Adolescent Medicine* 161: 684–689.

Daft, R.L. and Lengel, R.H. (1984) 'Information Richness: A New Approach to Managerial Behaviour and Organizational Design', *Research in Organizational Behaviour* 6: 191–233.

David, M., Hart, G., Bolding, G., Sherr, L., and Elford, J. (2006) 'Sex and the Internet: Gay Men, Risk Reduction and Serostatus', *Culture, health and Sexuality* 8(2): 161–174.

Deegan, M.J. and Kotarba, J.A. (1980) 'On Responsibility in Ethnography', *Qualitiative Sociology* 3(4): 323–331.

DeMasi, S. (2006) 'Shopping for Love: Online Dating and the Making of a Cyberculture of Romance', in Seidman S, Fischer, N., and Meeks, C. (eds.), *Handbook of the New Sexuality Studies, Routledge International Handbooks.* London: Routledge, pp. 223–232.

Dimmick, J., Kline S.L., and Stafford, L. (2000) 'The Gratification Niches of Personal E-Mail and the Telephone: Competititon, Displacement, and Complementarity', *Communication Research* 27(2): 227–248.

Dolan, A. (2011) 'Coroner Slams 'Vile' School Bullies Who Taunted Suicide Girl, 15, in Death', *Mail Online*, 22 July 2011. Available at: http://www.dailymail. co.uk/news/article-2017330/Natasha-MacBryde-Coroner-slams-bullies-taunt-suicide-girl-15-death.html (accessed 5 February 2012).

Donath, J. (1999) 'Identity and Deception in a Virtual Community', in Smith, M. and Kollock, P. (eds.), *Communities in Cyberspace.* London: Routledge, pp. 29–59.

Donath, J. (2007) 'Signals in Social Supernets', *Journal of Computer-Mediated Communication* 13(1: article 12). Available at: http://jcmc.indiana.edu/ vol13/issue1/donath.html?utm_source= twitterfeed&utm_medium= twitter (accessed 17 August 2012).

Donath, Judith and boyd, d. (2004) 'Public Displays of Connection', *BT Technology Journal* 22(4): 71–82.

du Bois-Reymond, M. (1998) ' "I Don't Want To Commit Myself Yet": Young People's Life Concepts', *Journal of Youth Studies* 1(1): 63–79.

Du Gay, P. (1996) 'Organising identity', in Hall, S. and Du Gay, P. (eds.), *Questions of Cultural Identity.* London: Sage, pp. 151–169.

Dunbar, R. (1996) *Grooming, Gossip, and the Evolution of Language.* Cambridge, MA: Harvard University Press.

Dunbar, R. (2010) *How Many Friends does One Person Need? Dunbar's Number and Other Evolutionary Quirks.* London: Faber and Faber.

Duncombe, J. and Marsden, D. (1993) 'Love and Intimacy: The Gender Division of Emotion and "Emotion Work", a Neglected Aspect of Sociological Discussion of Heterosexual Relationships', *Sociology* 27(2): 221–241.

Dunn, A. (2011) 'The Arab Spring: Revolution and Shifting Geopolitics: Unplugging a Nation: State Media Strategy During Egypt's January 25 Uprising', *The Fletcher Forum of World Affairs Journal* 35(15): 15–24.

Dwyer, C., Hiltz, S.R., and Passerini, K. (2007) 'Trust and Privacy Concern within Social Networking Sites: A comparison of Facebook and MySpace', *Proceedings of AMCIS 2007*, Keystone, CO. Available at: http:// lbsstorage.googlecode.com/svn/trunk/Drafts/Vu/Trust%20and%20privacy %20concern%20within%20social%20networking%20sites%20-%20A%20com parison%20of%20Facebook%20and%20MySpace.pdf (accessed 18 November 2012).

Economist (2011) 'Technology and Disorder: The Blackberry Riots'. 13ᵗʰ August 2011 August. Available at: http://www.economist.com/node/21525976 (accessed 15 August 2012).

Eckert, P. (1989) *Jocks and Burnouts: Social Categories and Identity in the High School.* New York: Teachers College.

Ellison, N., Heino, R., and Gibbs, J. (2006) 'Managing Impressions Online: Self-Presentation Process in the Online Dating Environment', *Journal of Computer-Mediated Communication* 11(2): Article 2. Available at: http://jcmc.indiana.edu/vol11/issue2/ellison.html (accessed 20 August 2012).

Ellison, N., Steinfeld, C., and Lampe, C. (2007) 'The benefits of Facebook "Friends": Exploring the relationship between College Students' Use of Online Social Networks and Social Capital', *Journal of Computer-Mediated Communication* 12(3): 1143–1168.

Ellison, N.B., Steinfield, C., and Lampe, C. (2011a) 'Connection Strategies: Social Capital Implications of Facebook-Enabled Communication Practices', *New Media and Society* 13(6): 873–892.

Ellison, N., Lampe, C., Steinfeld, C., and Vitak, J. (2011b) 'With a Little Help From My Friends: How Social Network Sites Affect Social Capital Processes', in Papacharissi, Z. (ed.), *A Networked Self: Identity, Community, and Culture on Social Network Sites.* New York: Routledge, pp. 124–145.

Eve, M. (2002) 'Is Friendship a Sociological Topic?' *European Journal of Sociology* 43(3): 386–409.

Facebook (2009) 'Friends for Sale: Info'. Available at: www.facebook.com/friendsforsale?v=info&viewas=0 (accessed 29 July 2012).

Facebook (2011a) 'Terms of service', Last updated 26 April. Available at: http://www.facebook.com/terms.php (accessed 27 September 2011).

Facebook (2011b) 'Report an Underage Child'. Available at: https://www.face book.com/help/contact.php?show_form=underage (accessed 27 September 2011).

Falicov, C.J. (2007) 'Working with Transnational Immigrants: Expanding Meanings of Family, Community, and Culture', *Family Process* 46(2): 157–171.

Farmer, J. (2009) '20bits: Notification Strategies for Social Networks'. Available at: http://20bits.com/articles/notification-strategies-for-social-networks/ (accessed 12 November 2011).

Featherstone, M., Hepworth, M., and Turner, B.S. (1991) *The Body: Social Processes and Cultural Theory.* London: Sage.

Flanagin, A.J. and Metzger, M.J. (2001) 'Internet Use in the Contemporary Media Environment', *Human Communication Research* 27: 153–181.

Fayard, A.L. and Weeks, J. (2007) 'Photocopiers and Water-Coolers: The Affordances of Information Interaction', *Organization Studies* 28: 605–634.

Fenton, N. (2012) 'The Internet and Social Networking', in Curran, J., Fenton, N., and Freedman, D. (eds.), *Misunderstanding the Internet.* London: Routledge, pp. 123–148.

Ferguson, N. (2012) 'The Rule of Law and Its Enemies: Civil and Uncivil Societies', *BBC Reith Lectures 2012*, BBC Radio 4, first broadcast 10 July 2012. Available at: http://www.bbc.co.uk/programmes/b01jms03 (accessed 17 July 2012).

Fernback, J. (2007) 'Beyond the Diluted Community Concept: A Symbolic Interactionist Perspective on Online Social Relations', *New Media & Society* 9(1): 49–69.

Fingerman, K.L. (2009) 'Consequential Strangers and Peripheral Partners: The Importance of Unimportant Relationships', *Journal of Family Theory and Review* 1: 69–82.

Fingerman, K.L., Hay, E.L., and Birditt, K.S. (2004) 'The Best of Ties, the Worst of Ties: Close, Problematic, and Ambivalent Relationships Across the Lifespan', *Journal of Marriage and Family* 66: 792–808.

Flanagin, A.J. and Metzger, M.J. (2001) 'Internet Use in the Contemporary Media Environment', *Human Communication Research* 27: 153–181.

Fogel, J. and Nehmad, E (2008) 'Internet Social Network Communities: Risk Taking, Trust, and Privacy Concerns', *Computers in Human Behaviour* 25: 153–160.

Foley, S. (2007) 'The Battle for Facebook', *The Independent*, 26 September 2007. Available at: http://www.independent.co.uk/news/business/analysis-and-features/the-battle-for-facebook-403557.html (accessed 19 August 2012).

Fortier A M. (2000) *Migrant Belongings: Memory, Space, Identity.* Oxford: Berg.

Foucault, B., Zhu, M., Huang, Y., Atrash Z., and Contractor, N. (2009) 'Will You be My Friends? An Exploration of Adolescent Friendship Formation online in Teen Second Life', *International Communication Association*, Chicago, IL. Available at: http://129.105.161.80/uploads/ICATSLPaper_2009_Final.pdf (accessed 15 April 2012).

Foucault, M. (1977) *Discipline and Punish.* London: Allen Lane.

Foucault, M. (1991) 'Governmentality', in Burchell, G., Gordon, C., and Miller, P. (eds.), *The Foucault Effect: Studies in Governmentality.* Hemel Hempstead: Harvester Wheatsheaf, pp. 87–104.

Fox, S. (2011) 'The Social Life of Health Information, 2011', *Pew Research Centre Internet and American Life Project.* Pew Research Centre, California Health Foundation. Available at: http://pewinternet.org/~/media//Files/Reports/2011/PIP_Social_Life_of_Health_Info.pdf

France, A. (2007) *Understanding Youth in Late Modernity.* Maidenhead: Open University Press.

Frohlick and Migliardi (2011) 'Heterosexual Profiling: Online Dating and "Becoming" Heterosexualities for Women Aged 30 and Older in the Digital Era', *Australian Feminist Studies*, 26(67): 73–88.

Fuchs, C. (2009) 'Some Reflections on Manuel Castell's Book "Communication Power" ', *tripleC* 7(1): 94–108.

Fulk, J. and Collin-Jarvis, L. (2001) Wired Meetings: Technological Mediation of Organisational Gatherings', in Jablin, F.M. and Putnam, L.L. (eds.), *The New Handbook of Organisational Communication: Advances in Theory, Research and Methods.* Thousand Oaks, CA: Sage, pp. 624–663

Gabb, J. (2008) *Researching Intimacy in Families.* Basingstoke: Palgrave Macmillan.

Garfinkel, S. (2001) *Database Nation: The Death of Privacy in the 21st Century.* Sebastopol, CA: O'Reilly Media.

Gerner, B. et al. (2005) 'The Relationship Between Friendship Factors and Adolescent Girls' Body Image Concern, Body Dissatisfaction, and Restrained Eating', *International Journal of Eating Disorders* 37(4): 313–320.

Gershon, I. (2010) *The Breakup 2.0: Disconnecting over New Media.* Ithica, NY and London: Cornell University Press.

Gibson, J.J. (1979) *The Ecological Approach to Visual Perception.* Boston, MA: Houghton Mifflin.

Giddens, A (1991) *Modernity and Self-identity: Self and Society in the Late Modern Age*. Cambridge: Polity.

Giddens, A. (1992) *The Transformation of Intimacy: Sexuality, Love and Eroticism in Modern Societies*. Oxford: Polity press.

Giddens, A. (1999) *Family*, Reith Lectures 4. BBC Radio 4.

Gilbert, E., Karahalios, K., and Sandvig, C. (2010) 'The Network in the Garden: Designing Social Media for Rural Life', *American Behavioral Scientist* 53(9): 1367–1388.

Gillies, V., Ribbens McCarthy, J., and Holland, J. (2001) *'Pulling Together, Pulling Apart': The Family Lives of Young People*. York: Family Policy Studies Centre/ Joseph Rowntree Foundation.

Goffman, E. (1959) *The Presentation of Self in Everyday Life*. New York: Anchor Books.

Goffman, E. (1961) *Asylums: Essays on the Social Situation of Mental Patients and Other Inmates*. New York: Doubleday. Anchor.

Goldenberg, J., Libai, B., and E. Muller (2001) 'Talk of the Network: A Complex Systems Look at the Underlying Process of Word-of-Mouth', *Marketing Letters* 12: 211–223.

Golder, S.A., Wilkinson, D., and Huberman, B.A. (2007, June) 'Rhythms of Social Interaction: Messaging within a Massive Online Network', in Steinfield, C., Pentland, B., Ackerman, M., and Contractor, N. (eds.), *Communities and Technologies 2007: Proceedings of the Third International Conference on Communities and Technologies*. London: Springer, pp. 41–66.

Goodchild, R. (2010) Eighty-Eight Dates: The Perilous Joys of Internet Dating, Michael Joseph.

Granovetter, M. (1973) 'The Strength of Weak Ties', *American Journal of Sociology* 78(6): 1160–1180.

Granovetter, M. (1983) 'The Strength of Weak Ties: A Network Theory Revisited', *Sociological Theory* 1: 201–233.

Graves, L. (2007) 'The Affordance of Blogging: A Case Study in Culture and Technological Effects', *Journal of Communication Inquiry* 31(4): 331–346.

Gray, M.L. (2009) *Out in the Country: Youth, Media, and the Queering of Rural America*. New York: NYU Press.

Griffiths, V. (1995) *Adolescent Girls and their Friends: A Feminist Ethnography*. Farnham: Ashgate.

Haddon, L. (2004) *Information and Communication Technologies in Everyday Life*. Oxford and New York: Berg.

Haley, M. (2006, Winter). 'Virtual Society: Facebook.com @ PLU., 2007'. Available at: http://www.plu.edu/scene/issue/2006/winter/features/virtual-society. html (accessed 21 August 2012).

Halliday, J. (20011a) 'London Riots: How BlackBerry Messenger Played a Key Role', *The Guardian*, 8 August 2011. Available at: http://www.guardian. co.uk/media/2011/aug/08/london-riots-facebook-twitter-blackberry (accessed 16 November 2012).

Halliday, J. (2011b) 'David Cameron Considers Banning Suspected Rioters from Social Media', 11 August, *The Guardian*. Available at: http://www.guardian. co.uk/media/2011/aug/11/david-cameron-rioters-social-media   (accessed 14 August 2012).

Hamel, Jean-Yves (2009) 'Information and Communication Technologies and Migration', Human Development Research Paper 2009/39, United Nations Development Programme, MPRA Paper No. 19175, posted 11 December 2009/16: 29. Available at: http://mpra.ub.uni-muenchen.de/19175/1/MPRA_paper_19175.pdf (accessed 12 February 2012).

Hampton, K., Lee, C-J., Her, E.J. (2011) 'How new media affords network diversity: Direct and mediated access to social capital through participation in local social settings', *New Media and Society*, online version, published 16 February 2011, 1–19.

Hampton, K. and Wellman B. (2003) 'Neighboring in Netville: How the Internet Supports Community and Social Capital in a Wired Suburb', *City and Community* 2(4): 277–311.

Hargittai, E. (2007) 'Whose Space? Differences among Users and Non-users of Social Network Sites', *Journal of Computer-Mediated Communication* 13(14): 276–297.

Hargittai, E. (2008) 'The Digital Reproduction of Inequality', in Grusky, D. (ed.), *Social Stratification*. Boulder, CO: Westview Press, pp. 936–944.

Hargittai, E. and Hsieh, Y.P. (2011) 'From Dabblers to Omnivors: A Typology of Social Netwrok Site Usage', in Papacharissi, Z. (ed.), *A Networked Self: Identity, Community, and Culture on Social Network Sites*. New York: Routledge, pp. 146–168.

Harris, K. (2003) 'Keep Your Distance: Remote Communication, Face-to-Face and the Nature of Community', *Journal of Community Work and Development* 1(4): 5–28.

Haythornthwaite, C. (2005) 'Social Networks and Internet Connectivity Effects', *Information, Communication and Society* 8(2): 125–147.

Hearn A (2008) ' "Meat, Mask, Burden": Probing the Contours of the Branded "Self" ', *Journal of Consumer Culture* 8(2): 197–217.

Heath, S. (2004) 'Peer-Shared Households, Quasi-Communes and Neo-Tribes', *Current Sociology* 52(2): 161–179.

Hechinger, J. (2008) 'College Applicants Beware: Your Facebook Page is Showing', *Wall Street Journal*, 18 September 2008. Available at: http://online.wsj.com/article/SB122170459104151023.html (accessed 30 July 2012).

Hennebry, J.L. (2006) *Report on Activities – 31 May 2006*. Ottawa: International Development Research Centre.

Heussner, Ki Mae (2011) 'Underage Facebook Members: 7.5 million Users Under Age 13', *ABC News* (10 May). Available at: http://abcnews.go.com/Technology/underage-facebook-members-75-million-users-age-13/story?id=13565619 (accessed 27 September 2011).

Hey, V. (1997) *The Company She Keeps: An Ethnography of Girls' Friendships*. Buckingham: Open University Press.

Hillier, Harrison and Bowditch (1999) ' "Neverending Love" and "Blowing Your Load": the Meaning of Sex to Rural Youth', *Sexualities* 2(1): 69–88.

Hillier, L. and Harrison, L. (2007) 'Building realities less limited than their own: Young people practicing same-sex attraction on the internet', *Sexualities* 10(1): 82–100.

Hird, M.J. and Jackson, S. (2001) ' "Where Angels and Wusses Fear to Tread": Sexual Coercion in Adolescent Dating Relationships', *Journal of Sociology* 37(1): 27–43.

Hjarvard, S. (2006) 'The Mediatization of Religion: A Theory of the Media as an Agent of Religious Change', paper presented at the 5th International Conference on Media, Religion and Culture, Sweden, 6–9 July 2006.

Hogan, R., Jones, W., and Cheek, J.M. (1985) 'Socioanalytic Theory: An Alternative to Armadillo Psychology', in Schlenker, B.R. (ed.), *The Self and Social Life*. New York: McGraw-Hill, pp. 175–198.

Holdsworth, C. and Morgan, D. (2007) 'Revisiting the Generalized Other: An Exploration', *Sociology* 41(3): 401–417.

Holland, D. and Skinner, S. (1987) 'Prestige and Intimacy: The Cultural Models Behind Americans' Talk about Gender Types', in Holland, D. and Quinn, N. (eds.), *Cultural Models in Language & Thought*. Cambridge: Cambridge University Press, pp. 78–111.

Holloway, S.L. and Valentine, G. (2003) *Cyberkids: Children in the Information Age*. London: Routledge Falmer.

Holmes, M. (2004) 'The Precariousness of Choice in the New Sentimental Order: A Response to Bawin-Legros', *Current Sociology* 52(2): 251–257.

Holmes, M. (2010) 'The Emotionalization of Reflexivity', *Sociology* 44(1): 139–154.

Holstein, J. and Gubrium, J. (2000) *The Self We Live By: Narrative Identity in a Postmodern World*. New York: Oxford University Press.

Hondagneu-Sotelo, P. and Avila, E. (1997) ' "I'm Here, But I'm There": The Meaning of Latina Transnational Motherhood', *Gender and Society* 11(5): 538–571.

Hoover, Stewart M., Lynn Schofield Clark, and Diane Alters (with Joseph G. Champ and Lee Hood) (2004) *Media, Home, and Family*. New York: Routledge.

Horst, H.A. (2006) 'The Blessings and Burdens of Communication: Cell Phones in Jamaican Transnational Social Fields', *Global Networks* 6(2): 143–159.

Horst, H.A. (2010a) 'Families', in Ito, M., Baumer, S., Bittanti, M., Boyd, D., Cody, R., Herr-Stevenson, B., Horst, H.A., Lange, P.G., Martinez, K.Z., Pasko, C.J., Perkel, D., Robinson, L.S., Sims, C., and Tripp, L. (eds.), *Hanging out, Messing Around, Geeking Out: Kids Living and Learning with New Media*. Cambridge, MA: The MIT Press, pp. 149–194.

Horst, H.A. (2010b) 'From MySpace to Facebook: Coming of Age in Networked Public Culture', in Ito, M., Baumer, S., Bittanti, M., boyd, d., Cody, R., Herr-Stephenson, B., Horst, H.A., Lange, P.G., Mahendran, D., Martinez, K.Z., Pascoe, C.J., Perkel, D., Robinson, L., Sims, C. and Tripp, L. (eds.), *Hanging Out, Messing Around, and Geeking Out: Kids Living and Learning with New Media*. Cambridge, MA: MIT Press, pp. 92–93.

Horst, H.A. and Miller, D. (2005) 'From Kinship to Link-Up: Cell Phones and Social Networking in Jamaica', *Current Anthropology* 6(5): 755–778.

Horst, H.A. and Miller, D. (2006) *The Cell Phone: An Anthropology of Communication*. Oxford: Berg.

Hsu, Shu-Ching (2011) *The Golden Rules of Online Dating, 6 Crucial Rules To Finding The Perfect Online Date* [Kindle Edition] Amazon Media EU S.à r.l.

Hutchby, I. (2001) 'Technologies, Texts and Affordances', *Sociology* 35: 441–456.

Infographic (2010) 'Infographic: Twitter Statistics, Facts and Figures'. Available at: http://www.digitalbuzzblog.com/infographic-twitter-statistics-facts-figures/ (accessed 17 August 2012).

Ito, M. (2008) 'Introduction', in Vernelis, K. (ed.), *Networked Publics*. Cambridge MA: MIT Press, pp. 1–14.

Ito, M., Baumer, S., Bittanti, M., boyd, d., Cody, R., Herr-Stephenson, B., Horst, H.A., Lange, P.G., Mahendran, D., Martinez, K.Z., Pascoe, C.J., Perkel, D., Robinson, L., Sims, C., and Tripp, L. (2010) *Hanging Out, Messing Around, and Geeking Out: Kids Living and Learning with New Media*. Cambridge, MA: MIT Press.

Ito, M. and Okabe, D. (2005) 'Intimate Connections: Contextualizing Japanese Youth and Mobile Messaging', in Harper R., Palen L., and Taylor, A. (eds.), *Inside the Text: Social, Cultural and Design Perspectives on SMS*. New York: Springer, pp. 127–143.

Jacobs, K. (2010) 'Lizzy Kinsey and the Adult Friendfienders: An Ethnographic Study of Internet Sex and Pornographic Self-Display in Hong Kong Culture', *Health and Sexuality* 12(6): 691–703.

Jackson, S. (1998) 'Heterosexuality and Feminist Theory', in Richardson, D. (ed.), *Theorising Heterosexuality*. Buckingham: Buckingham Open University Press, pp. 21–38.

James, A., Jenks, C., and Prout, A. (1998) *Theorizing Childhood*. Cambridge: Polity Press.

James, A. and Prout, A. (eds.) (1997) *Constructing and Reconstructing Childhood*, 2nd edn. London: Routledge/Falmer.

Jamieson, L. (1987) 'Theories of Family Development and the Experience of Being Brought Up', *Sociology* 21: 591–607.

Jamieson, L. (1998) *Intimacy: Personal Relationships in Modern Societies*. Cambridge and Malden, MA: Polity Press.

Jamieson, L. (1999) 'Intimacy Transformed? A Critical Look at the "Pure Relationship"', *Sociology* 33(3): 477–494.

Jamieson, L. (2005) 'Boundaries of Intimacy', in McKie, L. and Cunningham-Burley, S. (eds.), *Families in Society: Boundaries and Relationships*. Bristol: Policy Press, pp. 189–206.

Jamieson, L., Morgan, D., Crow, G., and Allan, G. (2007) 'Friends, Neighbours and Distant Partners: Extending or Decentring Family Relationships?' *Sociological Research Online* 11(3). Available at: http://www.socresonline.org.uk/11/3/jamieson.html

Jankowski, N.W. (2002) 'Creating Community with Media: History, Theories and Scientific Investigation', in Lievrouw, L. and Livingstone, S. (eds.), *The Handbook of New Media*. London: Sage, pp. 34–49.

Jenkins, H. (2006) *Convergence culture: Where Old and New Media Collide*. New York: New York University Press.

Joinson A.N. (2008) 'Looking at, Looking Up or Keeping up With People?: Motives and Use of Facebook', *Proceedings of the SIGCHI Conference on Human Factors in Computing Systems*. New York: ACM, pp. 1027–1036.

Jones, G.P. (1990) 'The Study of Intergenerational Intimacy in North America', *Journal of Homosexuality* 20(1/2): 275–295.

Kaplan test prep (2008) 'Facebook Checking is No Longer Unchartered Territory in College Admissions: Percentage of Admissions Officers Who Visited An Applicant's Profile On the Rise', Press release of Kaplan test Prep Survey. Available at: http://press.kaptest.com/press-releases/facebook-checking-is-no-longer-unchartered-territory-in-college-admissions-percentage-of-admissions-officers-who-visited-an-applicant%E2%80%99s-profile-on-the-rise   (accessed 30 July 2012).

Katz, J.E. and Rice, R.E. (2002) *Social Consequences of Internet Use: Access, Involvement, and Interaction*. Cambridge, MA: MIT.

Kavanaugh, A.L. and Patterson, S.J. (2002) 'The Impact of Community Computer Networks on Social Capital and Community Involvement in Blacksburg', in Wellman, B. and Haythornthwaite, C. (eds.), *The Internet in Everyday Life*. Malden, MA: Blackwell, pp. 325–344.

Keane, J. (2009) *The Life and Death of Democracy*. London: Simon and Schuster.

Kinkaid, J. (1998) *Erotic Innocence*. Durham, NC: Duke University Press.

Kinney, D.A. (1993) 'From Nerds to Normals: The Recovery of Identity among Adolescents from Middle School to High School', *Sociology of Education* 66(1): 21–40.

Kitsak, M. et al. (2010) 'Identification of Influential Spreaders in Complex Networks', *Nature Physics* 6: 888–93.

Kohut, A. (2008) 'Key News Audiences Now Blend Online and Traditional Sources: Audience Segments in a Changing News Environment', *Pew Research Centre for the People and the Press*. Available at: http://people-press.org/report/444/news-media (accessed 12 November 2012).

Korobov, N. and Thorne, A. (2006) 'Intimacy and Distancing: Young Men's Conversations about Romantic Relationships', *Journal of Adolescent Research* 21(1): 27–55.

Kotimo, L. (2011) 'Social Media and Migration: Virtual Community 2.0', *Journal of the American Society for Information Science and Technology* 62(6): 1075–1086.

Kraut, R, Patterson, M., Lunmark, V., Kiesler, S. Mukopadhyay, T., and Scherlis, W. (1998) Internet Paradox: A Social Technology that Reduces Social Involvement and Psychological Well-Being? *American Psychologist* 53: 1017–1031.

Kraut, R. et al. (2002a) 'Internet Paradoxes Revisited', *Journal of Social Issues* 58: 49–74.

Kraut, R.E., Fussell, S.R., Brennan, S.E., and Siegel, J. (2002b) 'Understanding Effects of Proximity on Collaboration: Implications for Technologies to Support Remote Collaborative Work', in Hinds, P. and Kiesler, S. (eds.), *Distributed Work*. Cambridge, MA: MIT Press, pp. 137–162.

Lampe, C., Ellison, N., and Steinfield, C. (2006) 'A Face(book) in the Crowd: Social Searching vs. Social Browsing', *Proceedings of the 2006 20th Anniversary Conference on Computer Supported Cooperative Work*. New York: ACM, pp. 167–170.

Lampe, C., Ellison, N.B., and Stenfield, C. (2007) 'A Familiar Face(book): Profile Elements as Signals in an Online Social Network', *Proceedings of the SIGCHI Conference on Human Factors in Computing Systems*. New York: ACM. pp. 435–444.

Lang K.J. (2009) 'Facebook Friend Turns into Big Brother', *LaCrosse Tribune*, 19 November. Available at: http://lacrossetribune.com/news/local/article_0ff40f7a-d4d1-11de-afb3-001cc4c002e0.html (accessed 5 April 2010).

Lareau, A. (2003) *Unequal Childhoods: Class, Race and Family Life*. Berkeley, CA: University of California Press.

Lash, S. (1994) 'Reflexivity and its Doubles, Structures, Aesthetics, Community''', in Beck, U., Giddens, A., and Lash, S. (eds.), *Reflexive Modernization: Politics,*

Tradition and Aesthetics in the Modern Social Order. Cambridge: Polity Press, pp. 110–173.

Lave, J. and Wenger, E. (1991) *Situated Learning: Legitimate Peripheral Participation.* Cambridge: University of Cambridge Press.

Lemert, C. and Branaman, A. (1997) *The Goffman Reader.* Oxford: Wiley-Blackwell.

Lenhart, A. (2009) 'Pew Internet Project Data memo', 14 January. Online. Available at: http://www.pewinternet.org/Reports/2009/Adults-and-Social-Network-Websites.aspx (accessed 18 November 2012).

Lin, N. (2001) 'Building a Network Theory of Social Capital', in Lin, N., Cook, K.S., and Burt, R.S. (eds.), *Social Capital: Theory and Research.* New York: Aldine de Gruyter, pp. 3–29.

Lenhart, Amanda and Madden, Mary (2007) 'Teens, Privacy and Online Social Networks. Pew Internet & American Life Project'. Available at: http://www.pewInternet.org/PPF/r/211/report_display.asp

Lenhart, A., Madden, M., Rankin macGill, A., and Smith, A. (2007) 'Teens and Social Media: The Use of Social Media Gains a Greater Foothold in Teen Life as They Embrace the Conversational Nature of Interactive Online Media', *Pew Internet & American Life Project.* Washington, DC: Pew/Internet. Available at: http://www.pewinternet.org/pdfs/PIP_Teens_Social_Media_Final.pdf (accessed 16 January 2012).

Lenhart, A., Madden, M., Smith, A., Purcell, K., Zickuhr, K., and Rainie, L. (2011) 'Teens, Kindness and Cruelty on Social Network Sites', Report of the Pew Research Center, *Cable in the Classroom and the Family Online Safety Institute.* Washington, DC (9 November 2011). Available at: http://pewinternet.org/Reports/2011/Teens-and-social-media/Summary.aspx (accessed 20 August 2012).

Lenhart, A., Purcell, K., Smith, A., and Zickuhr, K. (2010) 'Social Media & Mobile Internet Use Among Teens and Young Adults', *Pew Internet and American Life Project* report (3 February). Available at: http://www.pewinternet.org/~/media/Files/Reports/2010/PIP_Social_Media_and_Young_Adults_Report_Final_with_toplines.pdf (accessed 5 February 2012).

Levine, J. (2002) *Harmful to Minors: The Perils of Protecting Children from Sex.* Minneapolis, MN: University of Minnesota Press.

Lev-Ram, Michal (2011) 'Zuckerberg: Kids UNDER 13 Should Be Allowed on Facebook', *Fortune* (20 May). Available at: http://tech.fortune.cnn.com/2011/05/20/zuckerberg-kids-under-13-should-be-allowed-on-facebook/ (accessed 27 September 2011).

Lievrouw, L. (2011) *Alternative and Activist New Media.* Cambridge: Polity.

Little, L., Sillence, E., Sellen, A., and Taylor, A. (2009) 'The Family and Communication Technologies', *International Journal of Human Computer Studies* 67(2): 125–127.

Liu, H. (2007) 'Social Network Profiles as Taste Performances', *Journal of Computer-Mediated Communication* 13(1). Available at: http://jcmc.indiana.edu/vol13/issue1/liu.html?ref=SaglikAlani.Com (accessed 13 August 2012).

Livingstone, S. (2002) *Young People and New Media: Childhood and the Changing Media Environment.* London: Sage.

Livingstone, S. (2004) 'Media Literacy and the Challenge of New Information and Communication Technologies', *Communication Review* 7: 3–14.

Livingstone, S. (2005) *Audiences and Publics: When Cultural Engagement Matters for the Public Sphere*. Portland, OR: Intellect.

Livingstone, S. (2007) 'From Family Television to Bedroom Culture: Young People's Media at Home', in Devereux, E. (ed.), *Media Studies: Key Issues and Debates*. London: Sage, pp. 302–321.

Livingstone, S. (2008) 'Taking Risky Opportunities in Youthful Content Creation: Teenagers' Use of Social Networking Sites for Intimacy, Privacy and Self-Expression', *New Media and Society* 10(3): 393–411.

Livingstone, S. (2009a) 'On the Mediation of Everything', *Journal of Communication* 59(1): 1–18.

Livingstone, S. (2009b) *Children and the Internet*. Cambridge: Polity.

Livingstone, S. and Bovill, M. (2011) 'Families and the Internet: An Observational Study of Children and Young People's Internet Use'. Final report to BT, Media @ LSE: London School of Economics. Available at: http://eprints. lse.ac.uk/21164/1/Families_and_the_internet_-_an_observational_study_of_ children_and_young_people%27s_internet_use.pdf (accessed 16 November 2012).

Livingstone, S., Haddon, L., Görzig, A., and Ólafsson, K. (2011) *Risks and Safety on the Internet: The Perspective of European Children. Full Findings*. LSE, London: EU Kids Online. Available at: http://www2.lse.ac.uk/media lse/research/EUKidsOnline/EUKidsII%20(2009-11)/EUKidsOnlineIIReports/ D4FullFindings.pdf (accessed 10 February 2012).

Loader, B.D. and Mercea, D. (2012) *Social Media and Democracy: Innovations in Participatory Politics*. London: Routledge.

Lofland, L. (1989) 'Social Life in the Public Realm: A Review', *Journal of Contemporary Ethnography* 17(4): 453–482.

Ljung, A. and Wahlfross, E. (2008) *People, Profiles and Trust: On Interpersonal Trust in Web-Mediated Social Spaces*. Berlin and Heidelberg: Springer-Verlag GmbH & Co.

Mackenzie, D. and Wajcman, J. (1999) 'Introduction Essay', in Mackenzie, D. and Wajcman, J. (eds.), *The Social Shaping of Technology*, 2nd edn. Buckingham: Open University Press, pp. 3–27.

Maczewski, M. (2002) 'Exploring Identities through the Internet: Youth Experiences Online', *Child and Youth Care Forum* 31(2): 111–129.

Madianou, M. and Miller, D. (2012) *Migration and New Media: Trasnational Families and Polymedia*, London: Routledge.

Madden, M. and Lenhart, A. (2006) 'Online Dating, Pew Internet and American Life Project', Washington, DC: Pew/Internet. Available at: http://pewinternet. org/~/media//Files/Reports/2006/PIP_Online_Dating.pdf.pdf (accessed 15 July 2012).

Madden, M. and Smith, A. (2010) 'Reputation Management and Social Media: How People Monitor their Identity and Search for Others Online', *Pew Internet and American Life Project*, Washington: Pew Research Centre. Available at: http://pewinternet.org/Reports/2010/Reputation-Management.aspx (accessed 13 November 2011).

Mansour Tall Sr. (2004) 'Senegalese Migrants: New Information & Communication Technologies', *Review of African Political Economy* 31(99): 31–48.

Marks, M.J. and Fraley, R.C. (2006) 'Confirmation Bias and the Sexual Double Standard', *Sex Roles* 54: 19–25.

Martinez, K. (2010) 'Sharing snapshots of teen friendship and Love', in Ito, M.,
   Baumer, S., Bittanti, M., boyd, d., Cody, R., Herr-Stephenson, B., Horst, H.A.,
   Lange, P.G., Mahendran, D., Martinez, K.Z., Pascoe, C.J., Perkel, D., Robinson,
   L., Sims, C., and Tripp, L. (2010) *Hanging Out, Messing Around, and Geeking
   Out: Kids Living and Learning with New Media.* Cambridge, MA: MIT Press,
   pp. 85–88.
Marwick, A. (2005a) 'I'm a lot more interesting that a Friendster profile: iden-
   tity presentation, authenticity and Power in Social Networking Services.'
   Available at: http://microsoft.academia.edu/AliceMarwick/Papers/400480/
   IMa_Lot_More_Interesting_Than_a_Friendster_Profile_Identity_Presentation
   _Authenticity_and_Power_In_Social_Networking_Services (accessed 30 July
   2012).
Marwick, A.E. (2005b) *Selling Yourself: Online Identity in the Age of a Commodified
   Internet.* Washington, DC: University of Washington Press.
Marwick, A. (2008) 'To Catch a Predator? The MySpace Moral Panic', *First Monday*
   13(6). Available at: http://www.uic.edu/htbin/cgiwrap/bin/ojs/index.php/fm/
   article/view/2152/1966 (accessed 26 June 2008).
Marwick, A.E. and boyd, d. (2011) 'I Tweet Honestly, I Tweet Passionately: Twitter
   Users, Context Collapse, and the Imagined Audience', *New Media and Society*
   13(1): 114–133.
Matsuda, M. (2005) 'Mobile Communication and Selective Sociality', in Ito, M.,
   Okabe, D., and Matsuda, M. (eds.), *Personal, Portable, Pedestrian: Mobile Phones
   in Japanese Life.* Cambridge, MA: The MIT Press, pp. 123–142.
Mazer, J.P., Murphy, R.E., and Simonds, C.J. (2007) I'll See You on 'Facebook': The
   Effects of Computer-Mediated Teacher Self-Disclosure on Student Motivation,
   Affective Learning, and Classroom Climate. *Communication Education* 56: 1–17.
McGerevan, W. (2009) 'Disclosure, endorsement and identity in social market-
   ing', University of Illinois Law Review, 1105, Research Paper No. 09-04. Avail-
   able online at: http://papers.ssrn.com/sol3/papers.cfm?abstract_id= 1334406
   (accessed 17 August 2012).
McKay, D. (2010) 'On the Face of Facebook: Historical Images and Personhood in
   Filipino Social Networking', *History and Anthropology* 21(4): 479–498.
McKenna, K.Y.A., Green, A.S. and Gleason, M.E.J. (2002) Relationship Forma-
   tion on the Internet: What's the Big Attraction? *Journal of Social Issues* 58(1):
   9–31.
McLaughlin, C. and Vitak, J. (2012, March) 'Norm evolution and violation on
   Facebook' *New Media & Society* 14(2): 299–315.
McLuhan, M. (1964) *Understanding Media: The Extension of Man.* Mentor:
   New York.
Mead, G.H. (1934/1962) *Mind, Self, and Society: From the Standpoint of a Social
   Behaviourist.* Chicago: University of Chicago Press.
Mesch, G. and Talmud, I. (2006) The Quality of Online and Offline Relationships.
   The Information Society 22: 137–148.
Mesch, G.S. and Talmud, I. (2007a) 'Similarity and the Quality of Online and
   Offline Social Relations among Adolescents in Israel', *Journal of Research in
   Adolescence* 17(2): 455–66.
Mesch, G. and Talmud, I. (2007b) Special Issue on E-Relationships – The Blur-
   ring and Reconfiguration of Offline and Online Social Boundaries. *Information,
   Communication and Society,* 10(5): 585–589.

Miller, B.C. and Benson, B. (1999) 'Romantic and Sexual Relationship Development during Adolescence', in Furman, W., Brown, B.B., and Feiring, C. (eds.), *The development of Romantic Relationships in Adolescence*. Cambridge: Cambridge University Press, pp. 99–121.

Miller, D. (2008) *The Comfort of Things*. Cambridge: Polity.

Miller, D. (2011) *Tales from Facebook*. Cambridge: Polity.

Miller, D. and Slater, D. (2000) *The Internet: An Ethnographic Approach*. Oxford: Berg.

Milner, M. Jr. (2004) *Freaks, Geeks, and Cool Kids: American Teenagers, Schools, and the Culture of Consumption*. New York: Routledge.

Mitra, A. (2001) 'Diasporic Voices in Cyberspace', *New Media and Society* 3(1): 29–48.

Panagakos, A.N. and Horst, H.A. (2006) 'Return to Cyberia: Technology and the Social Worlds of Transnational Migrants', *Global Networks* 6(2): 109–124.

Modell, J. (1989) *Into One's Own: From Youth to Adulthood in the United States*. Berkeley, CA: University of California Press.

Montgomery, K. (2001) 'COPPA: The First Year, a Survey of Sites', *Report on Web Site Compliance by Center for Media Education* (April). Available at: http://www.uhoh.org/cme/coppa-rpt.pdf (accessed 27 September 2011).

Morgan, D. (2005) 'Revisiting "Communities in Britain"', *Sociological Review Monograph* 4(53): 641–657.

Morgan, D. (2009) *Acquaintances: The Space Between Intimates and Strangers*. Maidenhead: Open University Press.

Morgan, D. (2011) 'Conceptualising the Personal,' in May, V. (ed.), *A Sociology of Personal Life*. Basingstoke: Palgrave Macmillan, pp. 11–21.

Morley, D. (2000) *Media, Mobility and Identity*. New York: Psychology Press.

Morley, D. (2008) *Home Territories: Media, Mobility and Identity*. London: Routledge.

Morris, M.R., Teevan, J., and Panovich, K. (2010) 'What do people ask their social networks, and why? A survey study of status message Q&A behavior', *Proceedings of the ACM Conference on Human Factors in Computing Systems*. New York: ACM, pp. 1739–1748.

Muise, A., Christofides, E., and Desmarais, S. (2009) 'More Information than You Ever Wanted: Does Facebook Bring Out the Green-Eyed Monster of Jealousy?' *CyberPsychology & Behavior* 12(4): 441–444.

Nikken, P., Jansz, J., and Schouwstra, S. (2007). 'Parents' Interest in Video Game Ratings and Content Descriptors in Relation to Game Mediation', *European Journal of Communication* 22: 315–336.

Nosko, A., Wood, E., and Molema, S. (2010) 'All About Me: Disclosure in Online Social Networking Profiles: The Case of Facebook', *Computers in Human Behaviour* 26(2010): 406–418.

Ofcom (2009) 'Digital Lifestyles: Parents of Children Under 16'. Available at: http://stakeholders.ofcom.org.uk/market-data-research/media-literacy/medlitpub/medlitpubrss/digilifestyles/ (accessed 3 August 2010).

Oksman, V. and Turtainen, J. (2004) 'Mobile Communication as a Social Stage', *New Media & Society* 6(3): 319–339.

Oliker, S. (1998) 'The Modernization of Friendship: Individualism, Intimacy and Gender in the Nineteenth Century', in Adams, R. and Allan, G. (eds.), *Placing Friendship in Context*. Cambridge: Cambridge University Press, pp. 18–42.

Ortiz, S.M. (1994) 'Shopping for Sociability in the Mall', in Cahill, S.E. and Lofl, L.H. (eds.), *The Community of the Streets, Supplement 1, Research in Community Sociology*. Greenwich, CT: JAI Press, pp. 193–199.

Osgerby, B (2004) *Youth Media*. London: Routledge.

Pahl, R. (2005) 'Are all Communities, Communities in the Mind?' *Sociological Review Monograph* 4(53): 621–640.

Pahl, R. and Pevalin, D. (2005) 'Between Family and Friends: A Longitudinal Study of Friendship Choice', *British Journal of Sociology* 56(3): 433–450.

Pahl, R. and Spencer, L. (2004) Personal Communities: Not Simply Families of 'Fate' or or 'choice', *Current Sociology* 52 (2) 199-221.

Palfrey, J. and Gasser, U. (2008) *Born Digital: Understanding the First Generation of Digital Natives*. New York: Basic Books.

Papacharissi, Z. (2002) 'The Presentation of Self in Virtual Life: Characteristics of Personal Home Pages', *Journalism and Mass Communication Quarterly* 79(3): 643–660.

Papacharissi, Z. (2009) The Virtual Geographies of Social Networks: A Comparative Analysis of Facebook, LinkedIn and ASmallWorld', *New Media and Society* 11(1–2): 199–220.

Papacharissi, Z. (2010) *A Private Sphere: Democracy in a Digital Age*. Cambridge: Polity.

Parker, A. (2011) 'Suicide Girls' Dad Slams Web Sickos', *The Sun*, 23 February 2011. Available at: http://www.thesun.co.uk/sol/homepage/news/3427677/Suicide-girl-Natasha-MacBrydes-dad-slams-web-sickos.html (accessed 5 February 2012).

Parks, M. (2011) 'Social Network Sites as Virtual Communities', in Papacharissi, Z. (ed.), *A Networked Self: Identity, Community, and Culture on Social Network Sites*. New York: Routledge, pp. 105–123.

Pascoe, C.J. (2007) *'Dude, you're a Fag': Masculinity and Sexuality in High School*. Berkeley and Los Angeles, CA: University of California Press.

Pascoe, C.J. (2010) 'Intimacy', in Ito, M., Baumer, S., Bittanti, M., boyd, d., Cody, R., Herr-Stephenson, B., Horst, H.A., Lange, P.G., Mahendran, D., Martinez, K.Z., Pascoe, C.J., Perkel, D., Robinson, L., Sims, C., and Tripp, L. (eds.), *Hanging Out, Messing Around, and Geeking Out: Kids Living and Learning with New Media*. Cambridge, MA: MIT Press, pp. 117–148.

Patchin, J.W. and Hinduja, S. (2012) *Cyberbullying Prevention and Response: Expert Perspectives*. New York: Routledge.

Patulny, R. (2005) 'Social Capital and Welfare: Dependency or Division? Examining Bridging Trends by Welfare Regime, 1981 to 2000', Social Policy Research Centre, UNSW: Sydney. Available at: http://arrow.unsw.edu.au/vital/access/services/Download/unsworks:1960/SOURCE01?view=true

Perry, P. (2002) *Shades of White: White Kids and Racial Identities in High School*. Durham, NC: Duke University Press.

Pertierra, R. (ed.) (1992) *Remittances and Returnees: The Cultural Economy of Migration in Ilocos*. Quezon City: New Day Publishers.

Pertierra, R. (2006) *Transforming Technologies: Altered Selves – Mobile Phones and Internet Use in the Philippines*. Manila: De Salle University Press.

Pertierra, R. (2010) *The Anthropology of New Media in the Philippines*. Quezon City: Institute of Philippine Culture, Ateneo de Manila University.

Pertierra, R., Ugarte, E., Pingol, A., and Dacanay, N. (2002) *Txt-ing Selves: Cellphones and Philippine Modernity*. Manila: De La Salle Press.

Peters, T. (1997) 'The Brand Called You', *Fast Company* 10(83): 233–259.

Petronio, S. (2002) *Boundaries of Privacy: Dialectics of Disclosure*. Albany, NY: State University New York Press.

Plummer, K. (2003) *Intimate Citizenship: Private Decisions and Public Dialogues*. Seattle, WA and London: University of Washington Press.

Postman, N. (1982) *The Disappearance of Childhood*. New York: Delacorte Press.

Postman, N. (1993) *Technopoly: The Surrender of Culture to Technology*. New York: Vintage Books.

Putnam, R. (1995) 'Bowling Alone: America's Declining Social Capital', *Journal of Democracy* 6: 65–78.

Putnam, R. (2000) *Bowling Alone*. New York: Simon and Schuster.

Putman, R.D. and Feldstein, L.M. (2003) *Better Together: Restoring the American Community*. New York: Simon and Schuster.

Quan-Hasse, A. and Wellman, B. (2004) 'How Does the Internet Affect Social Capital?' in Huysman, M. and Wulf, V. (eds.), *Social Capital and Information Technology*. Cambridge, MA: MIT Press, pp. 113–135.

Raynes-Goldie, K. and Fono, D. (2005) 'Hyperfriendship and Beyond: Friendship and Social Norms on Livejournal', *Association of Internet Researchers (AOIR-6)*, Chicago.

Read more at Suite101: Internet & Anti-Social Behavior Theory Unfounded: Facebook, MySpace, Online: Research Refutes Cyber Socializing Fears | Suite101.com   http://suite101.com/article/internet–anti-social-behavior-theory-unfounded-a111897#ixzz227kABheq

Richtel, M. and Helft, M. (2011) 'Facebook Users Who Are Under Age Raise Concerns', *New York Times* (11 March). Available at: http://www.nytimes.com/2011/03/12/technology/internet/12underage.html (accessed 27 September 2011).

Rheingold, H. (1993) *The Virtual Community: Homesteading on the Electronic Frontier*. Reading: MA: Addison-Wesley.

Robinson, L. (2007) 'The Cyberself: The Self-Ing Project Goes Online, Symbolic Interaction in the Digital Age', *New Media and Society* 9: 93.

Rochman, B. (2011) 'Should Kids Under 13 Be on Facebook?' *Time* (24 May). Available at: http://healthland.time.com/2011/05/24/should-facebook-welcome-users-under-13/ (accessed 27 September 2011).

Rose, N. (1996) 'Identity, Genealogy, History', in Hall, S. and Du Gay, P. (eds.), *Questions of Cultural Identity*. London: Sage, pp. 128–150.

Rose, N. (1999) *Powers of Freedom*. Cambridge: Cambridge University Press.

Roseneil, S. (2000) 'Queer Frameworks and Queer Tendencies: Towards an Understanding of Postmodern Transformations of Sexuality', *Sociological Review Online* 5(3). Available at: http://www.leeds.ac.uk/cava/papers/wsp8 (accessed 18 November 2012).

Roseneil, S. and Budgeon, S. (2004) 'Cultures of Intimacy and Care Beyond 'the Family': Personal Life and Social Change in the Early 21st Century', *Current Sociology* 52(2): 135–159.

Rubin, Z. (1975) 'Disclosing Oneself to a Stranger: Reciprocity and Its Limits', *Journal of Experimental Social Psychology* 11(1975): 233–260.

Russell, A., Ito, M., Richmond, T., and Tuters, M. (2008) 'Culture: Media Convergence and Networked Participation', in Varnelis, K. (ed.), *Networked Publics*. Cambridge, MA: The MIT Press, pp. 43–76.

Sandfort, T. (1987) *Boys on their Contacts with Men*. Elmhurst, NY: Global Academic Publishers.

Savage, M. Bagnall, G., and Longhurst, B. (2005) *Globalisation and Belonging*. London: Sage.

Saxenian, A. (2006) *International Mobility of Engineers and the Rise of Entrepreneurship in the Periphery*. Helsinki: United Nations University, World Institute for Development Economics Research.

Schau, Hope Jensen, and Mary C. Gilly (2003) 'We Are What We Post? Self-Presentation in Personal Web Space', *Journal of Consumer Research* 30(3): 385–404.

Schor, J.B. (2004) *Born to Buy: The Commercialized Child and the New Consumer Culture*. New York: Scribner.

Schwartz, O. (2011) 'Who Moved My Conversation? Instant Messaging, Intertextuality and New Regimes of Intimacy and Truth', *Media, Culture and Society* 33(1): 71–87.

Seder, J.P. and Oishi, S. (2009) 'Ethnic/Racial Homogeneity in College Students' Facebook Friendship Networks and Subjective Well-Being', *Journal of Research in Personality* 43: 438–443.

Seib, P. (2011) *Real-Time Diplomacy: Politics and Power in the Social Media Era*. Basingstoke: Palgrave.

Seiter, E. (1993) *Sold Separately: Parents and Children in Consumer Culture*. New Brunswick, NJ: Rutgers University Press.

Seiter, E. (2005) *The Internet Playground: Children's Access, Entertainment, and Mis-Education*. New York: Peter Lang.

Seiter, E. (2008) 'Practicing at Home: Computers, Pianos, and Cultural Capital', in McPherson, T. (ed.), *Digital Youth, Innovations and the Unexpected*, Vol. 4. Cambridge, MA: MIT Press, pp. 27–52.

Senft, T.M. (2008) *Camgirls: Celebrity and Community in the Age of Social Networks*. New York: Peter Lang.

Shilling, C. (1993) *The Body and Social Theory*. London: Sage.

Siibak, A. (2010) 'Constructing Masculinity on a Social Networking Site: The Case-Study of Visual Self-Presentations of Young Men on the Profile Images of SNS Rate', *Young: Nordic Journal of Youth Research* 18(4): 403–425.

Silver, A. (1997) 'Two Different Types of Commerce: Friendship and Strangership', in Weintraub, J. and Kumar, K. (eds.), *Civil Society in Public and Private in Thought and Practice: Perspectives on a Grand Dichotomy*. Chicago: University of Chicago Press, pp. 43–74.

Silverstone, R. (2005) 'Mediation and Communication', in Calhoun, C. Rojek, R., and Turner, B. (eds.), *Handbook of Sociology*, London: Sage, pp. 188–207.

Silverstone, R. (2006) 'Domesticating domestication: Reflections on the life of a concept', in Berker T., Hartmann, M., Punie, Y., and Ward, K.J. (eds.), *The Domestication of Media and Technology*. Maidenhead: Open University Press, pp. 229–248.

Silverstone, R. and Hirsch, E. (1992) *Consuming Technologies: Media and Information in Domestic Spaces*. London: Routledge.

Silverstone, R. Hirsch, E., and Morley, D. (1992) 'The Moral Economy of the Household', in Silverstone, R. and Hirsh, E. (eds.), *Consuming Technologies: Media and Information in Domestic Spaces*. London: Routledge.

Simmel, G. (1950) *The Sociology of Georg Simmel*, trans. Wolff, K. New York: The Free Press.

Sims, C. (2007) 'Composed conversations: Teenage Practices of flirting with New media', *Society of the Social Studies of Science conference*, 11 October 2007, Montreal, Canada.

Sims, C. (2010) 'The Milvert Family: A Portrait of Rural California', in Ito, M., Baumer, S., Bittanti, M., Boyd, D., Cody, R., Herr-Stevenson, B., Horst, H.A., Lange, P.G., Martinez, K.Z., Pasko, C.J., Perkel, D., Robinson, L.S., Sims, C., and Tripp, L. (eds.), *Hanging Out, Messing Around, Geeking Out: Kids Living and Learning with New Media*. Cambridge, MA: The MIT Press, pp. 186–188.

Smart, C. (2007) *Personal Life*. Cambridge: Polity Press.

Smith, A. (2008) 'The Internet's Role in campaign 2008', Pew Internet and American Life Project. Available at: http://web.pewinternet.org/ ~/media/Files/Reports/2009/The_Internets_Role_in_Campaign_2008.pdf (accessed 16 August 2012).

Smith, H. (2011) 'Apple Fires Employee Over iPhone Facebook Rants', *Metro*, 30 November 2011. Available at: http://www.metro.co.uk/tech/883333-apple-sacks-worker-for-ranting-about-iphone-on-facebook (accessed 19 March 2012).

Smith, M.R. and Marx, L. (1998) *Does Technology Drive History? The Dilemma of Technological Determinism*. Cambridge, MA: MIT press.

Sohn, D. (2008) *Social Network Structures and the Internet: Collective Dynamics in Virtual Communities*. Amherst, NY: Cambria Press.

Solomon, Y. et al. (2002) 'Intimate Talk between Parents and their Teenage Children. Democratic Openness or Covert Control?' *Sociology* 36(4): 965–983.

Solove, D. (2007) ' "I've Got Nothing to Hide" and Other Misunderstandings of Privacy', *San Diego Law Review* 44: 757.

Spencer, L. and Pahl, R. (2006) *Rethinking Friendship: Hidden Solidarities Today*. Princeton, NJ: Princeton University Press.

Spigel, L. (2001) *Welcome to the Dreamhouse: Popular Media and Postwar Suburbs*. Durham and London: Duke University Press.

Spira, J. (2009) *The Perils of Cyber-Dating: Confessions of a Hopeful Romantic Looking for Love Online* [Kindle Edition]. New York: Morgan James Publishing.

Starker, S. (1989) *Evil Influences: Crusades Against the Mass Media*. New Brunswick, NJ: Transaction Books.

Statistics Canada (2008) 'Canadian Internet Use Survey'. Available at: http:// www.statcan.gc.ca

Stefanone, M., Lackaff, D., and Rosen, D. (2008) 'We're All Stars Now: Reality Television, Web 2.0,and Mediated Identities', *Proceedings of the ACM Conference on Hypertext and Hypermedia (HYPERTEXT '08)*, 19, 107–112. Los Alamitos, CA: IEEE Press. Available at: http://www.communication.buffalo.edu/contrib/ people/faculty/documents/stefanone_hypertext08_000.pdf (accessed9 July 12).

Stefanone, M., Lackaff, D., and Rosen, D. (2011) 'Contingencies of Self-worth and Social-Networking-Site Behavior', *Cyberpsychology, Behavior and Social Networking* 14(1–2): 41–50.

Steinfield, C., Ellison, N.B., and Lampe, C. (2008) 'Social Capital, Self-Esteem, and Use of Online Social Network Sites: A Longitudinal Analysis', *Journal of Applied Developmental Psychology* 29: 434–445.

Subrahmanyam, K. and Greenfield, P. (2008) 'Online Communication and Adolescent Relationships', *The Future of Children* 18(1): 119–46.

Sundén, J. (2003) *Material Virtualities: Approaching Online Textual Embodiment*. New York: Peter Lang.

Thompson, C. (2008) 'Brave New World of Digital Intimacy', *New York Times Magazine*, 5 September 2008. Available at: http://www.nytimes.com/2008/09/07/magazine/07awareness-t.html?pagewanted=all (accessed 22 March 2012).

Toma, C.L. and Hancock, J.T. (2012) 'What Lies Beneath: The Linguistic Traces of Deception in Online Dating Profiles', *Journal of Communication* 62: 78–97.

Toma, C. (2010) 'Looks and Lies: The Role of Physical Attractiveness in Online Dating Self-Presentation', *Communication Research* 37: 335–351.

Tong S.T, Van Der Heide, B., Langwell, L., and Walther, J. (2008) 'Too Much of a Good Thing? The Relationship Between Number of Friends and Interpersonal Impressions on Facebook', *Journal of Computer-mediated Communication* 13: 531–549.

Thorne, B. (1993) *Gender Play: Girls and Boys in School*. New Brunswick, NJ: Rutgers University Press.

Thorne, B. (2009) ' "Childhood": Changing and Dissonant Meanings', *International Journal of Learning and Media* 1(1): 19–27.

Tönnies, F. (1957) (reprinted 1974) *Community and Association*. London: Routledge.

Tufekci, Z. (2008) 'Grooming, Gossip, Facebook and Myspace', *Information, Communication and Society* 11(4): 544–564.

Turkle, S. (1995) *Life on the Screen: Identity in the Age of the Internet*. New York: Simon and Schuster.

Turner, B.S. (1996) *The Body and Society: Explorations in Social Theory*, 2nd edn. London: Sage.

Turow, J., King, J., Hoofnagle, C.J., Bleakley, A., and Hennessy, M. (2009) 'Contrary to What Marketers Say, Americans Reject Tailored Advertising and Three Activities That Enable It'. Available at: http://ssrn.com/abstract=1478214 (accessed 10 May 2011).

Twenge, J.M. and Campbell, W.K. (2009) *The Narcissism Epidemic: Living in the Age of Entitlement*. New York: Simon and Schuster.

Ulicsak, M. and Cranmer, S. (2010) *Gaming in Families: Final Report*. Bristol: Futurelab, Innovation in Education. Available at: http://www.futurelab.org.uk/resources/documents/project_reports/Games_Families_Final_Report.pdf (accessed 11 July 2010).

UNDP (2001) United Nations Development Programme (2001) *Human Development Report 2001: Making New Technologies Work for Human Development*. Oxford: Oxford University Press.

Uslaner, E.M. (1999a) 'Democracy and Social Capital', in Warren, M.E. (ed.), *Democracy Band Trust*. Cambridge: Cambridge University Press, pp. 121–150.

Uslaner, E.M. (1999b) 'Trust but Verify: Social Capital and Moral Behavior', *Social Science Information* 38(1): 29–55.

Valentine, G. (2004) *Public Space and the Culture of Childhood*. Hants: Ashgate.

Vazire, S. and Gosling, S.D. (2004) 'Personality Processes and Individual Differences: E-Perceptions: Personality Impressions Based on Personal Websites', *Journal of Personality and Social Psychology* 87(1): 123–132.

Vertovec, S. (2004) Migrant Transnationalism and Modes of Transformation. *International Migration Review* 38(3): 970–1001.

Vitak, J. and Ellison, N. (2012) ' "There's a Network Out There You Might As Well Tap": Exploring the Benefits of and Barriers to Exchanging Informational and Support-Based Resources on Facebook', *New Media & Society* 23 July 2012.

Verbrugge, L.M. (1977) 'The Structure of Adult Friendship Choices', *Social Forces* 56(2): 576–597.

Lee, W., Chan, B., Ho, K.C., Kluver, R., and Yang, K.C.C. (eds.) (2003) *Asia.com:Asia Encounters the Internet*. London: RoutledgeCurzon.

Wajcman, J., Bittman, M., and Brown, J. (2008) 'Intimate Connections: The Impact of the Mobile Phone on Work/Life Boundaries', in Goggin, G. and Hjorth, L. (eds.), *Mobile Technologies: From Telecommunications to Media*, New York: Routledge, pp. 9–22.

Walther JB (1992) Interpersonal Effects in Computer-Mediated Interaction: A Relational Perspective, *Communication Research* 19(1): 52–90.

Walther, J.B. (1994) 'Anticipated Ongoing Interaction Versus Channel Effects on Relational Communication in Computer-Mediated Interaction', *Human Communication Research* 20(4): 473–501.

Walther J.B. (1996) Computer-Mediated Communication: Impersonal, Interpersonal and Hyperpersonal Interaction, *Communication Research* 23(1): 3–43.

Walther, J.B., Anderson, J.F., and Park, D. (1994) 'Interpersonal Effects in Computer-Mediated Interaction: A Meta-Analysis of Social and Anti-Social Communication', *Communication Research* 21(4): 460–487.

Walther, J.B. and Parks, M. (2002) 'Cues Filtered Out, Cues Filtered in: Computer Mediated Communication and Realtionships', in Knapp, M.L., Daly, J.A. and Miller, G.R. (eds.), *The Handbook of Interpersonal Communication*, 3rd edn. Thousand Oaks, CA: Sage, pp. 529–563.

Walther, J.B., Van Der Heide, Kim, B., Westerman, D., and Tong, S.T. (2008) The Role of Friends' Appearance and Behavior on Evaluations of Individuals on Facebook: Are We Known by the Company We Keep? *Human Communication Research* 34: 28–49.

Wellman, B. (1979) 'The Community Question', *The American Journal of Sociology* 84: 1201–1231.

Wellman, B. (1982) 'Studying Personal Communities', in Marsden, P. and Lin, N. (eds.), *Social Structure and Network Analysis*. Beverley Hills, CA: Sage, pp. 61–80.

Wellman, B. (1993) 'An Egocentric Network Tale: Comment on Bien et al. (1991)', *Social Networks* 15(4): 423–436.

Wellman, B. (2002) 'Little Boxes, Glocalization, and Networked Individualism', Center for Urban & Community Studies, University of Toronto. Available at: http://homes.chass.utoronto.ca/~wellman/publications/littleboxes/littlebox.PDF (accessed 21 August 2012).

Wellman, B. and Guila, M. (1999) 'Virtual Communities as Communities: Net Surfers Don't Ride Alone', in Smith, M.A. and Kollock, P. (eds.), *Communities in Cyberspace*. London: Routledge, pp. 167–194.

Wellman, B., Quan Haase, A., Witte, J., and Hampton, K. (2001) 'Does the Internet Increase, Decrease, or Supplement Social Capital? Social Networks, Participation, and Community Commitment', *American Behavioral Scientist* 45: 437–456.

Wellman, B., Smith, A., Wells, A., and Kennedy, T. (2008) Networked Families, *Pew Research Centre Internet and American Life Project*. Pew Research Centre, California Health Foundation. Available at: http://www.pewinternet. org/~/media//Files/Reports/2008/PIP_Networked_Family.pdf.pdf (accessed 22 August 2012).

Weeks, J. (2000) *Making Sexual History*. Oxford: Polity Press.

Weeks, J., Donovan, C., and Heaphy, B. (1996) *Families of Choice: Patterns of Non-Heterosexual Relationships, a Literature Review*, No. 2. London: School of Education, Politics and Social Science, South Bank University.

Weeks, J., Heaphy, B., and Donovan, C. (2001) *Same Sex Intimacies: Families of Choice and Other Life Experiments*. London: Routledge.

Weintraub, J. and K. Kumar (1997) *Public and Private in Thought and Practice: Perspectives on a Grand Dichotomy*. Chicago: University of Chicago Press.

Weston, K. (1997) *Families We Choose: Lesbians, Gays, Kinship*. New York: Columbia University Press.

Wiederman, M.W. (2000) 'Women's Body Image Self-Consciousness During Physical Intimacy with a Partner', *Journal of Sex Research* 37(1): 60–68.

Wilding, R. (2006) '"Virtual" Intimacies? Families Communicating Across Transnational Contexts', *Global Networks* 6(2): 125–142.

Wilkinson, J. (2010) 'Personal Communities: Responsible Individualism or Another Fall for Public [man]', *Sociology* 44(3): 453–470.

Williams, D. (2006) 'On and Off the 'Net: Scales for Social Capital in an Online Era', *Journal of Computer-Mediated Communication* 11: 593–628.

Williams, R. (1974) *Television, Technology and Cultural Form*. London: Routledge.

Williamson, D. (2011) *Internet Dating, Are You Mad?* [Kindle Edition]. Amazon Media EU S.à r.l.

Willmott, H. (2007) Young Women, Routes through Education and Employment and Discursive Constructions of Love and Intimacy, *Current Sociology* 55(3): 446–466.

Wilkinson, J. (2010) 'Personal communities: Responsible Individualism or Another Fall for Public [man]', *Sociology* 44(3): 453–470.

Willson, M.A. (2006) *Technically Together: Rethinking Community within Techno-Society*. New York: Peter Lang.

Wilson, C., Boe, B., Sala, A., Puttaswamy, K.P.N., and Zhao, B.Y. (2009) User Interactions in Social Networks and the Implications, *EuroSystems*, 1–3 April 2009. Available at: http://www.cs.ucsb.edu/~alessandra/papers/interaction-eurosys09.pdf (accessed 30 July 2012).

Wolak, J., Finkelhor, D., Mitchell, K.J., and Ybarra, M.L. (2008) 'Online "Predators" and Their Victims: Myths, Realities, and Implications for Prevention and Treatment', *American Psychologist* 63(2): 111–128.

Wolak, J., Mitchell, K., and Finkelhor, D. (2006) *Online Victimization of Youth: Five Years Later*. Alexandria, VA: National Center for Missing and Exploited Children.

Wolak, J., Mitchell, K., and Finkelhor, D. (2007) 'Does Online Harassment Constitute Bullying? An Exploration of Online Harassment by Known Peers and Online-Only Contacts', *Journal of Adolescent Health* 41(6): S51–S58.

Wouters, C. (2004) 'Changing Regimes of Manners and Emotions: From Disciplining to Informalizing', in Loyal, S. and Quilley, S. (eds.), *The Sociology of Norbert Elias*. Cambridge: Cambridge University Press, pp. 193–211.

Wynne-Jones, J. (2009) 'Facebook and MySpace Can Lead Children to Commit Suicide, Warns Archbishop Nichols', *Telegraph.co.uk*, 1 August 2009. Available at: http://www.telegraph.co.uk/news/religion/5956719/Facebook-and-MySpace-can-lead-children-to-commit-suicide-warns-Archbishop-Nichols.html

Yabarra, M.L., Diener-West, M., and Leaf, P.J. (2007) 'Examining the Overlap in Internet Harassment and School Bullying: Implications for School Intervention', *Journal of Adolescent Health* 41(6): S42–S50.

Young, I.M. (1997) 'Asymmetrical Reciprocity: On Moral Respect, Wonder, and Enlarged Thought', *Constellations* 3(3): 340–363.

Zarbatany, L. et al. (2000) 'Gender-Differentiated Experience in the Peer Culture: Links to Intimacy in Preadolescence', *Social Development* 9(1): 62–79.

Zelizer, V. (2005) *The Purchase of Intimacy*. Princeton, NJ: Princeton University Press.

Ziehe, T. (1994) 'From Living Standard to Life Style', *Young: Nordic Journal of Youth Research* 2(2): 2–16.

Index

CPI Antony Rowe
Eastbourne, UK
August 08, 2019